CW00551077

Pullman Profile No 5

THE GOLDEN ARROW

Antony M Ford

Crécy Publishing Ltd

Pullman Profile No 5

THE GOLDEN ARROW

Antony M Ford

To Brendan Brabazon and Alec Hasenson, who for thirty years guided my hand and who both gave me, with so much else, the idea for this book.

First published 2018

© Antony Ford and Crécy Publishing Ltd 2018

ISBN 9781909328709

All rights reserved. Apart from any fair dealing for the purpose of private study, research, criticism or review, as permitted under the Copyright, Design and Patents Act 1988, no part of this publication may be reproduced, stored in a retrieval system, or transmitted in any form or by any means, electronic, electrical, chemical, mechanical, optical, photocopying, recording or otherwise, without prior written permission. All enquiries should be directed to the publisher.

Printed in Malta by Gutenberg Press Ltd

Crécy Publishing Ltd
1a Ringway Trading Estate, Shadowmoss Rd, Manchester M22 5LH
www.crecy.co.uk

Front cover: *The first post-War 'Golden Arrow' awaiting departure from Victoria behind* **No 21C1** *'Channel packet'.*
Preceeding page and back cover: *An atmospheric view of the cavernous interior of Dover Marine, c.1965. Electric locomotive* **E5015** *waits patiently for departure and immediately behind it is a general utility van, two green-liveried MK2 first-class coaches followed by the Pullmans.*

CONTENTS

Foreword

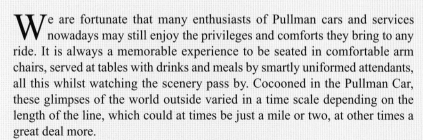

We are fortunate that many enthusiasts of Pullman cars and services nowadays may still enjoy the privileges and comforts they bring to any ride. It is always a memorable experience to be seated in comfortable arm chairs, served at tables with drinks and meals by smartly uniformed attendants, all this whilst watching the scenery pass by. Cocooned in the Pullman Car, these glimpses of the world outside varied in a time scale depending on the length of the line, which could at times be just a mile or two, at other times a great deal more.

The fact is though these latter-day services are all artificial, the play-acting child of the role-playing parent. To get a feeling for some of the real services that once ran in this country we can do no better than to read *Profile 5*, where Antony Ford has so painstakingly recreated for us in words and pictures the world of the Pullman Car as it existed so many decades ago in all four of his earlier Profile books. This particular edition, *No. 5*, brings back many memories for me, especially the luxurious nature of the 'Golden Arrow', a train I used to ride occasionally in my youth in the Forties and Fifties. The sheer nature of the ambience was in marked contrast to the austerity and rationing still in force. This was no afterthought. Even two decades earlier, we read, the new 'Flèche d'Or' of 1926 was gloriously compared in brochures to the 'age of pageantry and bejewelled magnificence', comparing it to Henry VIII and the Field of the Cloth of Gold, though perhaps that was stretching it a bit.

Nevertheless, standing on the platform in Victoria station in the days of post-World War 2 austerity, waiting to board our wonderful cars for the ride south (Pullmans were never known as Carriages), still gave pause for thought. I now realise how anyone with the appropriate ticket must have felt.

Antony Ford provides full details of the South-Eastern Pullman Services he mentions, the history of the individual cars and, not least, the politics involved.

Comprehensive references at the end of each chapter tell where to look for more information as well as an insight into the amount of work involved in compiling this latest part of his Pullman story. Antony Ford is to be congratulated on the scale and scope of his work, and *Profile No. 5* surely deserves a place on any enthusiast's book shelf, together with all his previous other ones.

Alec Hasenson

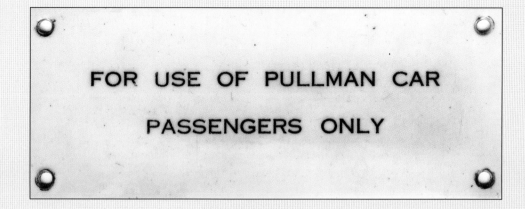

FOR USE OF PULLMAN CAR

PASSENGERS ONLY

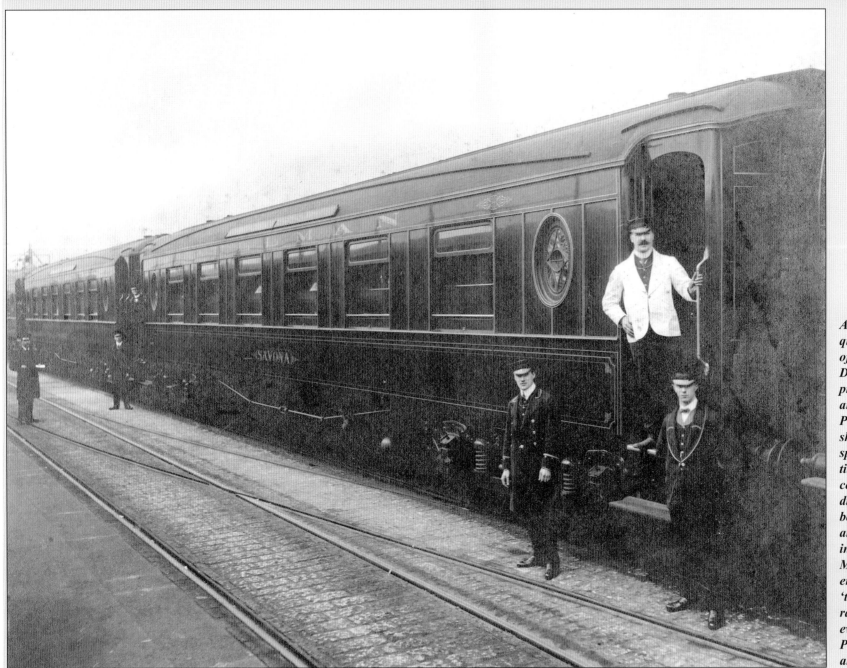

Although not of the best quality, a rare inaugural view of the first Pullman cars at Dover Pier with Savona prominently in view sporting an all-over crimson lake livery. Pullman attendants and staff show off their uniforms for this special occasion. Note: At this time, the Pullman Company coat of arms are not yet displayed on the match-boarding. In their special article a week after the inaugural trip of 21 March1910, The Graphic enthusiastically asserted that 'the disagreeable side of railway travelling decreases every day… The fitting of each Pullman car is most luxurious and yet it is always tasteful'.

The origins of luxury rail travel on the London to Paris route to 1939

By the middle of the 19th century, the combined rail and steamer journey from London to Paris took around 12 hours in the best of conditions, and was uncomfortable, tiring and to many a journey of endurance, while the railway company infrastructure and rolling stock on both sides of the Channel were generally rudimentary. Paris was only linked by rail to the seaport of Le Havre in 1847, Dieppe, Boulogne, Calais and Dunkirk a year later, in 1848.

The ships involved were then only small paddle steamers of around 200 gross tonnage. When the weather was fine their speed exceeded no more than 10 knots and the shortest crossing took at least 2 hours. Moreover, access to the ports of Dover and Folkestone, and vis-à-vis those of Calais and Boulogne, was dependant on the tides which frequently involved transferring passengers and mail off these ports by small boats. Furthermore, timetables were always only indicative and remained wholly dependent on the weather, tides and winds.[1]

In their endeavours to find gainful employment, the American-owned Pullman Company Limited introduced a luxury-type service in June 1882 on the London, Chatham & Dover Railway (LCDR) using a solitary 'parlor car', named *Jupiter*. Originally allocated to the London, Brighton & South Coast Railway and transferred probably on loan, this vehicle formed part of the 10 a.m. 'Dover Pullman Car Boat Train Express' service from London Victoria to Dover Pier, returning at 3.30 p.m. The service appears to have struggled to attract sustainable custom, and ran for the duration of the contract of two years, before being withdrawn in July 1884. (A surviving weekly statement of earnings for the week ending 7 May 1884, for example, records almost impecunious receipts of £7 and 6 shillings for the London-Dover service, compared with £32 and 18 shillings, on the corresponding London-Brighton route, similarly utilising one 'parlor car'.)[2]

Paris held its Great International Exhibition in 1889, and by the end of that year the railway reached the new harbour terminal and maritime station of Calais, offering in all weather conditions the precious ability of berthing ships independently from the state of the tide. Boulogne had opened earlier its own maritime station, in 1877; it only became fully operational in 1885, after dredging had reached the required draught. The best journey times via the short sea crossing had by then reduced to almost 7½ hours from London to Paris and vice versa; a timing which remained almost unchanged until the 20th century.[3]

Despite the short-lived Pullman car service, the railway companies serving Dover continued to

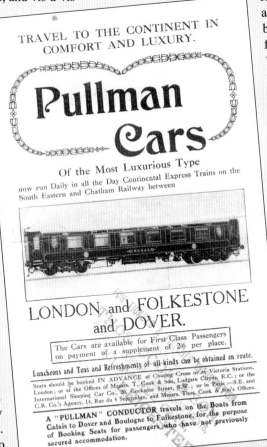

TRAVEL TO THE CONTINENT IN COMFORT AND LUXURY.

Pullman Cars

Of the Most Luxurious Type now run Daily in all the Day Continental Express Trains on the South Eastern and Chatham Railway between

LONDON and FOLKESTONE and DOVER.

The Cars are available for First Class Passengers on payment of a supplement of 2/6 per place.

Luncheons and Teas and Refreshments of all kinds can be obtained en route.

Seats should be booked IN ADVANCE at Charing Cross or at Victoria Stations, London; or at the Offices of Messrs. T. Cook & Son, Ludgate Circus, E.C.; or the International Sleeping Car Co., 20, Cockspur Street, S.W.; or in Paris:—S.E. and C.R. Co.'s Agency, 14, Rue du 4 Septembre, and Messrs. Thos. Cook & Son's Offices.

A "PULLMAN" CONDUCTOR travels on the Boats from Calais to Dover and Boulogne to Folkestone, for the purpose of Booking Seats for passengers who have not previously secured accommodation.

make concerted attempts to attract additional custom, by introducing 'club trains' offering superior appointments to connect with the Paris Exhibition. The first were supplementary-fare saloon-type vehicles belonging to La Compagnie Internationale des Wagons-Lits (Wagons Lits) which ran on the LCDR, while later, competing with a similar service running on the rival South Eastern Railway (SER); each of these trains arrived within minutes of the other at Dover. Sadly, in both cases they proved short-lived, loss-making experiences, but these have often been cited as the forerunners to the 'Golden Arrow' that was to come.

However, the SER continued to improve their standards by introducing another train, American in style but without any supplements, what became known as the 'Hastings Car Train': each vehicle elaborately furnished with open ends and platforms. Later still, another train the 'Folkestone Vestibuled Express' offered comfortable first-, second- and third-class accommodation, which, like its predecessors, proved to have only a fleeting existence (and the vehicles eventually found their way to Pullman ownership after World War 1).

By the time the SER and LCDR were transformed into the South Eastern and Chatham Railway (SECR) in 1898, the new managing committee appeared to be much in favour of developing luxury services to the Kentish sea ports, and links with its French counterparts. One of the first improvements on the short sea route took place in 1903 with the introduction of a powerful screw ship, christened the 'Queen'. According to contemporary reports, it proved a great success, whose introduction initiated the gradual elimination of paddle steamers on the Dover Straits; the last two, the grand vessels 'Nord' and the 'Pas de Calais' were withdrawn from service in 1923.[4]

During the following year, the SECR, Wagons Lits and La Compagnie du Nord each studied, in common, the possibility of creating a through de-luxe London-Paris link via Dover-Calais with the ambitious target of a 6¼ hours journey time between the two Capitals. The late Monsieur Roger Commault, one-time Historical Adviser and Wagons-Lits Archivist, advised the author that this initiative eventually became untenable and was soon disregarded due to the refusal of the British Customs to carry out their control formalities in the train between London-Dover and vice versa. It was only when the new owner of the British Pullman Company, the financier Davison Dalziel entered discussions to revive Pullman car services, that matters again seem to have generated interest with a reciprocal desire 'for the maximum of luxury at the minimum of cost' – a slogan used repeatedly in early Pullman Company literature.

By June 1909 negotiations were formally concluded between Pullman and the SECR, which resulted in an agreement to introduce, early the following year, six handsome British-built Pullman parlour and buffet cars, resplendent in a crimson lake (red Indian brown) livery favoured by the SECR. These were to run in pairs on selected boat train services to and from Dover.[5]

This appointment was seen by many observers as a promising step towards improving the travelling experience between London to the Kentish port and onward connections to Paris. The early encouraging signs of escalating receipts and demand for this type of accommodation at the booking offices was such that within a matter of just three years, supplemented by further batches of cars, practically all boat trains linking London stations with the South-East Coast ports included two or more Pullman cars.

By the end of 1913, the fastest timings between the two capitals had fallen to 6½ hours and Pullman patronage progressively improved annually, although it cannot be claimed that the advertised luxurious facilities were enthusiastically received by all travellers. *The Railway Gazette* commented on the absurdity of the advice given to passengers by a correspondent of *The Times* who objected to the supplement of 2 shillings and 6 pence for the Pullman cars on the Dover boat trains.

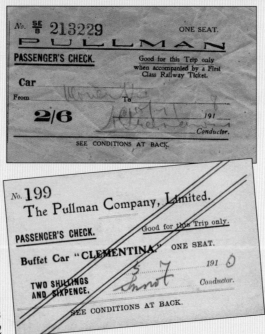

Another correspondent soon joined issue with him, putting the law and common sense of the matter in a short letter. The following extraction, quoted verbatim, makes for interesting reading:

He pertinently asks what it has to do with a passenger who is supplied with first-class statutory accommodation, that the Company may have chosen to licence some person to attach a superfluous carriage de-luxe to the train and make a charge for its use. As a matter of law, it is clear that private coaches were intended to run on railways as on ordinary highways, and that this arrangement only became practicable because the companies refused to work the signals. Subject to the assent of the railway concerned, such coaches can, therefore, run and carry passengers. If, however, these private carriages with an extra supplement were run in such a fashion as practically to exclude the ordinary statutory accommodation, then it might become a question whether the railway company was affording reasonable facilities for the carriage of passengers.

Later, in their article regarding another matter, namely 'Railway Companies as Public Caterers', *The Railway Gazette* outlined what were then considered by a correspondent, 'short-sighted reflections on Pullman car policy of the SECR'.[6]

'Why, for instance', asked the correspondent, 'should there be continued such an anachronistic and un-business-like absurdity as an almost empty Pullman diner on the evening Continental train from Victoria to Folkestone, available for first-class passengers only, at an increased fare?' *The Railway Gazette* remarked that 'before setting down all of this the writer might have taken the trouble to verify his statements … this "almost empty car" runs on the night service via Flushing, and during March, which is one of the quietest months, it averaged 11 passengers'.

The correspondent goes on to ask: 'Has not the South-Eastern management yet learnt that second-class passengers – not to speak of the democratic third – are even better paying customers in this direction than the few of the first-class?' Again, 'he has not realised', asserts *The Railway Gazette*, 'that there is an essential difference between the character of the Continental boat-train traffic and that of the ordinary long-distance express in England.[7]

With an expanded fleet of 20 cars allocated to the SECR workings, and the Pullman image and branding soon acquiring an almost household name synonymous with luxury travel in Britain and elsewhere, World War 1 abruptly interrupted any further development in this regard. The majority of Pullman cars were withdrawn and stored during the interregnum, although several including *Daphne* and *Ruby* were used for special trips to the South Coast by military and government officials often marshalled in troop trains.

With numerous accolades bestowed on him, Dalziel enjoyed much respect from the travelling public during his private ownership of the Pullman Company, to which it was widely recognised that significant inroads raising passenger standards were made. At an extraordinary meeting held at the Pullman offices, Moorgate Street, London, on 15 September 1915, a special resolution was agreed to change the name of the company to 'the Drawing Room Cars Company Limited'. For legal reasons, this allowed the company to be called 'The Pullman Car Company Limited', while a fortnight later, a public company was formed to take over all 'the cars, stock, work-in-hand and goodwill' with Dalziel holding a significant share in this new company and taking the position as Chairman.[8]

After the 11 November 1918 Armistice, civilian cross-Channel services gradually resumed between Boulogne and Folkestone some three months later, while over a year elapsed before services could commence between Dover and Calais on 8 January 1920. Although passenger traffic gradually increased to pre-war levels, the re-establishment of all the former Pullman services was not so immediate, but once they were fully phased in, the Pullman Car Company (as it was now known) experienced a considerable period of demand and growth. By July 1921, for instance, the company had arranged with the SECR for an all-Pullman service, the first in South-East England, to run to the popular resorts of Margate, Broadstairs and Ramsgate. This train was first-class only and given the title 'The Thanet Pullman Limited', departing from Victoria station every Sunday at 10.10 a.m.

The Pullman Chairman Davison Dalziel seated in car **Ruby** *c. 1923 showing an up-to-date version of a radiogram first introduced to the Pullman services (and to this vehicle) in 1914. Much later, this attractively-appointed vehicle decorated with Spanish mahogany elaborately inlaid to Pergolesi- inspired designs was damaged internally by enemy action on 12 September 1940. Following repairs, it was one of a handful of cars ready to return to revenue-earning service on cessation of hostilities.*

The 'Continental Pullman Express' at speed c 1924 hauling a mixture of 8- and 12-wheel cars in original crimson lake livery with a birdcage brake vehicle leading. **The Railway Gazette's** *January 1926 report regarding 'Pullman popularity' suggests that the British public's 'preference for compartment coaches must no longer be assumed to prevail among all classes of travellers. Indeed, the strong preference shown for the Pullman vehicles wherever they are available may be said to dispose of this formerly well-established principle among travellers in this country'.*

and running non-stop to Margate West in one hour and 30 minutes. The inaugural train was composed of six 'A-type' cars of 1910-14 vintage which were often rostered during weekdays on the London-Dover route: *Corunna, Daphne, Leghorn, Ruby, Sorrento* and *Topaz.*[9]

At this time, too, on the other side of the Channel improving *de-luxe* travel in France was still hampered by the massive war-time destruction of much of the railway infrastructure between Paris and Calais. The return to pre-war running conditions and timings remained severely delayed, yet remarkably by the time the newly-created Southern Railway Company regenerated in quick succession all the earlier SECR Pullman workings, including single car workings to South-East resorts in 1923, the French railways were running back to normal. This also brought about a reorganisation of the London-Paris Continental services with an improved timetable of sea crossings,

and for the Southern Railway the concentration of all such services from Victoria station, London.

A year later, the Southern Railway introduced the first all-Pullman service between London-Dover during November 1924, composed of six new all-first-class 'K-type' kitchen cars in a new umber and cream livery – as outlined in *Pullman Profile No.2* – together with two 'F-type' parlour cars with guard accommodation and hand brakes (of four constructed in 1923 per Chapter 8). These were often topping and tailing, and each ran momentarily in their original crimson lake livery. Occasionally, some of the older cars of 1910-14 were also in the composition (as well as ordinary vehicles), and these are shown to good effect in several illustrations within this profile.

This service was originally a relief departing at 10.50am from Victoria, arriving at Dover Marine at 12.32pm, and it was closely followed by the 11am ordinary train. This arrived at the port at 12.40pm where passengers from both trains boarded the 12.55 boat, arriving in Calais at 2.10pm (local time) and Paris at 6.15pm.

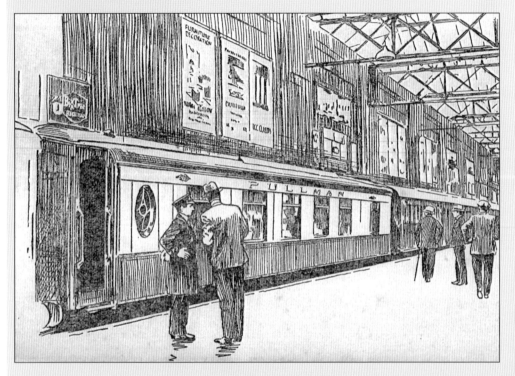

The 'Pullman Continental Express' was customarily hauled by 'King Arthur' locomotives (later by the more powerful 'Lord Nelson' class from 1928) and became colloquially known as the 'White Pullman' as the Pullman cars generally forming the train were in a livery not of the usual crimson lake in colour, but were increasingly seen in the new soon-to-be-standard umber and cream livery (with umber below the waist and cream above to the roof). Pullman travel, it seemed, was not only comfortable, but exclusive and secure; finding favour with royalty, diplomats and the rich. The Pullmans represented the height of luxury, with meals served to all passengers at their seats. Progressively in vogue with the public, this profile will show, the increased demand for *de-luxe* travel, including a dalliance with second- and third-class Pullman accommodation on selected Southern boat trains probably reached its zenith during the early inter-war period.

In France, comfortable first-class carriages of the Nord Railway introduced to trains connecting with the steamer at Calais had undoubtedly made the travelling experience that much more

pleasurable, but at the Paris headquarters of Wagons Lits, Davison Dalziel was already setting out an ambitious and daring plan, developing superior rail travel to extraordinary lengths and to dazzling effect.

On 25 October 1925, a letter appeared in *The Times* from Dalziel indicating the imminent introduction of new all-Pullman car services throughout Europe. The princely path to Paris was about to be established – and fully endorsed the following year by the delivery of new strikingly attractive all-steel cars running on French railways. These Pullman services soon promoted accelerated connections, swifter customs arrangements, where appropriate, and seamless high levels of comfort between London, the business centre of Europe, and Paris, the cultural capital (and beyond). The high pinnacle and culmination of Dalziel's visionary aspirations and investment, was the creation – among others – of one of the world's most celebrated trains: the cosmopolitan and fabulously chic 'Golden Arrow'.

Contemporary artist impression of the relaxed atmosphere of the French 'Golden Arrow' (1926) with a Customs official in discussion with a passenger: **Avez-vous quelque-chose à declarer, Monsieur?**

Lord Dalziel, as he soon became, acknowledged in publicity material the importance of the golden anniversary year of the founding of the Wagons-Lits Company and the historical significance, although exaggerated, of the Field of the Cloth of Gold with great aplomb. (At a ceremony, held two years later at the French Embassy, London, in recognition of the important contribution made to trade and industry by the Pullman Car Company, the French Ambassador presented Lord Dalziel with the Insignia of the Guard Officer of the Legion d'Honour. 16 February 1928).

For the inauguration, two trains were exclusively made up of British-built Pullman cars only, each with a lined livery of umber and cream and gold leaf arrow decoration, operated by two sets of five couplages (one parlour and one kitchen car); ten vehicles per train. There were also cars in reserve based in Paris and others at Calais. All of the vehicles, as detailed in Chapters 11, 12 and 13, were exquisitely decorated by leading furniture companies, including Morison, Martyn, Waring & Gillow and Maple's, whose latter Chairman, Sir John Blomdell, was a friend of Lord Dalziel.

As Dalziel once remarked: 'I think I am right in saying that no train in the world carries daily so many first-class passengers as the 10.45am London-Dover Pullman, and after that no other train in Europe so many are to be found on an average in the "Golden Arrow" between Calais and Paris'.

The furore and excitement shown by the new Pullman cars eventual arrival had to some extent been overshadowed by the earlier General Strike that swept through Britain during May 1926, and the costly delays experienced with their release from certain builders. The Dover and Folkestone Pullman services had at the time all been curtailed, and one of the few that ran, the Newhaven boat train, did so to revised timings.[10]

Reflecting on the impact the General Strike had made to Pullman business generally, Dalziel advised at the subsequent Ordinary General Meeting of the Company:

'… in all the circumstances, there is reason for congratulation that we have withstood the shock as well as we have done. First the railway strike, and subsequently the coal strike, brought the great bulk of our services to a standstill, while the working charges in all departments, with exception of the commissary supply, remained the same. Not only did we suffer from the abrupt and practically complete shutting down of our earnings, but it was unfortunately only by slow degrees that, even when peace was declared, we were able to recover our normal working conditions. While our services were the first to suffer from the general strike, it is only right to acknowledge the sympathy and encouragement we received at the hands of the railway companies with which we are associated and the generous effort on their part to make matters as easy as possible for us … In our case they temporarily arrested development and construction work of the new Golden Arrow cars.'[11]

Unfortunately, one of the transport mediums which began to pose a serious threat to Pullman revenue – air traffic – was one of the first to show significant increases in patronage during the industrial unrest, when the Parisian edition of *Matin* advised that the Nord and State Railways decided to suspend a number of passenger trains connecting with the cross-Channel boats. At

Le Bourget aerodrome, the traffic showed an increase of 45 per cent. over that of the previous week, while at Calais, the hotels were crowded with passengers held up by the strike.[12]

By 1927, French-built Pullmans with some furnishings acquired from England (and the final delayed batch of Leeds-built cars) were added to what had become more universally known, in French, as 'La Flèche d'Or' in addition to the Ètoile du Nord Pullman and other new de-luxe services then being introduced. These vehicles offered an even greater variety of interior décor – each exuberantly finished individually in designs that anticipated the bold colourings and visual impact that eventually became Art Deco.

Registered luggage and trunks were initially forwarded in luggage vans of the Nord Company (loaded off and on the ship). These were replaced in 1928 by three luggage vans constructed by Blanc Misseron (Nos. 1260-1262) to carry specially designed containers on either side of a central body. Featuring Wagons-Lits bogies 'type P' with oil boxes, these vehicles started their working careers painted in umber and cream colours, lined and lettered '*Fourgon*' and '*Pullman*' flanking the guard's compartment doors. Unfortunately, as they almost always ran next to the locomotive, the cream could not be kept clean, and in 1929 they were painted dark brown; by 1932 when the Pullman cars were progressively repainted in the standard blue livery, these vehicles were similarly treated.

Connecting with the French train and a new Brussels Pullman service, the 'Continental Express' ran with seven or more first-class cars, including some of the heavy 12-wheelers of 1920/21 in its formation. Now departing from Victoria at 10.45am, 15 minutes before the ordinary train, it enabled Pullman passengers to secure the seats of their choice on the steamer. Calais was reached at 2.10pm and Paris (and Brussels) at 5.40pm. These timetable arrangements lasted until May 1929.

Further improvements soon followed when the Southern Railway's own luxury vessel, the SS 'Canterbury' was launched in 1928, and designed specifically to suit the needs of its special clientele (outlined in detail later).

At a meeting on 25 January 1929, the Southern Railway Docks and Marine Committee were first apprised, by the General Manager, of the proposal to introduce an additional service between London and Paris. In conjunction with the special steamer, this train would be promoted as the London-Paris 'Golden Arrow Limited', the corresponding title already used by its esteemed French counterpart; a proposal which was to take place in the forthcoming timetable from 15 May.

The inaugural train departing at 11.0am from platform 2 at Victoria station was composed of the following 10 Pullmans with new roof boards, in order: *Aurora, Pauline, Chloria, Rosemary, Minerva, Zenobia, Cecilia, Niobe, Geraldine* and *Flora* (with *Montana, Aurelia* and *Juno* in reserve).[13]

From the ship's gangway direct to the waiting Pullman train. An artist impression that was used repeatedly in railway publicity. For those passengers wanting to buy a souvenir of their travels, the Southern Railway Company issued a colour picture of the 'Golden Arrow' in 1929 drawn by the locomotive **Sir Richard Grenville** *each costing one shilling. For five shillings, a jig-saw puzzle of the same image could be obtained from the Advertising Department at Waterloo Station and through WH Smith's bookstalls and shops.*

Change and continuity

In connection with the new 'Golden Arrow' an arrangement was successfully made by Pullman management, Southern Railway and the French Government for the Customs examination of hand baggage and for passport formalities to be carried out on the French train during its journey. By this means passengers were spared the inconvenience and delay at Calais. As a special feature, registered luggage could also be handed over to the care of the attendant on the train, who undertook to see it through Customs on arrival at Paris, and deliver it to any address within the city. Regrettably, the best their British counterparts could offer was a rapid examination at Dover for hand baggage, although luggage and trunks could be sealed, and for a small fee left in the care of a Southern Railway official for examination at Victoria, and conveniently delivered to addresses in London the same evening, or nationwide destinations the following day. (In France, to supplement the existing baggage vehicles, new all-steel brake vans, known as '*fourgons*', built by the Metropolitan Carriage, Wagon & Finance Co at Saltley, Birmingham in 1928/9 each featured wide sliding doors and staff accommodation. Habitually painted blue and cream they were often used on Pullman trains).

By July 1930, notable changes also took place with the rolling stock on the Southern train, when the Pullman Company introduced a reconditioned and refurbished set of eight cars that had at one time seen service on the Continent, as outlined in *Pullman Profile 2*. These were all painted in the new style of livery with their fascia panel painted umber, rather than cream. (For the record, these cars were: *Adrian, Diamond, Ibis, Lady Dalziel, Lydia, Onyx, Pearl* and *Princess Elizabeth*.) With just a few exceptions, almost all other vehicles rostered to the 'Golden Arrow' were transferred to other services and often to different operating lines. Some found themselves allocated to boat trains, for instance, running in pairs to Folkestone or on stopping services to South Coast resorts.

The 'Golden Arrow' by this time was generally operated by Maunsell 4-6-0 locomotives; the then new 'Lord Nelsons' became the usual motive power, with the occasional use of 'King Arthurs' taking their turn. The train departed daily from London Victoria at 11am, with the passengers scheduled to arrive in Paris at 5.35pm local time.

Unfortunately, as soon as travelling patterns had settled down successfully on both sides of the Channel, one of the seemingly cyclic trade depressions was beginning to grip the country, resulting in an overnight impact on luxury services where demand for Pullman accommodation plummeted. In the United States of America, the Wall Street Crash further compounded the difficulties on a global basis, which lasted for many years and made already demanding matters even worse.

As regard to luxury passenger services, only two years after the inauguration of the 'Golden Arrow', the Southern Railway announced that given the continued industrial depression and consequent loss of traffic, the all-in tariff from 15 May 1931 was reduced from £5 to £4 12 shillings and 6 pence. (The year 1932 was a particularly poor one for cross-Channel receipts compared to the previous year – 1,440,000 passengers reducing to 975,000 in 1932.)[14]

So desperate was the situation that ordinary rolling stock was introduced into the Victoria-Dover train (as well as combining the 11am and 11.15am services) with the 'Canterbury' accepting non-Pullman passengers for the first time. In the interim, single car workings on many South-East Coast services via Ashford, soon offered both first- and third-class accommodation following the rebuilding of numerous 'A-type' (now re-designated as 'G-type') Pullmans for that purpose into composites at Preston Park Works.[15] (*Clementina, Daphne, Florence, Mimosa, Regina, Savona* and *Valencia*, for instance, later reverted to first-class during 1946-47 when they were allocated to boat train service on the Western Section of the Southern Railway.)

By May 1932, the 'Flèche d'Or' incorporated remodelled Pullman cars offering second-class accommodation, which together with Wagons Lits Company sleeping cars were in direct connection with the 'Calais-Mediterranean Express' (Le Train Bleu), the 'Rome Express' and the 'Simplon-Orient-Express' (Trieste and Istanbul).

The Pullman supplement and meals on board were significantly reduced in order to attract custom: First-class was discounted by 37 per cent to 40 Frs fr and second-class by 22 per cent to 35 Frs fr. Set meals were advertised at 30 Frs fr, a reduction of 25 per cent on previous *prix des repas dans le Pullman*. Having weathered the most difficult of circumstances, the British counterpart continued with a reduced complement of just four first-class Pullman cars, as well as a host of ordinary first- and second-class carriages in its formation.

By contrast, the combination of sleeping cars into its composition – and Pullmans (of varying types) now running in a new blue and cream livery, displacing the umber and cream – the 'Flèche d'Or' remained completely a 'Wagons Lits Company' train, although to find economies of scale, it was deemed necessary to use just one train rather than two, and re-route it to Boulogne Ville and the Maritime stations for sea crossings to Folkestone. The service from London contrariwise continued to use the Dover to Calais route – a situation which remained unchanged until 1952.

For the many cinema goers of the 1930s, Pathé News regularly brought to their attention Pullman cars conveying visiting Heads of State, Royalty and film stars. One such occasion was a State visit made by their Majesties King George VI and Queen Elizabeth to France in July 1938. Landing at Boulogne from the Royal Yacht, the news bulletin captured their departure to Paris in a special train, including two Pullman cars (*Nos. 4147* and *4164*) which were later used in the 'Flèche d'Or', handled by the Nord Railway's streamlined Pacific Locomotive No. 31280. On their return journey (22 July), their Majesties travelled by a connecting Pullman train which ran from Dover Marine station to Victoria hauled by Schools Class Locomotive, No. 915 'Brighton'.

From 16 April 1939, the departure from Victoria was at 11am, with a scheduled arrival at Dover Marine at 12.35pm – with an allowance of 20 minutes to transfer passengers from train to ship, before sailing at 12.55pm.

Calais was reached at 2.10pm and the 'Flèche d'Or' departed at 2.30pm with an arrival at Paris Nord at 5.40pm.

The corresponding morning departure from Paris Nord was at 10.30am with a brief stop at Boulogne (Ville) at 1.05pm followed by the Maritime station at 1.10pm. The sailing for Folkestone departed at 1.45pm with a scheduled arrival at 3.15pm. 29 minutes were allowed for the transfer to the train departing at 3.44pm with an arrival at Victoria at 5.20pm.[16]

As with almost all Pullman services, the 'Golden Arrow' was abruptly withdrawn when war was declared. The last sailing of the 'Canterbury' took place on 3 September 1939, and the majority of cars went into store. Many Pullmans languished locked-up in lonely sidings, and some were later damaged by enemy action. *Flora, Pearl, Philomel, Plato, Rosemary, Viking* and *Medusa*, all regular cars at one time or another on the Dover and Folkestone boat trains, found themselves rostered to special services, including secretive trips to Bournemouth, and elsewhere, as detailed later.

After the severe hardships and destruction brought about by years of relentless war, the early reinstatement of refreshment facilities in peacetime on most Eastern Section trains – excepting at this stage Continental services – was seen as a welcome return, with the catering provided by the Pullman Car Company. By additional arrangement, several non-supplement Pullman buffet cars were also introduced on the relief Dover Boat Trains operating progressively from December 1945 and, in respect of catering on their own services, an agreement was formally approved to ensure that no percentage rental in respect of catering receipts would be charged against Pullman. As was always the case, the company would nevertheless pay the Railway Company the usual buffet car rental of £10 per annum, plus cleaning charges with regard to extra-fare accommodation.[17]

On 3 January 1946, the Southern Railway released its eagerly awaited timetable for cross-Channel Services between England and the Continent and the Channel Islands.[18] Unfortunately, as it transpired, there was some disappointment for the Railway Company's ability to reintroduce all the familiar services were not so extensive as had been hoped. The explanations given were:

Only some of the Southern Railway steamers had been returned from war service.

Only partial reconditioning had been possible.

The Channel ports had not yet been freed from some of the war-time obstructions to normal working.

Longer sea passages were necessary.

More time would be required for examination of passports and baggage.

The Continental Railway systems were still suffering from the effects of war damage.

However, according to the Railway's Traffic Officers' Conference minutes just three weeks later, significant and meaningful progress had been made during the interim.[19] The railway company's own restaurant and buffet cars would be used, where possible, on the Dover/Sandwich and Chatham/Ramsgate routes (many of which in pre-war days featured extra-fare Pullman services which were not reinstated) and although this arrangement was regarded as temporary for an experimental period – it later in fact became permanent – and without prejudice to the Pullman Car Company's agreements already in place.

An example of one of the first post-war boat train tariffs for non-supplement Pullman buffet cars. The footnote declares that 'By order of the Ministry of Food, no passenger may be served with a meal of more than three courses and exceeding 5/- in price'.

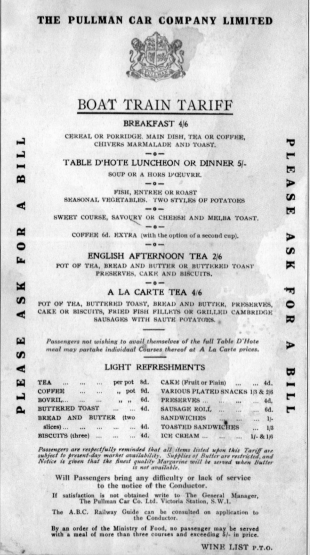

PLEASE ASK FOR A BILL

THE PULLMAN CAR COMPANY LIMITED

BOAT TRAIN TARIFF

BREAKFAST 4/6

CEREAL OR PORRIDGE, MAIN DISH, TEA OR COFFEE, CHIVERS MARMALADE AND TOAST.

— o —

TABLE D'HOTE LUNCHEON OR DINNER 5/-

SOUP OR A HORS D'ŒUVRE.

— o —

FISH, ENTRÉE OR ROAST

SEASONAL VEGETABLES. TWO STYLES OF POTATOES

— o —

SWEET COURSE, SAVOURY OR CHEESE AND MELBA TOAST.

— o —

COFFEE 6d. EXTRA (with the option of a second cup).

ENGLISH AFTERNOON TEA 2/6

POT OF TEA, BREAD AND BUTTER OR BUTTERED TOAST PRESERVES, CAKE AND BISCUITS.

— o —

A LA CARTE TEA 4/6

POT OF TEA, BUTTERED TOAST, BREAD AND BUTTER, PRESERVES, CAKE OR BISCUITS, FRIED FISH FILLETS OR GRILLED CAMBRIDGE SAUSAGES WITH SAUTE POTATOES.

Passengers not wishing to avail themselves of the full Table D'Hote meal may partake individual Courses thereof at A La Carte prices.

LIGHT REFRESHMENTS

TEA ... ... per pot 8d.	CAKE (Fruit or Plain) ... ... 4d.
COFFEE ... ... ,, pot 9d.	VARIOUS PLATED SNACKS 1/3 & 2/6
BOVRIL... ... ,, ,, 6d.	PRESERVES ... ... 4d.
BUTTERED TOAST ... ... 4d.	SAUSAGE ROLL ... ... 6d.
BREAD AND BUTTER (two	SANDWICHES 1/-
slices) ... ... 4d.	TOASTED SANDWICHES ... 1/3
BISCUITS (three) ... ... 4d.	ICE CREAM ... ... 1/- & 1/6

Passengers are respectfully reminded that all items listed upon this Tariff are subject to present-day market availability. Supplies of Butter are restricted, and Notice is given that the finest quality Margarine will be served when Butter is not available.

Will Passengers bring any difficulty or lack of service to the notice of the Conductor.

If satisfaction is not obtained write to The General Manager, The Pullman Car Co. Ltd. Victoria Station, S.W.1.

The A.B.C. Railway Guide can be consulted on application to the Conductor.

By an order of the Ministry of Food, no passenger may be served with a meal of more than three courses and exceeding 5/- in price.

WINE LIST P.T.O.

PLEASE ASK FOR A BILL

GOLDEN ARROW

LONDON —PARIS PULLMAN SERVICE

with " TRIANON " Bar

MAXIMUM COMFORT SHORT SEA CROSSING DOVER — CALAIS BY NEW STEAMER "INVICTA"

SOUTHERN RAILWAY

It was also widely reported by 15 January that preliminary arrangements were already in-hand to resume a passenger service between England and France via Dover-Calais, aimed precisely three months later, from 15 April. The minutes also record that the officers were hopeful of securing the release of the SS 'Canterbury' from Ministry of War Transport charter to cover the sailings.[20]

A daily de-luxe passenger service was vigorously promoted far and wide (by the printing of 10,000 leaflets, repeated in several tranches, together with posters and handbills vibrantly coloured in tango orange, similar to ephemera produced originally in 1929), announcing that on and from Monday, 15 April, 1946, the restoration of the famous 'Golden Arrow' London-Paris Pullman Car services would take place, once again, to and from the Continent via Dover-Calais.[21]

Also from that date, direct connection at Calais would allow for a daily through train (first-, second- and third-class, and second-class sleeping car) between Calais and Basle, with the 'Simplon-Orient Express'. One first-class Pullman car, and one composite first- and second-class coach of the Calais-Paris Boat train would be worked through to Paris (Lyon) enabling passengers to join principal night trains to the south of France, Switzerland, Italy, etc without change of stations in Paris.

Arrangements were also in place for reservations in advance of first-class Pullman seats on the 'Calais-Paris Boat Train'. An echo of pre-war civilised travel, supplementary tickets could again be obtained in advance from the Continental Enquiry Office, Victoria Station on payment of 15 shillings. (First- and second-class Pullman seats on the 'Golden Arrow' between Victoria-Dover Marine and vice versa could also be reserved on payment of a supplement of 5 shillings first-class, and 3 shillings second-class.)[22] If spare Pullman seats were available on any of these services just prior to departure, the supplement could be collected directly by the Conductor on-board.

supported on either side by the Union Jack and the Tricolour flags, hauled the glittering train with Driver James Peck and Fireman Drewitt of Stewarts Lane in charge, under the supervision of Inspector F. Hillman. A magnificent start was reported from the crowded platform end 'at the stroke of ten o'clock from Victoria' and continued for much of the journey, with the train eventually reaching speeds of 70 mph along the unique stretch of 25 miles or so of practically dead straight lines between Tonbridge, Westenhanger and Ashford.[24]

Unfortunately, the addition of the revamped 12-wheel buffet car (*No. 5* of 1917 vintage) known as the plastics bar car – fitted out in previous months with an ultra-modern Warerite laminated plastic interior of grey and pink, and designed by Architect Mr Richard Levin of Bakelite Ltd – ran hot necessitating an emergency stop at Folkestone Central to cool it off.[25]

Elsewhere, matters were also improving, too. Although a heavily restricted Newhaven-Dieppe service had resumed during the latter part of the War from 15 January 1945, a three-class service was introduced a year later with onward connections to Paris (St. Lazare) which also included a first-class Pullman car between Victoria to Newhaven. As this service was a tidal one, it was not possible to provide a timetable, and details were only provided from the Continental Enquiry Office at Victoria station.

Another important link – the tri-weekly service between Folkestone and Ostend which was one of the first to resume on 23 October 1945 – became a year later a London-Brussels service via Folkestone-Ostend featuring one or two first-class Pullman cars running (from Victoria to Folkestone) every Tuesday, Thursday and Saturday, traversing down the steep 1 in 30 harbour branch line.[23]

Just prior to the momentous occasion of re-introducing the 'Golden Arrow', Sir Eustace Missenden, the Southern Railway's General Manager, and Mr Stanley Adams, the Pullman Chairman (and opportunely also board member of Bakelite Ltd., whose marketing division was known as Warerite), agreed to a special 'dress rehearsal' run on Saturday, 13 April. Members of the press, BBC and newsreels were invited to travel in the stately comforts of refurbished Pullman cars: *Niobe, Onyx, Cecilia*, in addition to a new cocktail bar car named *Trianon* adjoined to another new vehicle – a plastics bar car – specially included, on what might also be called the 'press', 'demonstration' or 'trial' run, as variously described in contemporary popular press and railway literature.

Fittingly, the Southern Railway 'Merchant Navy' Class locomotive '21C1 Channel Packet' bearing a large golden arrow on each side, and decorated for the occasion with a golden 'V'

One of the six-wheel bogies of the 'plastics bar car' being inspected at Dover Marine by a repair gang following the development of a hot box experienced on the 'Press Trip' down to Dover.

Unusually, it had neither exterior Pullman fascia branding nor centrally located running name or number at this time – except fine lining and coats of arms. Interestingly enough, this car was one of a number of vehicles earmarked by the Pullman management post-war for modernisation, the work being undertaken primarily by polymer specialists Bakelite Ltd, although in collaboration with other outside contractors who possessed specialist knowledge with metalwork and modernist tendencies, such as J. Starkie Gardner of Wandsworth.

The décor was doubtless seen as a portent of a brighter, brave new world, but understandably, too, there must have been some misgivings from a commercial point of view about the consequential loss of 12 first-class seats in the 'Arrow' if it were to be used regularly. Pullman's General Manager, Mr Frank Harding (who travelled on the trial and inaugural runs), observed that for this trip the 'plastic car' would offer extra bar accommodation and would make 'a very convenient "press room" in which the [Southern Railway's] Public Relations Officer could make his contacts'.[26] (It is also intriguing to note, the Southern's Deputy General Manager who visited Preston Park Works to enthusiastically endorse the conversion work of *Car No. 5* was none other than Mr John Elliot – later Sir John – destined 13 years later to become the Pullman Company's last Chairman.)

At Dover Marine a repair gang got to work on the hot-box, but apparently the matter was too serious, and the car had to be removed from the train and shunted into a siding on the quay before the return journey.[27] However, on 1 May (rather than 25 April as had been widely anticipated by the Pullman Company management), this attractive vehicle once fully repaired at Preston Park Works, Brighton, returned again to the 'Golden Arrow' which it served until 11 June 1951.[28] Officially labelled as the *Trianon Bar* (II), it replaced the former *Trianon* (I) bar car (ex *Diamond*), which following a repaint cascaded to other services and became, briefly, *The One Hundred Bar*, to mark the centenary of Belgian Marine and, from July, *The New Century Bar* – the latter name which was very fleetingly once given to *Trianon Bar* (II).[29]

Even though the arrival of the train was five minutes late behind schedule, the special guests were however given an enthusiastic reception at Dover Marine station by a representative gathering of Dover people, headed by the Mayor, Councillor A.T. Goodfellow, reported the *Dover Express*.[30] The SS 'Canterbury' was berthed alongside the Marine station which as sumptuous as the 'Golden Arrow' train would provide from the following Monday, the second stage of the 8¾-hours service to Paris.

Mr H.A. Short, Deputy Traffic Manager of the Southern Railway, who had travelled with the train and his party were welcomed by the Mayor and other members of the Dover Town Council, as well as by Mr R.E. Sinfield, the Divisional Marine Manager at Dover, Mr H.A. Jewell, Chief Immigration Officer, Borough officials, and many others.

After a brief inspection of the Customs Shed, the party walked onto a gang-plank with specially decorated 'Golden Arrow' fabric covers, and joined others aboard the 'Canterbury'. This vessel had been thoroughly refitted after notable war service, and transformed again into a luxurious vessel from those who knew her at the Dunkirk beaches or carrying landing craft to the

Normandy coast. The 'Canterbury' was newly fitted with radar, and as reported by the *Dover Express* correspondent 'as she lay alongside the Admiralty Pier, it was possible to see quite clearly on the fluorescent screen a complete panoramic view of the surroundings. In the centre was the plan of the harbour with the SS 'Stuyvessant' just inside the Eastern Entrance. To the west, Shakespeare Cliff was the limit of "vision", sheltering as it does everything beyond'.[31]

In the main saloon on the 'Canterbury', the Mayor gave an official welcome.

The Public Relations Officer of the Southern Railway, Mr C. Grasemann, expressed his admiration advising that resumption of this service was probably one of the most vigorous signs that he had seen of getting back to some sort of peace and normality.

The Mayor proposed the toast of the 'Golden Arrow' service and the Southern Railway, and declared to everyone present that it had been one of the most encouraging mornings he had experienced for years. He further explained:

> '…when one had lived in Dover during the war years, when one knew something of the wreckage and devastation that the war left, and when one faced up to the problems of the future immediate and distant, to come to that glorious ship and to see the bright colour and decoration of the "Golden Arrow" train, was a tonic which had been the best I had for years.'[32]

The Mayor added that he looked upon that meeting as an earnest of the co-operation which would exist between the Town Council and the Southern Railway in the days which lie ahead.

Mr H.A. Short, in response, is recorded to have said: 'In the long years of war, the "Canterbury" had been almost continuously on active service. She started off with service in the Channel, and was in the hell of Dunkirk beaches. Then, in the dark years of 1941 to 1943 she saw service in northern waters, and had the honour of bringing over the first American troops to set foot in the British Isles, in Northern Ireland. From D-Day she played an important part in taking the British and Allies advancing armies to the Normandy beachhead. Later still, she was back on the short sea route bringing soldiers home on leave from the Continent.'[33]

During the later years of the vessel's war service, including D-Day, the vessel was under the command of Captain G.D .Walker, who was formerly in command of the Company's 'Maid of Orleans', which, like the 'Canterbury', was throughout the war officered and crewed by members of the Southern Railway staff. Captain Walker was in command of the 'Maid of Orleans' which was lost just after D-Day, at Dunkirk, where he won the Distinguished Service Cross (DSC) military decoration. Through her record at Dunkirk, the 'Maid of Orleans' would go down in history as one the most famous vessels in the Mercantile Marine. The steam locomotive 'Channel Packet', which hauled the 'Golden Arrow' train that day, was so named as a tribute to the sea-going staff of the Southern Railway.[34]

Captain Walker expressed the thanks of the ship's company for the messages of good will they had received 'with such a marvellous send-off he was sure the service would reach its former popularity and efficiency'.[35]

Arrival of the first post-war 'Golden Arrow' at Dover Marine.

After the ceremony on board the 'Canterbury', lunch was subsequently served to the special guests and other attendees on the stationary train which was almost to full capacity, by Pullman-attendants now sporting all-over white cotton monkey jackets onto which were pinned special 'Golden Arrow' lapel badges. The train had been backed onto the Admiralty Pier for the purpose – prior to its return trip to London. Despite rationing that was very much in force, the party enjoyed a menu which included soup, creamed Sussex chicken and mushrooms, and fruit salad, before returning to Victoria with an arrival at 4.40pm.

To great acclaim, and euphoric reports by the press, the 'Golden Arrow' resumed public service the following Monday, 15 April, seen off on its first post-war departure at 10am by Mr Alfred Barnes, Minister of Transport.[36] The BBC Home Service broadcast a world-wide Dover-Calais feature that evening (and subsequently) from Dover Castle and the quayside to mark the train's re-inauguration. The special programme also included interviews with the long-standing and well-respected Pullman Inspector Badger, and also people from Dover and Calais, on the conditions in the two towns, as outlined in the appendix – The return of the 'Golden Arrow' – at your service once more.

At first 100 minutes were allowed for the journey to Dover, but this timing was soon cut to 95 minutes. And by 1952, it was cut again to 92 minutes.

For April 1946, the train consisted of eight Pullman cars offering accommodation for 130 first-class (later reduced to 118) and 77 second-class. In the direction of Dover from Victoria and for the purpose of seat reservations, the cars were labelled 'H'-'A': *Lady Dalziel, Adrian, Niobe, Trianon, Onyx, Cecilia, No. 193* and *No. 154*. Spare cars *Montana, Chloria, Sappho* and *No. 194* all included arrow transfers except *Chloria*.

Reporting for *Modern Motoring and Travel*, Lindsay Shankland thoughtfully reflected upon the changeover from the austerity of war to the modified comforts of peace. In his view, the change was immortalised by the English poet and playwright, Algernon Charles Swinburne's line '… and blossom by blossom the Spring begins'.[37]

'To many passengers', Shankland explained, the pre-war 'Golden Arrow' was the last word in trans-Channel comfort, 'and even if one were not travelling oneself, it was a pleasure to go and see one's friends off at the Gare du Nord station, catching, vicariously, a whiff of French coffee and "Corporal" cigarettes, a glimpse of the Bois in spring and the strong Parisian sunlight … and the first swallow of what we hope will be, someday, a complete traveller's summer, lies in the restarting of the "Golden Arrow" service'.[38]

The 'Golden Arrow' cars at Dover Marine awaiting the arrival of incoming passengers. Car Flora of 1923 shows off its aluminium flag, No. '2', for seat reservation purposes. These flags were at one-time letters rather than numbers, before finally reverting permanently to numbers during the 1960s.

Beautifully painted and highly glossed, the 'Golden Arrow' Pullman cars had probably recaptured some of their former exclusiveness with their five first- and two second-class cars together with a novel bar car for the first time in public service, known as Trianon, as previously outlined, making eight cars in all. Interestingly, the *Trianon* Bar car (I) named after the grand and petit pavilions in the grounds of the Palace of Versailles, West of Paris, built for the enjoyment of Queen Marie Antoinette and her court, was available to all passengers on the train irrespective of class. (Originally a first-class kitchen car, named *Diamond*, half of the vehicle was specially redesigned to give the greatest possible counter space with 'stand-up seats' upholstered in 'Dunlopillo'. These provided a comfortable perch for passengers without obstructing the gangways. The other half featured a first-class saloon with armchairs together with a coupé compartment.) The interior floral decoration facing the bar area was finished in smoke blue with woven asbestos fabric for both the bar walls and curtains, as previously outlined in *Pullman Profile No. 2*, but much of its original exquisite mahogany marquetry panelling continued to adorn most of the walls, in addition to a prominent name panel behind the bar and above the Pullman coat of arms. Included for the first time, were two second-class cars, simply labelled in a central cartouche 'Second-Class' – or later occasionally obscured for no explicable reason with a plain running board (one vehicle had been swiftly converted from a first-class car named *Flora* to *No. 154* and featured 35 loose dining chairs rather than fixed seating, while another, a 12-wheeler, ran briefly with no identifiable running number).

A further novelty provided by the Pullman Company was radio 'public address' through 40 Vitavox loudspeakers fitted and dispersed throughout the train. These were supplied by the Acoustical Manufacturing Company, and operated by the conductor in charge, who, from time to time made announcements regarding passports, customs and the amenities of the train. (By the late 1940s, Miss Elaine Morley, the only 'stewardess' as she was called, rather than the habitual 'attendant', was employed on the train to broadcast information in French and English). On the first public trip down to Dover, light music was played intermittently, but this was soon dropped due to licence requirements and passenger complaints.

The train was notably resplendent with arrow and flag embellishments on the rostered locomotive, and huge painted arrows adorned the Pullman cars. These permanent arrows were visually attractive, but plainly inhibited the cars movement to other services, if transfers were necessary. As far as can be determined, they were progressively replaced from January 1949 when cars required repainting, by removable wooden and aluminium signs with spring clips.

The travel writer the late George Behrend once remarked that on his return home from North Africa and Italy after an absence of many years, he caught a glimpse of the 'Golden Arrow' at the Marine station. He was apparently 'overwhelmed with joy', and said so ardently in his correspondence to the author. 'What a marvellous sight it was to behold … everything about Pullman travel was first-rate … even the arrows adorning the cars all pointed in the right direction. "Flèche d'Or" faced France and "Golden Arrow" in the opposite direction pointed to London.'

*A glimpse inside Pullman kitchen car **Argus** of 1924, seen here in a refurbished state in 1946. Note: the partition panels have lost their intricate mirror beading, possibly due to war-time damage, as shown to great effect in **Profile 2**.*

At Victoria station, a new gated archway, brightly painted and similar in graphic design to one later erected for the famous 'Brighton Belle', was situated at the entrance to platform 8, the new Continental arrivals and departures platform instead of 2 as in pre-war days. It greeted intending passengers with the words 'Golden Arrow' in bold letters, 'Flèche d'Or' immediately below, and 'London' and 'Paris' flanking the tip of an inverted arrow. This archway proudly promoted the unique character of Pullman travel for many years, and later was refurbished with neon strip lights, until replaced during the mid-1960s by a simplified illuminated entrance board, using British Railways standard typeface.

While heavy military traffic continued to require accommodation, restoration of civilian traffic was still partially handicapped, and considerable use had been made of the port of Folkestone. That said, 1946 was a momentous year in the revival of once famous and well-known services,

Above: **Zenobia**, *with large painted arrows, photographed at Preston Park Works, Brighton, on 23 March 1949. The car is next to one of the observations cars used on the 'Devon Belle', although observation cars were never used with the 'Golden Arrow'.*
Above left: **Onyx**, *repainted and featuring new removable signage as photographed at Preston Park Works, Brighton, on 15 March 1949.*
Left: *A close study of the painted legend 'Flèche d'Or' of car* Cecilia *and arrow pointing in the direction of France. 10 March 1949.*

including: the 'Nord Express' by 6 May to Germany and Scandinavia; the 'Orient Express' by 12 July extended to Warsaw; the 'Arlberg Express' by 6 August extended to Budapest; and 16 December, the 'Engadine and Oberland Express' sleeping car train established once again from and to Calais. On 11 October 1946, just six months since its re-inauguration, the 'Golden Arrow' carried its 100,000th passenger. A small gold brooch suitably in the shape of an arrow was presented by Conductor Badger to passenger, Mrs Evelyn Steele, who happened to be the daughter of Sir Bernard Spilsbury, the pioneer forensic pathologist.

As reported in the *Dover Express* of 19 July, plans were afoot to return the 'Canterbury' to Folkestone when the Southern Railway had the 'Invicta' in service at Dover. This was scheduled for 12 December, when the 'Canterbury' introduced a completely new service between Folkestone and Calais.[39]

The 'Golden Arrow' gated archway was originally brightly painted in 1946, and as this May 1964 photograph shows, neon strip lighting has subsequently been fitted, illuminated when the train was at the station. The two ladies – Marilyn Hoggan (left) and Caroline Kirkpatrick (right) ran the London Tourist Board's information bureau at Victoria station.

In what was a mutilated Europe, the Pullman link and the improvements being made to rail travel became to many observers at least, a symbol that peace had again returned. And in their desire to welcome visitors to the devastated Calais, a temporary maritime station was constructed (later replaced by a purpose-built larger structure in 1954, while Boulogne re-opened a newly constructed station building in 1952). Bomb-damaged Dover and Folkestone looked forward to the future with promising civic plans to rejuvenate the town centres, as outlined in Chapter 22.

With fluctuating demand, all second-class cars were taken off on 4 May 1947, and the train's formation became all-first-class momentarily with cars *Zenobia*, *Chloria* and *Montana* being added, noted for forming part of the inaugural 'Golden Arrow Limited' in 1929. Seven months later, the London-Paris 'Night Ferry' restarted on 15 December, and included Pullman refreshment facilities as before, with a 16-seat 12-wheel kitchen car named *Monaco* marshalled in the non-sleeping car portion of the train.

The re-inauguration of the 'Night Ferry' with the Pullman car seen in the faint distance. This train was hauled by 'Battle of Britain' class locomotive 21C 156 'Croydon'. 15 December 1947.

23

Unusually, the Southern's Newhaven Boat trains were still steam powered over the electrified lines between Newhaven and London. This was because the formation of these trains continued to vary considerably, and required more van accommodation than was available in the normal multiple-unit electric sets which could work from the Harbour Station at Newhaven and not from the quayside. The second anniversary of the 'Golden Arrow' in 1948 was celebrated in style on both sides of the Channel with locomotive crew exchanges (repeated from the previous year); an on-board fashion parade with mannequins showing off furs, stoles and winter capes by Seigal, Jaeger and Harrods (during summer!); a buttonhole for every female passenger; long-awaited replacement badged crockery and embroidered napery; all this in addition to the presiding Miss Paris and Miss London flagging away their respective trains.[40]

In October 1949, second-class accommodation was re-established and formed a regular part of the train's composition until May 1965. A set of second-class Pullmans consisting of no more than two parlour cars running together in the 'Arrow' at any one time was supported by three additional cars in reserve (see appendix). Two of these vehicles were originally third-class, while the remainder were formerly first-class suitably rebuilt and remodelled.

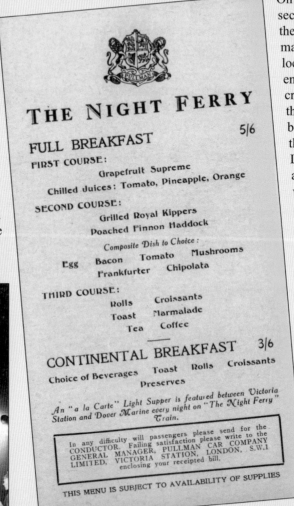

THE NIGHT FERRY

FULL BREAKFAST 5/6

FIRST COURSE:
Grapefruit Supreme
Chilled Juices: Tomato, Pineapple, Orange

SECOND COURSE:
Grilled Royal Kippers
Poached Finnon Haddock

Composite Dish to Choice:
Egg   Bacon   Tomato   Mushrooms
Frankfurter   Chipolata

THIRD COURSE:
Rolls   Croissants
Toast   Marmalade
Tea   Coffee

CONTINENTAL BREAKFAST 3/6
Choice of Beverages   Toast   Rolls   Croissants
Preserves

An "a la Carte" Light Supper is featured between Victoria Station and Dover Marine every night on "The Night Ferry" Train.

In any difficulty will passengers please send for the CONDUCTOR. Failing satisfaction please write to the GENERAL MANAGER, PULLMAN CAR COMPANY LIMITED, VICTORIA STATION, LONDON, S.W.1 enclosing your receipted bill.

THIS MENU IS SUBJECT TO AVAILABILITY OF SUPPLIES

On 9 December, several of the 12-wheel second-class cars running in the formation at the time, sustained superficial damage to their matchboard lower panels having struck a locomotive outside Victoria Station. The light-engine, a 'Battle of Britain' type, which was crossing from the main line to a relief line, ran through a signal at danger, and derailed before being struck by the empty stock working of the 'Golden Arrow' returning to Stewarts Lane Depot. The engine tilted over at an angle of 35 degrees after the collision, and was subsequently run into by an electric train leaving Victoria for West Croydon at 6.40pm.

All the Pullman cars remained on the rails, but the locomotive pulling the train received damage to its main frame, and a left-hand cylinder casting was broken. Eight passengers travelling in the electric train and three railwaymen were injured, but according to *The Railway Gazette* and the subsequent report on the collision, none were detained in hospital. By 20 December, Lt.- Colonel G.R.S. Wilson, Chief Inspecting Officer of Railways, Ministry of Transport, opened an inquiry into the collision.[41] The train was composed of the following vehicles: 'Battle of Britain' Class Pacific Locomotive No. 34084 '253 Squadron', Baggage van No. 1293, Conflat No. 39636 with *Car No. 99*, *Car No. 294*, *Malaga*, *Onyx*, *Zenobia*, *Trianon Bar*, *Chloria*, *Flora*.

The 'Golden Arrow' in collision outside Victoria station on 9 December 1949. The boat train and the derailed light engine which, after tilting over, was hit by a local train. The Pullman car nearest the camera is Car No. 294.

The post-war revival, 1946-1949

On 1 December, the 'Canterbury' went back into service after an extensive refit at Southampton. The vessel had latterly operated between Folkestone and Calais, in connection with the 1.30pm daily service from Victoria. At Calais, the 'Engadine-Oberland Express' connected with this service, providing through sleeping cars to Interlaken, and serving also the principal winter sports centres. In the inwards direction, the 'Canterbury' now left Calais at 12.35pm connecting with an early morning departure from Paris and an overnight departure from Switzerland. Passengers were due at Victoria at 3.19pm.

In the interim, the 'Invicta' sailing from Dover began to convey motor vehicles with their petrol tanks filled to capacity; previously it had been necessary to empty tanks before shipment of passenger vehicles. Only cars not exceeding 16ft. 9in. in length were acceptable for shipment by the 'Invicta'.[42]

Special fares from 15 May 1949, which included first-class Pullman reservations on both sides of the Channel, were widely promoted at £6 18s 7d single (available one month in advance) or £13 17s 2d return (available two months). Departure time from Victoria was at 10.30am with an arrival at Dover at 12.05pm. At this time, half an hour was required to transfer passengers from train to ship, and only 18 minutes upon arrival at Calais Maritime from ship to train. Paris Nord was reached by the 'Flèche d'Or' at 5.30pm.

The 'Flèche d'Or' awaiting passengers at Calais Maritime station, photographed from the TS 'Invicta' (1947).

Period of change and uncertainty, 1950-1960

By June 1951, a new modern-looking train with double glazing and 'New-Look' interiors had been introduced in England, as outlined in Chapter 26, which happily and fortuitously coincided with the Festival of Britain Exhibition held on the South Bank of the Thames. While in France, several *grand-luxe* 'Côte d'Azur-type' Pullman cars of 1929 with their huge reclining armchairs, spacious accommodation and extravagant Lalique and Prou interiors continued to work with some of the original 1926 cars on the 'Flèche d'Or' maintaining high levels of comfort, style and cuisine. (In fact, the last time a full complement of 'Flèche d'Or-type' cars were used, took place in the winter of 1934 between Paris-Calais and vice versa. The Pullman allocation thereafter included a mix of so-called 'Sud Express' 'Etoile du Nord' and 'Côte d'Azur' types until the outbreak of World War 2).

At this time, boat train services from Victoria were evidently still in much demand and, working to complex schedules and often utilising Pullman cars that first saw service on the SECR Dover and Folkestone workings 40 years before. Despite a great deal of discussion between senior management, the pre-war 'extra fare' Kent Coast single, and sometimes double car workings to Ashford, Dover Priory, Walmer, Deal and Sandwich and mid-Sussex line (before electrification in 1938), were not reinstated, other than specials or the nominally all-Pullman service the 'Thanet Belle' to Margate and Ramsgate introduced in 1948 (later becoming the 'Kentish Belle').

Even though the older vehicles were dated in their styling and construction, they each had a varied and often distinguished career. The 1910-built parlour cars, *Corunna, Emerald, Palermo, Sapphire, Savona* and *Sorrento,* were all previously rebuilt in 1924 to include a kitchen, pantry, saloon, two coupé compartments – one centrally-positioned – accommodating in total 16 passengers. Two cars particularly were unusual according to the Pullman works records. *Savona* briefly became a supply car and was used on excursion trains – being one of the last vehicles still retaining its original lake livery, as late as 1936, prior to being painted all-over umber.[43] *Corunna* was further remodelled with first- and third-class accommodation in 1933, and finally after N.A.A.F.I. service at the end of the war, both cars reverted back to first-class. Unlike any of its sisters, *Corunna* retained not only its original coupé compartment, but also the central coupé, which was later converted into a makeshift bar area with shelving and stand-up seats. Upon conversion in February 1953, it advertised the 'bar' facility by the application of large blue coloured transfers affixed to the corridor windows. In addition, *Corunna* received 14 new low-back dining car chairs and extending tables, working thereafter as an unclassed bar car on the overnight Channel Islands/St Malo Boat train from/to Southampton Docks. It was later withdrawn in February 1962.

Above: *A specially-wrapped packet of Abdulla cigarettes as sold to passengers on board the 'Golden Arrow'. Three varieties were always available: Turkish, Egyptian and Virginia.*
Left: *A glimpse inside the third-class saloon of* Cosmo Bonsor *following its 1930s remodelling to a composite. This vehicle reverted to first-class by the end of 1946 for boat trains and other special duties.*

Car **Corunna** *at Preston Park, March 1950. By some coincidence, during the four weeks ended 25 March, passenger train punctuality on the Southern Region reached the highest level for that month since the war.*

As regards the other cars of this type, *Palermo, Sapphire* and *Sorrento* each lost their central coupé much earlier in 1937, making one large saloon of 12 armchairs and another (original) coupé for four passengers, with the exception of *Emerald* which was remodelled as early as March 1930. Several were painted green and used by N.A.A.F.I. working in pairs as third and ninth vehicles in 11-car trains at the end of the war. The 1912-built cars *Alicante, Cosmo Bonsor* and *Seville*, as well as the 1914-built kitchen cars, *Daphne, Hawthorn* and *Ruby* (with the older *Clementina*), were concurrently remodelled to composite in April 1933 accommodating 12 first- and 14 third-class passengers, and again most reverting to first-class by the end of 1946 for boat trains and other special duties.[44] (*Alicante, Hawthorn* and *Seville* were similarly remodelled to their original nomenclature during the early 1950s.) The only exception by way of interior furnishings appears to have been *Ruby* which retained ten small dining car chairs in one saloon, with eight full-size armchairs featured in the adjacent saloon for much of its post-war existence. (At least until 1947, *Ruby* was listed officially as a composite car, but thereafter reverted again to first-class and employed on the 'Normandy Express' via Southampton Docks. It was finally withdrawn from service in January 1961.) In most other cases, only small cosmetic changes were made to the interiors of these older cars during the 1940s and 50s, such as the removal of the central door between saloons, while special tables and partitions were progressively fitted at seats 7 and 18, i.e. those facing a corridor door and Formica panelling progressively featured in the lavatories.

According to Pullman works memoranda, the original sets of 'Type C' table lamps first allocated to these vehicles generally remained a feature in most instances, although some replacements, were necessary during the early post-war period due to loss, damage or theft: *Emerald* was allocated a new (or reconditioned) set of 'Type D' table lamps; *Mimosa* 'Type A'; *Ruby* 'Type A' and *Seville* a mixture of both 'Types B and C'.

Throughout the 1950s many 'G-type' cars formed part of a boat train pool for services to Folkestone and Dover, although several worked at one time or another on all three divisions of the Southern Region as it was then known, in quick succession, either to 'The Cunarder' from Southampton Docks, for instance, or working on other special services, occasionally noted with some modern up-to-date vehicles, including 'U-type' *Car No. 303* (of 1952). Earlier during the period 1948-51, two cars were pressed into service on the 'Golden Arrow', each fitted with removable arrow boards, running with a mixture of 8- and 12-wheel vehicles. Other vehicles including *Daphne, Leghorn, Seville, Valencia,* and *Rainbow* (ex *Cosmo Bonsor*) had their timber equalised 'American-type' beam bogies replaced with standard Southern – or British Railways– steel 'leaf-spring type', as illustrated. (At least three of the four 'F-type' cars of 1923 were also similarly treated, as outlined separately. In line with periodic overhauls, the original timber bogies of these cars all required complete dismantling, and Pullman Company maintenance records reflect that costs were almost 50 per cent. higher compared to steel cars.) Rebuilt, modified and many reclassed as travelling conditions changed, this invariably led to individual variations appearing at the time, particularly as regard to interior and underframe detail.

Above: *Car* Valencia *at Preston Park Yard, 1957.*
Left: *The state arrival of Emperor Haile Salassi and his son, the Duke of Harar of Ethiopia, at the start of their three-day State visit during October 1954.*
Opposite: **Ruby** *photographed awaiting attention at Preston Park Works, Brighton, 1953.*

Unlike the all-timber 12-wheel cars which were earmarked for full or partial body sheathing of their matchboarding, the surviving record reflects that none of the 'G-type' cars were similarly treated with aluminium panels. Another interesting point appears to be a quite random feature with the fitting of replacement vestibule doors and sliding lights. During the 1920s, all the cars received new sliding lights, of three or sometimes four segments. While several vehicles were later fitted with Pilkington double glazing in the early 1950s, possibly as an experiment, others remained unaltered until withdrawn from service. *Florence* and *Regina* are noted for their three-segment sliding lights, contrasting with *Mimosa, Seville* and *Valencia*, which were each fitted with four.

During late June 1949, *Alicante* and *Mimosa* caught fire together in sidings, each sustaining extensive damage at the kitchen ends and adjoining saloons. Following full repair and renovation, they reappeared in service with simplified panelled interiors without any marquetry, re-profiled Pilkington windows, calor gas cooking and an eclectic mix of replacement furnishings from store. *Emerald* was almost completely gutted by fire in September 1955, but at great expense was later repaired and used as a training room, replacing *Sorrento*.

Mimosa *at Preston Park Works awaiting attention following fire damage to one vestibule, its kitchen, pantry and one saloon.*
Mimosa *(to the left) and* **Alicante** *(to the right) showing the extent of fire damage to each vehicle. Several saloon panels removed are noted in the foreground. Both cars were photographed on 1 July 1949.*

Mimosa and *Sorrento* appear to have been the only 'G-type' cars fitted with replacement vestibule doors featuring large oval panes of plate glass, in common with almost all other Pullmans built from 1924. In the case of *Mimosa*, two types of door were evidently used (in Pullman parlance types 'D' and 'E'): a wide flange type adjacent to the kitchen, and at the opposite end examples with simplified beading, possibly by reason of experimentation or recycling available spares. By 1957, many cars were ultimately allocated to a pool of almost 30 vehicles for the special Waterloo-Southampton ocean liner services. The exceptions were *Sapphire* and *Palermo* (and reserve cars *Savona* and *Sorrento*) and those cars running on the Channel Island boat train, with *Topaz* on the 'Bournemouth Belle'. These arrangements were in accordance with existing stipulations by the British Transport Commission, who had earlier purchased the controlling interest of the Pullman Car Company as governed by an agreement dated 1 January 1953 (and due to expire by 30 September 1962). Notwithstanding the provision of Pullman accommodation, the Company remained the train caterers on the South Eastern & Central Sections of the Southern Region.

The 'Golden Arrow' continued to remain as a daily service in each direction throughout the 1950s, and one, two or sometimes three 'extra fare' Pullman cars, providing a train refreshment service, continued to be featured in most of the Continental boat trains via the short sea routes. However, by 1955, the financial results for these services (listed below), made abundantly clear the increasing difficulties being experienced with these long-established services, and how their patterns and profitability had changed since their post-war reintroduction. Inevitably questions were periodically raised about their viability and prospects.

Golden Arrow	Continental boat train Services	Havre & Channel Islands Services
Receipts: £31,755	Receipts: £44,229	Receipts: £5,582
Operating costs: £14,756	Operating costs: £41,509	Operating Costs: £5,291
Overheads: £9,785	Overheads: £25,333	Overheads: £2,386
Net profit: £7,214	Net *loss*: £22,613	Net *loss*: £2,095

While the 'Golden Arrow' results were financially better than the catering services provided in trains formed mainly or wholly of railway owned stock, the British Transport Commission highlighted some of the misgivings of running Pullman services in general.

In truth, the real crux of the problem appeared to be service timing and an ageing stock. At various times, an approach had been made to the French railway authorities to alter the timing of the poorly patronised 'Golden Arrow' outwards service. This was considered 'not likely to be successful' and both the Railways and the International Services & Shipping Sub-Commissions closely reflected upon the Pullman Car Company position. While it was presumed that the British Transport Commission would decide global future policy, the Southern Region management considered they should make up their own mind and recommend to the Commission what was the most desirable form of catering service for the Region, not only for the forthcoming Eastern Section electrification but on the other lines as well. The question was put to the Traffic Officers, with recommendations on what form of service would best serve public needs and trains service requirements.[45]

Unhappily, the 'Golden Arrow' departure times continued to fluctuate considerably during the early 1950s – varying at the London end between 9am, 10am and 10.30am and, for the winter of 1952/53, an afternoon departure was introduced as late as 2pm (1pm from the end of British Summer Time), resulting in the outward journey being made via Folkestone to Boulogne. With the inward journey now being made from Calais to Dover again, the pre-war arrangements had been totally reversed, and a great deal of manoeuvring was additionally required to relay the stock from the outward arrival destination of Folkestone Harbour to the inward port of Dover Marine, a distance of almost 10 miles. The heavy train of eight Pullmans and two or more luggage vans required at least two, and sometimes three, small 0-6-0 tank locomotives to haul it up the 1 in 30 branch-line from the harbour station to Folkestone Junction station, which connected with the mainline. (Note: during this episode of change, *Car No. 54* a third-class parlour brake vehicle with van accommodation – remodelled from a kitchen car during 1946 and earmarked to run in the 'Devon Belle' – was briefly marshalled into the 'Golden Arrow'. The surviving records do not explain the reason for its inclusion, although generally neither brake parlour cars of this type, nor for that matter third/second-class kitchen cars, were rostered or listed in reserve to this specific service.)

During September 1954, the Pullman General Manager, Frank Harding, released information to attendees of an informal meeting of Chief Regional Managers, identifying the allocation/composition of boat trains, in addition to available spare vehicles.[46]

Golden Arrow	Extra Continental Services
1 First-class Brake	9 First-class kitchens
3 First-class kitchens	1 First-class half saloon/bar (Newhaven)
3 First-class parlours	1 Second-class kitchen
1 First-class half saloon/bar	
1 Second-class parlour	
1 Second-class brake	

Channel Islands, Le Havre & St Malo Services

4 Declassed non-supplement buffet cars

4 Composite First/Third kitchens*

(*These cars had probably already been remodelled to first-class by the time this information had been released)

By this time, too, the mainline motive power was variable. From 11 October 1951, for instance, British Rail standard 'Britannia' locomotives – normally No.70004 'William Shakespeare' which had previously been on display at the 'Festival of Britain', or No.70014 'Iron Duke', were immaculately turned out with small arrows fitted on the smoke deflectors. These were replaced by other Pacific locomotives from Stewarts Lane shed, often a 'Merchant Navy', supplemented occasionally by a lighter 'West Country' or 'Battle of Britain' locomotive. During February 1954 and March 1955, two British Railways experimental 1,750hp diesel electric locomotives, on trials, were used for a week, featuring a new oblong headboard with an arrow facing upwards made specially for the purpose.

However, receipts continued to decline and the results were considered serious enough to prompt a full study of the 'Golden Arrow' loadings in April and May 1956. These findings showed that the train continued to be very lightly loaded in the down direction, and although receipts were much better in the up direction, it was not a full train by any means, and the provision of a composite train carrying 'Golden Arrow' Calais passengers was at this time seriously considered to economise the mileage, engine power and train crews.

In the management meetings that followed, questions arose as to whether figures could be produced by the French authorities to establish if an altered timing made to suit them would materially improve the position on inward journeys. If not, consideration was given to reverting to the old timing and persuading French authorities accordingly. During the course of their enquiries, it became abundantly clear that the older Pullman cars (of 1910-1923 vintage) were far from favourable because of their bad running and amenities, while any conversion work 'would still have too much timber about them'. Indeed, the Chief Carriage & Wagon Engineering Officer on 7 May 1956 'certainly does *not* recommend that vehicles of wooden construction be renovated and covered with steel or alloy sheeting as suggested by Mr Adams [the Pullman Chairman]'[47]

The talks concluded that in light of a general policy in mind for Pullman services, the (1951 'Golden Arrow') cars, if available, might be better replacing older cars operating on established Pullman services elsewhere. In the circumstances, and upon guidance received from the Region's Chief Engineer, it was considered not possible for the 'Golden Arrow' set to be usefully employed as an additional Pullman train in another Region.

Furthermore, the management noted that in view of French feelings, they did not think it would be of any use to raise again the question of re-timing of this service which involved two sets of Wagons-Lits stock. It was suggested that in the future, consideration might be made of running new Grand Express European diesels in connection with the 'Golden Arrow' – concluding that enquiry should be pursued as to whether the service justifiably formed part of future Pullman policy.[48]

On reflection, with a generally perceived view recognising that the conditions confronting the Southern Region and the Pullman Car Company were due to the change in the type and habit of passengers travelling in residential and Continental services, it was found that passengers who travelled daily fuelled the pressure of rising costs more than did passengers travelling on business, and the character of passengers travelling in Continental services in particular had notably changed by the mid-1950s.

That said, there still remained a sufficient number of Pullman passengers to justify the 'Golden Arrow' and boat services, but passengers travelling in corridor coaches formed in these services were restrained in their spending. Other factors which completely changed the face of Pullman services were the greatly increased operating costs, including higher staff wages, very high maintenance costs, increased costs of all supplies and the heavy increase in the cost of fuel, and, not least, a marked reluctance on the part of passengers to recognise the true cost of Rail services. Under these conditions, all the Pullman services on the Southern Region taken together at this time were operated at a net loss of £30,489.[49] Catering on trains, claimed the Pullman management, 'has never been known to pay unsupported by a supplement revenue large enough to cover costs of maintenance, and amortisation and to provide a subsidy to the actual catering'[50] It recognised that in

Opposite: *The elegant lines of Pullman kitchen car Aquila, as new, 1951, is shown to good effect in this photograph reproduced countless times in popular travel magazines, and the combined press releases by the Pullman Car Company and Southern Region.*

Many years later, during severe icy conditions in December 1962, Aquila *again made news when a broken iron rod trailed on the track, causing short-circuits and the electric locomotive had to be replaced by a diesel. Although the* Daily Telegraph *reported that the 'Golden Arrow was stationary at Sevenoaks for nearly two hours, it incorrectly claimed that there were more than 1,000 passengers aboard, at a time when passenger numbers in the Pullmans averaged only 95. (28 December 1962).*

Left: *Unusual motive power – 1-Co+Co-1 Diesel Electric, No. 10202, hauling the 'Golden Arrow' passing Beckenham Junction. 8 February 1954.*

Several 'Flèche d'Or' Pullman cars (type Cote D'Azur) at the Gare du Nord, Paris, waiting for passengers prior to departure for Calais. 1963.

Merchant Navy class 4-6-2 No. 35028 'Clan Line' heading the 9.30am Victoria to Dover Marine 'Continental Express' for Calais through the cutting south of Knockholt on the 1 in 170 bank. 31 March 1951. A 1914-vintage Pullman car is the third vehicle in the formation.

addition to their responsibilities as a public company with private preference shareholders, they had a duty to the British Transport Commission who held all the equity, and expected them to maintain the services on a profit basis. Unless of course there was some very early reduction in costs of building, maintenance and operating, and unless the travelling public were prepared to pay more for the services they desired, Pullman could not hope to build and operate new cars successfully.

The Continental boat train services, in which were included railway special and sundry services, also operated at a continuing loss. Maintenance and depreciation alone accounted for £20,035 and Pullman claimed that 'it was impossible to reduce the administrative and labour costs any further'.

The principal difficulties attaching to this were the short runs to the coast, compounded with the problems of corridor service. Pullman cars were in the first instance not built or equipped for this type of composite service, and it was deemed impossible to carry sufficient equipment to serve a whole train. Proper service could be given to passengers travelling in a Pullman car, but even if the corridors were unimpeded, it proved difficult to give an adequate service to passengers

in corridors. It was subsequently suggested that these services could best be covered by buffet bars at which light refreshments could be served at the buffet bar, and that no attempt should be made to provide service in the corridor.

The new (1951) cars on the 'Golden Arrow' were valued four years later at £126,941 and, thankfully, continued to operate at a small profit, despite the late timing of the train on the down journey. The 'Flèche d'Or' connection from Calais operated with only three or sometimes four first-class Pullman cars by this time (and ordinary SNCF carriages and restaurant car), and it remained questionable as to whether the 'Golden Arrow' should be kept on the afternoon timing for the sake of this connection. If instead it were re-instated in the morning timing, with the normal connection Dover to Calais, it was viewed as potentially more popular with passengers who wished to get to Paris in good time, and perhaps no sacrifices would be made in abandoning the 'Flèche d'Or' link to Paris.[51]

In the event, the Continental Superintendent at Victoria corresponded with the General Manager at Waterloo outlining his increasing concerns and 'talking points' for future discussions. His closing remarks indicated the seriousness of the situation in light of the poor patronage of the

'Golden Arrow' which had been 'hastened by the SNCF/CIWL action to retire … frankly [making it] difficult to justify the continuance of an all-Pullman train London/Folkestone-Dover/London. Generally, the down service is very poor, and worse in Summer when the train departs at 2pm, i.e. after lunch-time'.

Later still, the issues regarding measures of economy came back again (and again) to be addressed, where it had been firmly suggested the 'Golden Arrow' could be made into a composite train with four Pullmans and the balance with ordinary carriages. While it had not been agreed by the Chief Operating Superintendent, it appeared on the face of it, to be a solution. However, it was also recognised that such a change could deliver a blow to the character (and snobbish appeal) of the train, and despite an agitated exchange of correspondence, such a solution was not immediately recommended. Needless to say, the Pullman General Manager, Mr Harding, was always against the idea of a composite train.

At the Superintendent's office, it was generally felt that the service should be advertised solely as between London and Calais, and that the outwards 'Golden Arrow' should revert to the morning departure and serve, for example, the 'Blue Train' serving Nice, Monte Carlo and other Mediterranean resorts. This proposition 'would please the Pullman Car Company, but would it please the French? … we must not let the name of "Golden Arrow" go; at least it has an advertising value'. The correspondent further remarks: "I cannot help wondering if we should not do better by cutting the Pullman cars out altogether and substituting buffet cars. We advertise in our publications that passengers in ordinary carriages can obtain meals, the idea being that this should be done from Pullman cars. In practice, it does not work satisfactorily – and we get many complaints, the up (Calais) Folkestone-Victoria service being a specially bad case. This subject raises an important principle…."

By 1957, further more poignant questions were raised at Sub-Commission meetings regarding the continued losses sustained by the Pullman Car Company on the Southern Region. (The figure for 1956 had increased to a net loss of £36,894.)[52]

Other than the Ocean liner Pullman services from Southampton – which will be covered in *Profile 6* – it was felt that the Continental and Special Services should in future be divided into two parts. It was understood that the Continental services, apart from the 'Golden Arrow', would be serviced by new British Railways Buffet Cars in which the Pullman Car Company agreed to operate. As an expression of opinion only, it was assumed that 'these vehicles would be non-supplement, but if they were attractively furnished and serviced with interesting snacks at a reasonable price, the services should become popular'.[53]

At a subsequent meeting between Pullman's General Manager and the Assistant General Manager on 13 February 1957 it was agreed that the Dover/Folkestone boat trains, except the comparatively modern 'Golden Arrow', would continue to be steam hauled until Stage II of the Kent Coast electrification scheme, in June 1962, when they would be fully replaced by multiple-unit trains with buffet cars. 'The present Pullman cars are old and will need replacement before then. It is proposed that they be replaced by new British Railways standard buffet cars, on temporary loan until the electric stock is available in 1962'.[54] On the Newhaven service, it was recognised the cars were also very elderly and 'must be replaced very soon'.[55] In sum, 10 Pullman cars would be withdrawn immediately from the Kentish services and no Pullman replacements were required, plus an additional 34 vehicles on other Southern-based services, making at this stage, 44 cars requiring replacement at this time, although a total of 56 were later converted into holiday 'Camping Coaches'.[56]

As far as the Pullman Car Company were concerned, the key to the replacement programme lay in new building of Pullman cars for the Northern Regions (from London King's Cross) and cascading all-steel cars built in 1928/30 (among others) from those services to the Southern. It was considered that this new building should be completed by 1960. 'Any later programme of building might well mean that old Pullman cars at present running on the Southern Region would have to be "stopped" as being unfit for further running and no stock of any kind would be available for replacing the "stopped" cars'.[57]

Pullman Camping Coach, CC165 ex **Montana** *waiting outside Preston Park Works, Brighton, to commence a new life in East Anglia. 1960. Note replacement vestibule door, removal of gangway and just in view a fitted flue pipe. This is also the first time that the new coat of arms has been displayed on a 'F-type' vehicle.*

The final years, 1960-1972

During 1959 and early 1960 considerable thought had been given to forming three five-car electric units, each consisting of two motor brakes and three Pullman cars for an electrically operated 'Golden Arrow' service. This suggestion had been prompted by the Traffic Assistant General Manager at Waterloo in an endeavour to stem escalating costs, proposing the transfer of some Central Section Electric composite Pullman cars for the purpose. It was also claimed that potentially this substitution 'would give a certain amount of second-class accommodation similar to the present arrangement, would minimise expense and labour and, give a most desirable feature in providing an electrically operated multiple-unit "Golden Arrow", with one spare unit'.[58] Protracted discussions continued on the subject for many months; all to no avail. In the event, having again sought the guidance of the Region's Carriage & Wagon Engineer, the practicability of converting the 1932-built Pullman cars was deemed an unnecessary and expensive cost, especially as the cars themselves were almost life-expired – having less than an anticipated five years or so remaining in revenue-earning service.

The steam operation of boat trains to and from Dover via the ex-London, Chatham & Dover Railway ceased with electrification on 15 June 1959, although as alluded elsewhere, the ex-South Eastern Railway route through Tonbridge and Ashford, to both Dover and Folkestone, went over to electric traction later, on 12 June 1961, including the 'Golden Arrow'.[59] Thereafter, immaculately turned out 2,550hp electric locomotives (later designated Class 71) with illuminated head code '46', took over the prestigious workings, which were soon accelerated the following summer, resulting in a 15 minutes saving off the southbound schedule and a similar improvement northbound. The first electric train was composed of the following vehicles, in order arriving at Dover Marine: *Isle of Thanet, Car No. 73, Aquila, Aries, Pegasus, Phoenix, Carina* and *Car No. 208* together with several ordinary Southern Region coaches and general utility vans.

At Dover and Folkestone, Pullman composite boat trains had almost all but disappeared by this time, and while several 1923-built cars continued to work on the Western Section boat train

The first day of the electric service – The 'Golden Arrow' leaving Victoria bound for Dover Marine behind Bo-Bo electric, E5015. 12 June 1961.

As outlined later in a **Modern Railways** *editorial during February 1963, a correspondent argued that the principal users of Pullman services continued to be businessmen travelling on expense accounts, who both ate and worked on such trains in order to waste as little time as possible. Although there might have been a strong case for more Pullmans on the long business routes elsewhere, the new Southern electric services with their improved timings came too late, as the popularity of the 'Golden Arrow' had already declined considerably by the early 1960s as most of its former business clientele went by air. (Modern Railways, Vol. XVII No.173, p.143)*

services, all were eventually withdrawn by the end of 1962; the majority had in fact been progressively converted to luxury 'Holiday' and 'Camping Coaches' during 1960/61. The remodelling work was undertaken at Preston Park and Lancing works, and the 'coaches', as they had become, were sold in batches to various railway Regions, often residing at specific beauty spots. A small number survive today in preservation.

Increasing air competition, rapidly expanding private motoring, cheap international coach services, compounded with the ongoing operating difficulties of the 'Golden Arrow', all took their toll on Pullman passenger numbers, not just in England, but also in France, where the once celebrated *Voiture Salon Pullman*, an icon of a beautiful age, was slowly and progressively being displaced by ordinary carriages. Up to December 1967, only two parlour cars were generally allocated to 'Flèche d'Or' (*Le train 19/82*) workings (and a number in reserve), served from an adjacent restaurant car, and more often than not the Pullmans attracted little custom. Since 29 May 1960, passengers wishing to alight at the Gare de Lyon for onward international connections could do so, for an extra supplementary fare of 1 shilling and six pence, following the stop at Gare du Nord. Although this extension had been previously introduced, and subsequently suspended during the winter of 1946, the cars were again propelled around to the XII arrondissement, in the east of Paris, by a tank engine, or more usually by a diesel shunter via the Petite Ceinture, a journey lasting about 30 minutes. Due to dwindling patronage from Calais, the two cars were withdrawn and substituted by a solitary Pullman car – a low density 'Côte d'Azur-type' with kitchen – which served light meals and refreshments only, while ordinary passengers were served from a Wagons-Lits voiture bar.[60]

The solitary Pullman kitchen car in the 'Flèche d'Or', photographed near Calais, 1968. Although trains 19 and 82 (as they were timetabled post-war) were often hauled by a type 231 steam locomotive to/from Calais Maritime, a change of traction took place from the summer of 1960 at Amiens, where an electric engine took over the final section to/from Paris.

Meanwhile, by 1963 the Pullman Car Company was now fully absorbed by British Rail and became a division of Hotels and Catering Services, prompting the new owner to find economies of scale.[61] An early casualty was the bar car *Pegasus*, which was removed from the 'Golden Arrow' during May, and transferred almost immediately to the London Midland Region. It operated in original livery on the London-Glasgow overnight sleeping car services, rebranded as the *Nightcap Bar*, while still retaining its running name and 'Trianon Bar' legend – prior to a full repaint in Corporate colours. Although occasionally required for Royal and V.I.P. workings, *Aquila* was allocated to work the 'Bournemouth Belle', while *Hercules* and *Aries* were briefly transferred on loan to the Eastern Region. *Minerva* and *Isle of Thanet*, which formed part of a dedicated pool of spares for the 'Golden Arrow' by this time, were each withdrawn in July 1967 and later earmarked for preservation.

Apart from the departure time from Paris being advanced to 12.21pm each winter, and the predictable out-of-step summer time dates from England and France which had invariably hampered the service with an hour's difference for certain dates, these times went unchanged until 30 May 1965 when 12.30pm became the departure from Paris throughout the year. Concurrently second-class accommodation was now deemed unnecessary and withdrawn permanently between London and Dover, which left the 'Golden Arrow' becoming a composite train of four or sometimes three first-class Pullmans (running in almost original condition) and ordinary second-class carriages outnumbering the Pullmans in its composition.

A day after the Southern Region's all-Pullman train the 'Bournemouth Belle' was withdrawn from service on 10 July 1967, the 'Golden Arrow' was berthed at Clapham Junction for the first time,

The 'Golden Arrow' waits patiently for passengers at Dover Marine station. Pullman car Isle of Thanet *is prominently in view in this June 1966 photograph. By 31 October, until 17 November of the same year, dredging work in the Western Docks at Dover Harbour prevented cross-Channel boats from using Admiralty Pier. The associated boat trains including the 'Golden Arrow' were transferred briefly to Folkestone Harbour. During this period, as reported by* Modern Railways *(Vol. XXII No.219 December 1966, p.682), the train was powered by an electro-diesel locomotive, which worked it through to Folkestone Harbour; on the up journey the locomotive took the train of 11 vehicles up the Harbour incline unassisted.*

Blue and grey liveried S307S ex **Carina** *at Clapham Junction yard attached to S308S ex* **Cygnus**. *Barely legible on the vehicle waist, the legend 'Pullman' can just be seen far right in this 1969 photograph.*

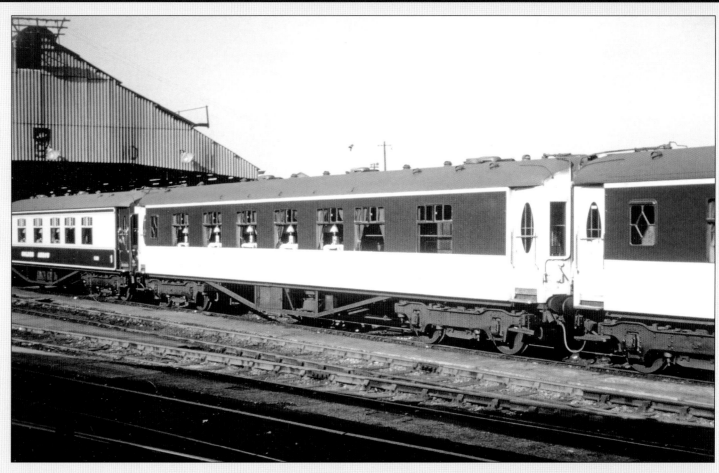

relocated from Stewart's Lane depot where the train had been victualled for much of its life. Other far-reaching changes had taken effect, too, including the on-board catering service, now provided by British Rail Catering, later known as Travellers Fare, a wholly separate company from the railway. Notable conspicuous variations included the title 'Steward' rather than 'Attendant' and a change of on-board uniforms – from the familiar monkey jackets with royal blue lapels first introduced in the late 1940s, altered to a light turquoise. Gone, too, were the special Pullman 'Golden Arrow' badges, replaced by brass convex 'discs' and buttons incorporating the new British Railways double-arrow symbol. The menu no longer proudly sported the Pullman coat of arms, but was replaced by the new British Rail symbol, heading what appeared to be a cost-saving exercise, by contrast to the elaborate bill of fare previously existing under Pullman auspices. Sensibly, an à la carte service still offered an enticing array of cold collation, grills and Dover sole, as well as sandwiches, buttered toast and cake. Blended coffee and speciality teas, champagne and a host of other drinks were also obtainable, but no longer listed was the habitual aspirin to help with the rigours of potential *mal de mer*. Refreshment receipts, similar to those used on the 'Brighton Belle', were also no longer issued on 'Pullman Division' headed paper, but displayed 'British Rail Catering' as noted in bold print, at the foot of each menu card.

The same month Horwich works undertook the task of modifying the last pre-war Pullman in service, *Car No. 208* – the former *Leona* (II) – a 1927-built vehicle, allocated as a spare 'Golden Arrow' car, which in keeping with the Modernisation Plan of British Railways (BR), adopted the new colour scheme intended for all nominated first-class Pullman cars. In the case of *S208S*, as it now became known, the former fixed 2+1 second-class seating layout it latterly possessed remained unaltered, but having been remodelled to first-class (again), a new aisle carpet was fitted, although it appears the original 1940s fixed curtains and table lamps (Type-A) were retained.

The new house colours which reflected the British national colours were to be monastral (or rail) blue, pearl grey and flame red. The blue and pearl grey colours were to be applied generally, but the flame red was to be restricted to smaller areas and used to emphasise the new symbol. With regard to the new satin-finished Pullman livery, a case was made for a special arrangement of the same basic colours to be used, allowing the standard scheme reversing the conventional disposition of the colour masses, with a broad blue band along the body side at window level, and pearl grey as the dominant colour below, including vestibule doors and car ends, as illustrated, removing the well-loved running names (and numbers) in the process, but retaining at lower body level the legend 'Pullman' in white lettering.

Although a shadow of its former glory, to many casual observers this new livery might have worked particularly well on the modern and air-conditioned vehicles that had been introduced to the 'Manchester and Liverpool Pullman' in April 1966, but quite clearly did not suit the traditional cars, including those of the 'Golden Arrow' where the care and meticulous attention previously given was now evidently disappearing fast. Even the occasional use of arrow carriage body boards (painted all-over umber) against a grey background gave a haphazard approach to business, and a lack of pride that was so lovingly bestowed on this once flagship-train. Incredulous as it might seem, the prevailing Pullman policy was misguided, for there was a mixture of two, and then three less than flattering old and new liveries used in formation together – from 1967 to early 1969. Initially, at least, the 'Pullman' branding and the cars numerical identity were evidenced on the newly-painted body sides in white standard font, but unfortunately this soon weathered against the pale pearl grey background becoming so faint that it was almost illegible. *Car No. 208, Cygnus* and *Carina* each received this revised BR institutionalised livery running with *Orion* and *Phoenix* still fully lined and in their glossy Pullman umber and cream.

Later, as a meagre concession to general reaction, the Southern Region management partially disregarded the strict Corporate ethos, and some might say thoughtfully adopted a modified livery of the same new colours by introducing simplified white lining in the old style and, in recognition of their special character, standard artwork to distinguish them from ordinary rolling stock. When *Perseus* was sent to Eastleigh railway works for refurbishment, a non-standard block Egyptian typeface wording advertising the service to which the car belonged – 'Golden Arrow' – was centred on the body sides with a blue background and flanked by '1' indicating first-class, as similarly adopted by the 'Brighton Belle' Pullman cars during late 1968/9. Sadly, something was lost in the process. Towards the end of the decade, only the Eastern and Western Regions retained the 'Pullman' brand name on their vehicles and advertisements, the Southern Region preferring, where possible, minimal descriptive language on timetables. Publicity material, including the 1968 leaflet 'Shipping Services between London and Paris-Brussels', for instance, discarded altogether for the first time the 'Golden Arrow' title, replacing it with 'I Cl. Pullmans and 2 Cl' together with a symbol to indicate 'Light refreshments available on train'.[62] However, all London-Dover (and vice-versa) supplementary tickets – now increased to 8 shillings or 40 new pence per single journey – continued to promote 'Golden Arrow' in very small print and headed with the words 'British Railways Pullman Services'. In his book 'Southern Titled Trains', D.W. Winkworth argued that the 'livery change failed to make a clear enough distinction between first-class and first-class Pullman, there being no indication [latterly] that these were Pullman cars'.[63]

With the exception of *Car No. 208,* which retained a 2+1 arrangement and its intricate marquetry panelling (and retiring later in 1969), the interiors of the other cars all received new metal framed and black lacquered tables and specially made dark mustard-coloured seating with adjustable white sponge headrests to a similar, but smaller, profile to those seats designed by

The modified 'Golden Arrow' livery. S302S ex Phoenix *awaits disposal outside Brighton at Lovers Walk, October 1972, following withdrawal.*

Wilkes & Ashmore in the new BR-built Pullman cars running on the London Midland Region. The kitchen cars now had increased accommodation for 28 passengers and the parlour cars 32, with just a few coupé compartments designated as 'non-smoking'.

As the seat density was fixed two and one abreast in the main saloons, all central partitions were by necessity removed to allow for more room, effectively creating one large saloon. The single seats facing corridors still featured small screens for added privacy, while the decorative mirrors and brass features on the bulkheads and mullion panels were retained, as too were collage panels designed by celebrated artist Mary Adshead in S302S (ex *Phoenix*). Dark blue-coloured moveable curtains were now prominent, which matched an even darker fitted carpet covering the whole floor space in each saloon, coupé and corridor.

Unusually, original armchairs survived in all the coupé compartments seating four, while that symbol of luxury travel, the brass table lamp, continued to be an attractive feature throughout, although each car gradually received a full set of yellow-coloured cylindrical plastic shades, displacing all the original celluloid tulip-type by late 1970.

The service requirement consisted of just four Pullmans, and another two cars as spare. A total of six were therefore selected for refurbishment:

S208S	Ex *Car No.208* (ex *Leona*)	parlour brake	(1927)
S301S	Ex *Perseus*	parlour car	(1951)
S302S	Ex *Phoenix*	parlour car	(1952)
S306S	Ex *Orion*	kitchen car	(1951)
S307S	Ex *Carina*	kitchen car	(1951)
S308S	Ex *Cygnus*	parlour car	(1951)

Almost by the time *Orion* proudly showed off the Pullman livery, coat of arms and running name for the very last time, prior to being outshopped in the new colour scheme, the solitary Wagons Lits Company Pullman car, a veteran of almost 40 years old with kitchen and 20 seats (*No. 4132*) was withdrawn from the Paris-bound 'Flèche d'Or' (*Le train 82*) on 1 July 1969. This day marked the end of *de-luxe* supplementary fare accommodation on the French train, although several other Pullman services from Paris lingered on for a few more years until 1971, including one to Lyon, and another as part of the famous 'Sud Express' to Hendaye/Irun on the Spanish border. Thereafter, the only other reminder of past glories at the Gare du Nord station, was an attractively appointed restaurant overlooking the grand concourse for many years, suitably called 'La Flèche d'Or'.

During 1970, both S307S (ex *Carina*) and S308S (ex *Cygnus*) were again repainted in what appears to be the more acceptable blue and grey livery, with full lining to match the other cars, although visibly the 'Pullman' brand name on the car exteriors had finally been abandoned. British Railways (Southern Region) continued to operate the service for another two years with sometimes only three, and briefly two cars running together, until 30 September 1972 when four 1951/2 vehicles made their last noble trips together – five months after another famous Southern train the 'Brighton Belle', per *Pullman Profile 4*, retired from service.

Throughout the last week in service the train was hauled by Class 71 No E5013 adorned with the arrows on its sides and the headboard with fluttering flags – and on occasion with all five remaining cars running together – but there were no prolonged celebrations on the scale given to the 'Brighton Belle' months earlier. That said, the final return workings, full with sentimental passengers and well-wishers, recognised that the end of a glorious era was nigh. British Rail produced special souvenir first-day railway covers; Champagne flowed and photographic interludes with on-board staff took place on the platforms to mark the end. The highlight of the

The final return trip to Victoria with a lady passenger being served coffee with hot milk at her seat by a Pullman steward. 30 September 1972.

trip included a number of BBC conducted interviews with notable passengers on the run down to Dover Marine, including one detailed discussion with Dr Alec Hasenson – well-known for his meticulously detailed published history of the 'Golden Arrow' in 1970, and who gave the author a great deal of encouragement and inspiration for this Profile.

Something clearly was now lost and assigned to history. No longer were there any regular Pullman services on the Southern Region, which in the past had been the true bastion of the Pullman Car Company. The tradition of personal service, the cossetting and the sense of something special had gone.[64] The handsome vehicles had not only disappeared, but so had the famous celebrities, stars of stage and screen and royalty, with their hat boxes, suitcases and trunks, who now preferred to take the jet aeroplane. Pullman travel on British Railways throughout the 1970s was generally viewed as an anachronism and had no place in the projected new image given by its management. The Pullmans were wholly displaced by nondescript electric multiple-unit trains which ran swiftly to the ports, and the customer – rather than the passenger – now took their own luggage, aver sacks and carrier bags aboard the Sea Link ferry, hovercraft or hydrofoil for destinations to Paris, Brussels and beyond. And epicurean meals were no longer a matter of choice on the rails; quick snacks, crisps and packets of sandwiches, and drinks from buffet counters were seen as the way forward.

Thankfully, the last five 'Golden Arrow' vehicles in service were purchased from British Railways after a spell in sidings at Brighton, in the company of a number of 'Brighton Belle' cars also put up for sale, of which three (*Cygnus, Perseus* and *Phoenix*) have been beautifully restored and are in regular weekly service on the incomparable 'British Pullman'. Recalling the so-called golden age of steam trains and the hubbub of boat train departures, they are invariably noted departing from London Victoria for the South Coast port of Folkestone in connection with the 'Venice Simplon-Orient Express', and with their 'New Look' interiors they are some regular passengers' favourites.

In a bid to save the remaining cars for posterity, several 'K- and U-type' 'Golden Arrow' Pullmans were at one time shipped over to France and used as static displays, and others of varying age are today on display at the British and French National Railway Museums in York and Mulhouse respectively. At Longueville in the Canton of Provins, North-Central France, three different types of British- and French-built Pullman cars in varying states of restoration, can be seen and admired. In recent years, many Pullmans have changed ownership, finding new homes often on heritage steam railways, such as the Colne Valley Railway, Halstead or the Kent & East Sussex Railway, Tenterden. At the time of writing, *Orion,* for instance, still resides immaculately preserved in East Devon, and is 'active in retirement'. Although it has sat majestically on a purpose-built track for almost 40 years – looking polished, serene and as grand as ever – it offers the visitor cream teas, light lunches and is licenced to serve alcoholic drinks to diners.[65]

Today there are other reminders, too, of the glorious and luxurious railway past. In Folkestone town is a small, unpretentious public house, appropriately named the 'Golden Arrow', which at one time sold local ale. And in the world of numismatics, the Bailiwick of Jersey released a commemorative copper-nickel £5 coin in 1994, designed by Ian Rank-Broadley, with an illustration of a 'Golden Arrow' locomotive carrying full regalia, whereas the Royal Mail issued their famous trains series of stamps in January 1985, one of which, a 22 pence stamp, featured the train at speed. On the Continent, luxury travel has not been forgotten either. The national postal service of Switzerland, a public company owned by the Swiss Confederation, issued a 1 franc 40 centimes postage stamp in 1997 depicting a 'Golden Arrow-type' Pullman car to celebrate 150 years of Swiss railways. More appropriately, perhaps, the Bluebell Railway in the heart of Sussex has promoted for many years their fully operational, steam-hauled 'Golden Arrow' train which runs regularly, and comprises beautifully preserved Pullman cars, matched by attentive attendants and silver service. One vehicle which has been painstakingly and immaculately restored at great expense, and is often cited in preservation as the 'jewel in the crown', is the one time 'Golden Arrow' kitchen car *Fingall* of 1924.

What of tomorrow? With increasing demands put upon the railways for improved and much faster train services to suit the business and leisure markets more than ever before, and potential possibilities offered via the Channel Tunnel, could perchance we one day see a dedicated 'de-luxe Eurostar' train promoting a *'Princely Path to Paris by the Golden Arrow'*?[66] Only time will give good advice.

A poignant reminder of the final 'Golden Arrow', 30 September 1972, with headboard, flags and arrows waiting to be mounted to the Class 71 locomotive No 5013.

The South Eastern & Chatham Railway Company Pullman services, 1910-1914

The running of luxury trains in the early part of the 20th century was nothing new on the London-Dover route. Comfortable 'voiture-salon' cars built by the Belgian Wagons-Lits Company for a 'Continental Club Train' had been introduced in the 1890s, while a short-lived Pullman service with a solitary car worked on the London, Chatham & Dover Railway a decade before. Despite great optimism, both services proved to be commercially unsuccessful. However, the extraordinary extent to which luxury travel had progressed following the acquisition of the English Pullman Company in 1907, by Mr Davison Dalziel, M.P. for Brixton, as he then was, Chairman of the Pullman Company and President du Conseil of the Wagons-Lits Company, is perhaps a matter of some surprise to the average person.[67]

In 1909, the Pullman Company management successfully negotiated an agreement with the South Eastern & Chatham Railway (SECR) to provide new and opulently appointed vehicles for service in selected Continental boat trains to and from the Channel port of Dover. These were intended to connect with the steamers to France, and in their distinctive style and handsome amenities became the forerunner to the 'Golden Arrow'. Billed under the slogan 'Pullman and Perfection', these services offered first-class passengers a far superior and pleasurable travelling experience to the Continent than hitherto known. The supplementary tariff was pitched at an affordable price, over and above the first-class fare, and was initially fixed at two shillings and six pence per journey.[68]

Savona *outside Preston Park Works, 1951. Note the distinct kitchen and pantry windows, and 'Continental Express' roof boards.*

Clementina *awaits in sidings for its return journey to London. For comparison purposes note the two types of vestibule doors used at this time on Pullman cars on Southern metals. Note too –just visible – the junior attendant sitting on the step immediate left.*

The inaugural special train comprising cars 'Corunna', 'Florence', 'Savona' and 'Valencia', together with a composite bogie coach hauled by SECR locomotive No 516.

From Monday, 21 March 1910 three parlour and three buffet Pullman cars were introduced to the Continental boat-train services, running in pairs, departing from London (Charing Cross) at 9 a.m. and London (Victoria) at 11 a.m. bound for Dover Pier, with return services scheduled at 3.20 p.m. and 5.20 p.m. respectively. The cars worked in three sets and almost all were given running names after cities in southern Europe: *Corunna* and *Florence*, *Savona* and *Valencia*, *Clementina* and *Sorrento*.

The total number of seats available in each train was 43. These were numbered and could be reserved in advance and, according to the contemporary report in *The Railway Gazette,* it was anticipated 'that there will be great demand for refreshment and drawing-room cars by passengers travelling to the various Continental cities'. It further suggested that the 'revival' in Pullman travel was due to the luxurious vehicles themselves 'than what the travelling public have hitherto known as Pullman cars [and] whilst people may hesitate before paying an extra fee to travel in

a vehicle really little better than an ordinary first-class compartment, they will gladly pay the small super-fare demanded to ride in a really luxurious saloon'.[69]

The Railway Magazine correspondent, Mr W.T. Perkins explained in his comprehensive article that an inaugural special train comprising cars *Corunna, Florence, Savona* and *Valencia*, together with a composite bogie coach, was hauled by SECR locomotive No. 516, previously exhibited at the Shepherd's Bush 1908 Franco-British Exhibition.[70] During formal proceedings taking place prior to departure, the Chairman of the Managing Committee, Mr Cosmo Bonsor, announced that 'if the public appreciated the new cars, the directors were prepared to add to the number, in order that they might form special trains and be used in express boat services other than those between London and Dover'.[71]

Valencia in almost original external condition at Preston Park yard awaiting attention. All blinds are lowered in this 1953 photograph.

Only a month later, it was reported that 'all cars had been almost full every journey … indeed throughout the Easter holidays, the demand for seats exceeded the number available'; and so successful was the experiment that facilities were later extended to all the London-Dover-Folkestone boat expresses, as well as to certain ordinary fast trains between London and the Kentish coast – under supplemental and enhanced agreements of 31 May 1912, 13 January 1914, 1 January 1919 and 23 October 1922.[72]

At a cost of almost £30,000 the contract for supplying the first batch of vehicles was awarded to Messrs W.S. Laycock Ltd of Victoria Works, Millhouses, Sheffield, while the timber body building and running gear were sub-contracted to the Birmingham Railway Carriage & Wagon Co, Ltd., Smethwick.[73]

Both parlour and buffet cars were exactly the same as regards their overall size, the principal dimensions and other features being as follows:

Length over buffers:	60ft
Extreme width:	8ft 7½ in
Height from rail to top of roof:	12ft 6⅜in
Wheel-base of bogies:	8ft
Vacuum brakes	
Centre couplings and adjustable side buffers	

As originally built, each vehicle weighed approximately 30 tons and became known by the Pullman Company as their registered 'Type A' (later becoming 'Type G' in 1932 to differentiate between the many other vehicles in their expanding fleet).[74] The hard timber and pitch pine bodies and underframes were built in one, on very similar lines to two Pullmans constructed the previous year for the Metropolitan Railway, but with spring improvements to suit the conditions of express service for which these cars had been built. Diagonal bracings were fitted beneath the waistrail, and these were constructed of ash. Between the cantrail and waistrail the body side was constructed in block form to ensure rigidity and to prevent creaking, with pads of felt running the full length of all the floor and side members. The floor framing was of teak and consisted of two layers of tongued and grooved boards covered with felt, laid diagonally and in opposite directions.[75]

The exterior dado boards and match boarding below the waist were of mahogany, and 'Sundeala' panels were used above, painted all-over in a 'crimson lake' colour (i.e. glossy deep red-brown) favoured by the SECR to match their ordinary carriages. All the cars were relieved with gold lining, and typical shaded lettering using stencils, but at this stage no Pullman coat of arms were carried.

The entrance vestibules, corridors and lavatories were panelled in figured mahogany, as standard, and a floor surface covered with black and white coloured interlocking rubber tiles, a familiar feature of almost all Pullman cars regardless of the lot, the only difference being the colours rendered from time to time.

The lavatories (of which there were two in each parlour car, and one in each buffet car) were complete with hot and cold-water supply, and fitted with a dressing table and mirror. The flooring was covered all round by 'Decolite', a hardwearing material then renowned for its robust and hygienic qualities. The wall panelling was invariably of mahogany, polished to a rich dark tone, and the pedestal washbasin and hopper were of white porcelain, forming 'a pleasant contrast with the panelling'. All fixtures were in lacquered brass.[76]

The heating throughout the saloons and coupes was arranged so that sections could be cut out to suit the requirements of the passengers using W.M. Still and Sons' 'atmospheric-type' controls.

An equipment of electric bells located in the main saloons and coupé compartment(s) were positioned flanking each window, as well as a bell push located in the lavatory. These were provided for the benefit of passengers who could readily communicate with the Pullman attendants.

The ventilation was carried out by Laycock's torpedo air extractors evenly spaced on the roof, in addition to exposed electric ceiling fans located in each saloon. For these cars, a novel reversing arrangement offered a constant circulation of fresh (moving) air – although prior to the fitting of brass framed sliding lights in the early 1920s, the large saloon windows each with clear plate glass could be opened upwards in two parts, using pinch levers and small handles.

The buffet cars, with a seating capacity for 19 passengers (24 seats in the parlour cars), were divided into two large saloons (one with a neat corner bar from which tea and light refreshments could be served), one coupé, kitchen, pantry and lavatory. The coupé compartment was considered likely to be of great demand for those passengers requiring extra privacy, and was placed next to the lavatory at one end of the car, arranged to seat four. Next to this was a larger saloon compartment, seating eight passengers, from which access could be gained to the other saloon, which accommodated seven. At the far end, a handsome lockable glass cabinet, for the storage of 'specially wrapped' cigars, confectionary, glassware and silver, was surmounted by a brass clock featuring Roman numerals. The top doors of the cabinet were in glass, and the lower doors of mahogany, all the woodwork being richly inlaid to various designs. Next to this was the 'butler's pantry', as it was termed in 1910, in which storage was provided for fine cut glass, crockery, wine, spirits and other refreshments. A sink with hot and cold-water supply was also provided from a copper tank located above the ceiling. The kitchen situated at the far end of the vehicle featured a gas cooking stove, together with shelves, cupboards, sink and preparing surfaces. As similarly noted in Pullman buffet or dining cars progressively introduced to other company lines, the kitchen and pantry floors were also finished in 'Decolite' for hygiene reasons and to aid easy cleaning, while a sliding shutter was arranged so that teas or other refreshments could be served from the corridor, if required, without having to open the (sliding) kitchen door. In the corner of the corridor, and opposite to the kitchen entrance, a large floor to ceiling ice chest was fitted, complete with numerous moveable shelves and racks for the cold storage of wines and fresh food supplies.

The decoration of each car offered a variable mix of rich and exuberant schemes based on the Pullman Company's interpretations of classical and historical designs, as per the appendix. *The Railway Magazine* correspondent went so far as to claim that at least four cars 'reproduced the predominant features of ancient French and Spanish castles. The periods adopted are the Renaissance, Georgian, Louis XVI, Adam and Louis XV.'[77]

In correspondence between the Author and the Curator of Drawings at the Soane Museum, London, it transpires that such schemes became increasingly popular at this time when a great revival of interest particularly in Adam and the decorative work of the 18th century is noted. (Adam had published a series of plates which were collected together between 1773 and 1779 and called *The Works in Architecture of Robert and James Adam*. Extracts showing the decorative elements were published in 1889-92 by J.A. Heaton in his very influential *Furniture and Decoration in England in the eighteenth century*. Pergolesi-inspired decorations were also re-published during the same period. His prints were collected together in two series, published between 1777 and 1785, and also 1788 to 1801, called *Original designs of vases, figures, medallions, friezes, pilasters, panels and other ornaments in the Etruscan and Grotesque style*.)[78] The reproduction of Adam and later Pergolesi plates, among others, became increasingly popular with the furnishing trades, and as detailed in other *Pullman Profiles* these were used to good effect in almost all Pullman car interior decoration from c.1910-1923, as well as other forms of transport, especially ocean liners.

The various and often unique interior schemes were all lavishly executed, and several cars including *Corunna* and *Sorrento* were recurring features in the *Illustrated London News* and more particularly the in-house magazine *The Pullman Car Guide*, all in an effort by company management to shape public opinion.[79] The following contemporary descriptions illustrate the vehicles' numerous design elements, in supposedly recognisable styles and used to great effect in press releases – sometimes erroneously labelled when describing the schemes – as specific representations of the growing interest in the 'English' (and by association the 'French') past.[80] Chapter 8 probes the Pullman Car Company's growing business acumen at this time, using such elements as marquetry to identify its personality, self-expression and values:

*Buffet car *Clementina* was described with a framework of mahogany and satiné quartered panels, inlaid with satinwood and green decorations in the apparent style of Louis XV. The carpet was a deep red velvet pile and the armchairs were covered in a soft morocco leather of a similar colour to match.

*Parlour car *Corunna* was panelled in fine wainscot oak, inlaid with holly wood in the style of the Renaissance. The carpet was originally a deep velvet crimson pile and a corresponding material was used for the armchairs.

*Buffet car *Florence* was finished in rich mahogany with panels of Spanish curled veneer, quartered and inlaid with satinwood marquetry in the Georgian style on the panels, friezes and pilasters. The carpet was a green velvet pile and the armchairs covered in green dyed morocco leather.

*Parlour car *Savona* featured finely marked satinwood, with quartered panels, inlaid with a green and red floral decoration in the Louis XVI style. It had a red velvet pile carpet and armchairs covered in red velvet embossed with a 'Fleur-de-Lys' pattern.

*Parlour car *Sorrento* was distinguished by its mottled pear tree panelling inlaid with shaded holly in a style known as 'Adamesque'. A deep blue velvet pile carpet covered the floor and the armchairs were originally covered in blue velvet to match.

*Buffet car *Valencia* was complete with a rose-coloured, fiddle-back pattern mahogany which was quartered and inlaid with satinwood floral decorations of the Louis XVI period. The carpet was a green velvet pile and the armchairs covered in green dyed morocco leather.

Unlike other vehicles forming part of the Pullman fleet at this time, one completely new feature, fitted from November 1910, was an electric lamp fitted over each vestibule entrance (inward-opening) door, which, by the aid of a reflector, threw a light on to the steps, proving useful during evening trips to assist boarding or alighting passengers.[81] Laycock's patented combined arrangement of centre coupler and adjustable side buffers, and compensated Pullman vestibules made it possible for the cars to couple up with other rolling stock fitted with either automatic centre couplings or ordinary drawgear and side buffers. The braking arrangements were of the vacuum type and the bogies, finished black, were of the four-wheel 8-ft so-called 'American-type' – to a new profile constructed wholly of hard woods including teak, fletched with steel plates.

The exterior paintwork of each car was finished in the standard SECR lake colour, lined with gold, while the running name was centrally located within a decorative cartouche. By very late 1910, one of the first of the Pullman Company's experimental circular coat of arms – flanking the name and positioned above the body ends – were indicated on each side.

In all cases, the work had been carried out under the close supervision of Mr. Thomas Powell, Secretary and Manager of the Pullman Company, and met with the approval of Mr. H.S. Wainwright, the SECR Company's Locomotive and Carriage Engineer.

Within eight months of the introduction of these services, *The Railway Gazette* claimed that the popularity of the Pullmans on the London-Dover boat train services 'induced the SECR to extend the provision of this development in passenger comfort'. Four additional Pullman cars supplemented the vehicles already allocated. The running names were: *Emerald, Palermo* and *Sapphire* (Parlour cars) together with *Regina* (Buffet car) which had been built at the works of the Birmingham Railway Carriage & Wagon Co., to similar dimensions and interior appointments, and furnished throughout by Messrs W.S. Laycock Ltd of Sheffield and London.[82]

Introduced initially to the 2.20 p.m. down and 9.5 p.m. up Folkestone Continental Expresses from 15 November 1910, these four cars worked in pairs (one parlour and one kitchen car) but more often than not, three cars were combined, offering light teas and other refreshments *en route*. Owing to the increasing popularity of Pullman facilities, a new service was introduced by

Original interior view of Clementina with a predominance of mahogany wall panelling reportedly decorated in the Louis XV style. Note the buffet counter and cabinet in the background. As with all the cars built between 1910-1913, Morison & Co. (under the control of William Robert Reid), were responsible for the entire interior for marquetry, panelling, ceiling panelling and carpets.

Original interior view of **Corunna** *with a predominance of wainscot oak wall panelling reportedly decorated in the Georgian style.*

The South Eastern & Chatham Railway Company Pullman services, 1910-1914

Original interior view of **Florence** *with a predominance of mahogany wall panelling reportedly decorated in the Georgian style. During the 1914-18 conflict, this car, with engine and brake van were stored in sidings at Victoria Station ready to start at a moment's notice with important persons on their way to the front. In addition, among others, a special leave train with Pullmans departed from Charing Cross.*

According to Inspector Badger, 'when the leave boat with the soldiers came alongside the quay at Folkestone Harbour, there was one big cheer and a rush to the cars. They said it was jolly good to see an old friend, the Pullman car, as it reminded them of peace time. Buttons were taken off the attendants' coats for luck'.

Original interior view of Savona with a predominance of satinwood wall panelling reportedly decorated in the Louis XVI style.

A 1948 interior view of Sorrento featuring pear-tree panelling, replacement arm chairs and 'type D' table lamps.

A 1948 interior view of Valencia with mahogany wall panelling reportedly decorated in the Louis XVI style. By this time, sliding lights, celluloid lamp shades and high-back fluted armchairs were standard. Note that each saloon has armchairs unusually finished in two distinctly different patterned moquettes. The furniture, including armchairs and gilded hat and umbrella racks with panels of brass treillage ornamentation, was identical throughout, although as noted above, each car offered different finishes of upholstery rendered in either soft morocco leather or fine cut 'Fleur-de-Lys' pattern moquette, the former finished off with gilt nails. The thick pile carpets were at this time laid in a variety of colours to harmonise with the panelling, while each table received a chased ormolu electric lamp with Adam-style embellishments of festoons, ram heads, swags and acanthus leaves complete with silk shade. (Only later, in 1919, were these lamps catalogued by the Pullman Car Company as their standard 'Type C' – with a weighted base notably of smaller dimension, compared to those introduced to the 'Southern Belle' just two years before, in 1908, per Pullman Profile No. 1.)

A 1911 exterior view of parlour car Emerald *showing off its experimental circular coats of arms and lined crimson lake livery.*

*A contrasting 1957 exterior view of kitchen car **Regina** with 'Ocean Liner Express' roof boards at Preston Parks Works, Brighton. The vehicle retains its original bogies, together with sliding lights of four segments fitted during the 1920s.*

*Although often seen in and around Southampton Docks, during a tug crew strike in April 1953, a 10-car train including **Regina** ran to Plymouth Millbay to collect incoming Cunard passengers. The train ran via Oakhampton, Exeter to Waterloo.*

February 1911 connecting with the 10 a.m. Continental boat train from London Charing Cross (via Boulogne) to Paris. A contemporary reporter observed that landing passengers, having experienced the rigours of a Channel crossing on one of the steamers, encountered a welcome 'daintily-served tea ready for them as they take their reserved seats in the Pullmans – marking a welcome advance upon the old-fashioned tea basket with its more or less uninviting contents'.[83]

However, even Pullman cars were not immune to unpredictable and adverse weather conditions. Forming part of the 1 p.m. boat express during late October 1911, *Savona* was partly wrecked whilst stationary on the Dover Admiralty Pier Extension by heavy seas. As a result of large waves breaking over the wall, damage to the value of £12 and 9 shillings recorded in the Company's Statement of Accounts was due to 'several [broken] windows and interior furnishings requiring attention' – the latter, apparently, were 'all afloat' momentarily in the saloons.[84]

Within a matter of two years, traffic on the Continental trains and Pullman receipts had steadily increased, to such extent that the number of cars employed was 'still insufficient' and would-be Pullman passengers were being turned away as all accommodation had been taken. According to *The Railway Gazette,* the boat trains were strengthened with four additional vehicles to meet 'the constantly increasing demand for this luxurious mode of transport'.[85]

The new cars with running names *Alicante* and *Leghorn* (Parlour cars), together with *Cosmo Bonsor* and *Seville* (Buffet cars), were built by the Sheffield based company, Cravens Ltd., with interior decoration and furnishings having been supplied by Messrs. W.S. Laycock, and again under the critical eye and approval of the SECR Locomotive and Carriage Engineer, Mr Harry S. Wainwright.

The first vehicle delivered from the Builders' was buffet car, *Cosmo Bonsor,* which formed part of a ceremony held at Charing Cross Station, having been specially named after Sir Henry Cosmo Orme Bonsor (1848-1929), 1st Baronet, DL, an English brewer, businessman and a Conservative politician who sat in the House of Commons from 1885 to 1900. A friend of Davison Dalziel, Bonsor was credited with the arranging the amalgamation of the South-Eastern Railway and the London, Chatham & Dover Railway in 1899, and became Chairman of the Managing Committee and an advocator of Pullman travel. The car was named in his honour, and decorated throughout in 'richly inlaid figured mahogany and satinwood of Pergolesi treatment'.[86]

In general design, this and the other vehicles differed very little from those constructed by the Birmingham Company during 1910, although the standard Pullman coat of arms introduced only in 1911 was now in evidence flanking the running name. All the interior decorations were reportedly rich in silk damask, with a new design of ormolu hat rack and high-quality upholstery, while the mahogany vestibule doors and end windows featured noticeably wider bevelled edge plate glass than previously known, with the car identity noted in fine large gold script on the inside of each door, in a font approximating 'Italicised Arial'. For the record, the remaining cars were decorated in the following known styles:

*Buffet car *Seville* was finished 'in fine mahogany with beautiful oval panels of curl veneer, giving a rich effect; the panelling enriched with shaded inlays in Georgian style, the principal motifs being oval in form with shaded festoons of flowers'. The chairs were covered with dyed green leather with gilt nails to match the deep pile green carpet. A feature of the saloon was the bow front show cabinet surmounted by a clock.

*Parlour car *Alicante* was 'panelled throughout in pear tree with shaded holly inlays. A new feature is introduced by the adoption of Louis XV as the style of decoration, and the exquisitely designed panels are taken in this instance the whole height of the panelling'. The chairs were upholstered in a blue velour and the carpets in the same harmonious colouring.

*Parlour car *Leghorn* provided 'an entirely new feature in the use of grey sycamore for the panelling, inlaid with a white wood richly shaded. The style of the car is of Louis XVI period and the essence of refinement. The details of the inlaid work have been carried out with great care, so as to preserve purity of style'. The chairs were upholstered in crimson velvet of Louis XVI design and the carpet was of the same design.

Pullman cars were first introduced into the London (Charing Cross)-Folkestone Harbour boat trains initially with *Cosmo Bonsor* on 7 May 1912, and the remaining cars followed in phases, prior to year-end. Several were allocated to the daily 2.20 p.m. service, returning from Folkestone at 9.5 p.m. Seats could be booked in advance at Charing Cross or at Victoria stations; the offices of Messrs Thos. Cook & Son, Ludgate Circus; the International Sleeping Car Co, 20 Cockspur Street, London; or overseas, in Paris, at the SECR Co.'s Agency at Rue du 4 Septembre, and Messrs. Thos. Cook & Son's Offices.

*A 1912 exterior view of **Cosmo Bonsor**, as built, in original crimson lake livery, sporting the Pullman Company coat of arms. Interesting features include roof rain strips, brass window bars (removed following the fitting of sliding lights) and shaded running name within the decorative cartouche. Much later, during October 1936, this vehicle is recorded to have received 8,550 hours of work at Preston Park at a cost of £81 – almost half its valuation a year later.*

A 1948 interior view of Seville with a predominance of mahogany panelling and decoration reportedly in the Georgian style. By this time, sliding lights, celluloid lamp shades and high-back fluted armchairs were standard. Note that each saloon has armchairs unusually finished in two distinctly different patterned moquettes. This was probably due to post-war shortages of luxury fabric (see a similar arrangement on page 54).

A 1950s exterior of Seville *at Preston Park Works, Brighton. As expected by this time, of course, there is no trace of damage sustained by enemy action involving this (and many other cars including* Emerald, Palermo *and* Sorrento) *at Preston Park Yard, 25 May 1943.*

A 1951 interior view of the restored and wholly redecorated Alicante following significant fire damage in 1949. The wall panels are devoid of costly marquetry and replacement hat racks, to a similar pattern used in some third-class cars, are now evident.

Above: *An original interior view of* **Leghorn** *with a predominance of grey sycamore panelling reportedly decorated in the Louis XVI style. The marketing efforts made by the Pullman Company and railway company extended to the uniform cleanliness of the cars both inside and out.*

Left: *A 1948 exterior view of* **Alicante** *at Preston Park Works, Brighton. At this time, this vehicle still retained its original bogies, but these were replaced by 1951.*

A Pullman Conductor travelled daily on the boats from Calais to Dover and Boulogne to Folkestone for the purpose of booking seats for passengers who had not previously secured accommodation.

By December 1912, the total number of Pullman cars running on the SECR, including the dining car *Shamrock* (outlined in a subsequent chapter), had increased to 15.

For the care and maintenance of the cars once in service, one of the surviving Articles of Agreement between the Pullman Company and the SECR Companies' Managing Committee, makes for fascinating reading. Dated 13 January 1914 (supplementing Clause 16 of the Principal Agreement of 31 May 1912, and cancelled with effect from 4 December 1925) it states:

A 1950s exterior view of **Leghorn** *at Battersea.*

The South Eastern & Chatham Railway Company Pullman services, 1910-1914

'… it was agreed that for the first twelve months after delivery of any new car thereunder at the expense of the Pullman Company and thereafter at their own expense, keep the bodies of the said cars and the wheels, trucks, platforms, drawbars, buffers, vestibules, automatic brakes and couplings in good order and repair.[87]

The Pullman Company were now 'desirous of themselves painting and varnishing the exteriors of the said cars and of being credited by the Managing Committee with the cost of such work'. It transpired that as from 1 January 1914, this work would be conducted by the Pullman Company, and 'that a sum of £17 per car per annum shall be payable to them, 12 months after delivery of such car'.[88]

And unlike agreements already in place with other railway companies existing at the time, the 'South Eastern contract is somewhat different, it runs as a whole until 1931 [later revised], but it provides that all new cars supplied shall have a life under the full terms of the contract for seventeen years from the date of delivery of such cars to the Company'.[89]

Just prior to the outbreak of the Great War in 1914, five additional cars of similar dimension and livery were delivered by the Birmingham Railway Carriage & Wagon Company Ltd., to satisfy the growing demand for Pullman facilities on boat train service. The SECR allocation of vehicles had now increased to an optimum of 20 and a joint concerted effort by the railway company and the Pullman Company was made to market the various services. These up-to-date cars were given running names after genus species of herb or laurel, as

Right: *An original interior view of* Topaz *with a predominance of satinwood panelling and furniture in view.*

An original 1914 exterior view of Topaz *as new. Note particularly the saloon and coupé windows are constructed of one section; rather than the usual two portions. In order to open these, grab rails, as faintly seen allowed for a slight tilting and raising of the window mechanism for fresh air. An unusual short-lived feature for this last batch of 'A-type cars'.*

A glimpse inside the coupé compartment of **Topaz** *highlighting its delicate floral inlays of dyed veneers and sandalwood. The 1930s armchairs are covered with a post-war cut moquette shown to good effect also on page 61.*

well as cardinal gemstones: *Mimosa* and *Topaz* (Parlour cars) together with *Daphne, Hawthorn* and *Ruby* (Buffet cars), each with a tare weight of between 31 and 32 tonnes, with 'strikingly attractive almond wood and satinwood interiors for the parlour cars, and Spanish mahogany in the Pergolesi style for the buffet cars'. They all entered revenue-earning service by March 1914.[90]

One of the first recorded journeys that gave prominence to this final set of 'A-type' cars was on the occasion when the Pullman Chairman, Davison Dalziel, in his capacity as M.P. for Brixton made a trip from Brussels to London to take part in the division on the second reading of the Welsh Disestablishment Bill at the House of Commons. (The Bill was in fact politically and historically significant as one of the first pieces of legislation to apply specifically to Wales, as opposed to the wider legal entity of England and Wales.) Dalziel travelled in *Ruby,* which had just been fitted with a short-lived, 'experimental wireless telephone' (sic) offering light musical entertainment for passengers. The car formed a special, coupled to two bogie brakes drawn by engine No. 36, and ran from Dover Pier to Charing Cross, the train reaching its destination in 1 hour and 23 minutes at an average speed of 57.29 mph.[91]

With war looming, all the SECR Pullman services were promptly withdrawn by the end of July and many cars stored for the duration. With the completion of the Admiralty Harbour at Dover, which almost immediately played host to the Dover Patrol – a Royal Navy command forming a discreet unit to prevent enemy German shipping from entering the English Channel *en route* to the Atlantic – and was the departure point for many thousands of soldiers leaving British soil for the last time, a group of Pullmans (*Daphne* and *Regina* recorded among others) were made readily available to convey the Prime Minister, ministerial and military top brass, including Sir Douglas (Earl) Haig, Commander of the British Expeditionary Force, on their various visits to the Western Front. Often marshalled into troop trains, these were also used by members of the royal family, especially King George V for special journeys to the Kentish ports.[92]

A mid 1950s exterior view of **Mimosa** *at Preston Park Works, Brighton, awaiting attention.*

A 1950 interior view of Mimosa *with framed panels depicting sprays of mimosa flowers and background panelling painted yellow and cream. Just months later on 5 August, the vehicle became derailed at the entry of the Clapham Junction carriage and wagon shop yard with one bogie dropping off the track. Rerailing was achieved with a local crane, possibly that from Nine Elms, and a gang of about a dozen men.*

A 1950s exterior view of **Daphne** *at Preston Park Works, Brighton.*

The Queenborough Pier Pullman dining car service

On 1 April 1911, a new Pullman car, specifically labelled 'a dining car', resplendent in crimson-lake livery, elaborately lined and given the running name of *Shamrock*, was attached to the 8.35 pm down SECR's Continental express from Victoria to Queenborough Pier on the Isle of Sheppey. It was advertised to return the following day on the 6.25 am up Continental express, serving breakfast. The contemporary notice by *The Railway Gazette* claimed this new arrangement was specially made for the convenience of passengers travelling to and from the Netherlands, Germany and Northern Europe with the Zeeland Steamship Company's service to the Dutch harbour town of Vlissingen (historically called 'Flushing' in English).[93]

With a tare weight of 33 tons and riding on American-style equalised 4-wheel bogies, *Shamrock* was designed with a similar exterior profile to *Clementina, Florence* and *Valencia* introduced a year before on the London-Dover boat trains, and built at the works of the Birmingham Railway Carriage & Wagon Company at Smethwick, but unlike most other similar-type Pullman car interiors at that time, it featured no private coupé compartment. Otherwise furnished and lavishly decorated in unmistakeable Pullman-style, it possessed just one large open saloon from end to end measuring 27 ft. 5¼ in. in length, fitted with tables and moveable upright dining chairs to accommodate 24 first-class passengers, 2+1 abreast in four bays.

In addition, there was a mahogany panelled lavatory with oval light, located at the opposite end to the kitchen, complete with w.c., hot and cold-water supply and vanity unit and a pantry 7 ft. 10¾ in. long, fitted with cabinets, shelving and ice chest. Adjoining the pantry was a kitchen with gas cooking range, shelving, a side board and cupboards.

The interior wall panels of the saloon featured richly figured mahogany with shaded satinwood, to a design said to be 'Chippendale' in character. The ceiling was painted white with a lightly decorated flat panel centre. The plate glass top tables were of mahogany and each complete with a table lamp (later designated as 'Type-C') featuring Adam-style embellishments, together with green and rose coloured pleated silk shade. The small moveable dining-type chairs were finished in soft Morocco leather, dyed green, buttoned and held in place by large gilt studs. A deep red pile carpet and green figured blinds of fine damask silk gave contrast and colour to the interior.

Electric lighting throughout using bracket lamps (S-shaped, torpedo-type) and recessed ceiling bulbs spaced out at equal intervals with glass tulip shades, 'brilliantly lit the car interior'.

Just a month after introducing the new facility, the Zeeland Company's vessels moved from Queenborough to Folkestone (and, later still, to Harwich in 1927), all for strategic reasons. Although known surviving Pullman records appear nebulous at this time, photographic evidence

A rather poor, but rare, interior view of Shamrock, dimly showing the passenger saloon and seating arrangement. The vehicle dimensions for the record were 57 ft. 6 in. over vestibules in length; 8 ft. 6 in. wide and from rail to the top of roof 12 ft. 6⅞ in.

suggests that *Shamrock* continued to operate briefly on the Flushing day services, but within months moved operation to and from Folkestone where the service finally ceased. The car was thereafter noted as withdrawn from service in 1916, and apparently saw the remainder of the Great War in store. After the hostilities, *Shamrock* was earmarked for 'light refurbishment' and, within a short time given its availability, was offered by the Pullman Company to the Caledonian Railway Traffic Committee as 'a temporary transfer' (at first), supplementing their fleet of cars running in Scotland under contract on various circuits. The Caledonian agreed, and with a new identity it became *Duchess of Gordon,* finished-off with the new Pullman livery of umber and cream, and delivered to the railway company during August 1919. Upon arrival modifications are recorded to the buffers and brakes at the expense of the Pullman Car Company. Later, in 1927, the vehicle was apparently remodelled internally and, under the auspices and eventual ownership of the London, Midland & Scottish Railway in 1933, it became one of a fleet of ex- Pullmans running as a 'restaurant car' until late 1937. It survived as a store into the 1960s before being condemned.[94]

An artist's impression of the bulkhead panelling and decorative scheme, annotated as 'Chippendale' in character (1910).

The Continental services – seafaring vessels

A complete range of Continental services between London and Dover, Folkestone and Newhaven promoted at one time or another either first-, second- and third-class Pullman car facilities during the 1920s, which in turn connected with increasing numbers of first- and later first- and second-class Pullman expresses from Calais, Boulogne and Dieppe to either Paris, Brussels, Cologne and other destinations.

The Southern Railway's 'Continental Pullman Express' (and its later incarnation into the 'Golden Arrow') was familiar to many travellers on the short-sea route, as they ran in connection with the various sleeping car expresses to all parts of Europe. The SS 'Canterbury' used in conjunction with the 'Golden Arrow' from 1929 was considered one of the finest vessels' on the English Channel, and in the early 1930s was joined by the 'Côte d'Azur', which coincided with the introduction of a night service between Folkestone and Dunkirk. Steamers of the A.L.A. Steamship Company maintained the passage across the Channel and sleeping accommodation was provided on board these vessels. Express trains of the Southern Railway, invariably with Pullman facilities, conveyed passengers between London (Victoria) and Folkestone Harbour, while through trains also ran from Dunkirk to Paris, Brussels and Basel, and vice versa.

In connection with the Dover-Ostend steamer services, two, three or more Pullman cars ran together or, dependant on class, were dispersed in all the Continental services to and from Dover. The 'Ostend-Cologne Pullman Express' which ran from Ostend quay in connection with the morning service from London via Dover enabled the journey between Ostend and the Belgian capital to be made in about an hour, and, moreover, was the quickest – and only Pullman – service to penetrate Germany.[95]

The steamers, *Princess Astrid, Prince Leopold, Prince Charles* and *Prinses Josephine-Charlotte,* ran frequently between Dover and Ostend.

The scheme of renewing the Dover-Ostend fleet started in 1929 with the introduction of *Prince Baudouin* which was the first motor mail vessel to be used in a Cross-Channel service. This vessel, the 28th built by Messrs. Cockerill for the Dover-Ostend Line, had a gross tonnage of 2,750 and was fitted with two 12-cylinder motors, each capable of reaching a power of 8,500 h.p. Increased passenger accommodation had been provided on this new vessel, and a particular feature was a roomy verandah, or garden lounge, affording a direct view of the sea forward of the vessel, through large bay windows.[96]

Another new vessel for the Dover-Ostend route, the *Prins Albert*, constructed in Antwerp, on similar lines to the *Prins Baudouin*, entered service in late 1937.

Pullman cars also increasingly ran on special Ocean Liner Expresses between London Waterloo and Southampton Docks, and many of the vehicles used particularly after World War 2 were some of the company's veterans, having previously seen service on the London-Dover boat trains between 1910 and 1939. The journey of 79 miles was covered in one hour thirty-five minutes and details of these service will be covered in *Pullman Profile 6*.

A novel Cross-Channel train and motor-car ferry service operated between Dover and Dunkirk for the conveyance of both passengers and merchandise. Three new 'Train Ferry' steamers, the *Twickenham Ferry, Hampton Ferry*, and *Shepperton Ferry*, each with accommodation for 500 passengers, had been constructed specially for this ferry service. Embodying all the requirements of modern sea travel of the mid-1930s, these vessels included luxurious private cabins, lounges and restaurants. Through first- and second-class sleeping cars ran every night from London (Victoria) to Paris (Nord) and vice versa, via the 'Train Ferry', and light meals or refreshments

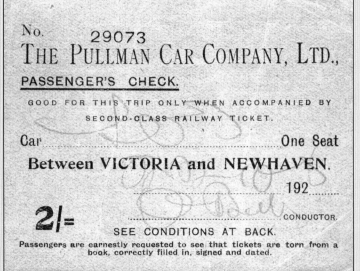

were provided in a Pullman car which was taken off at Dover (from 1936-1939 and 1947-1949). At one time or another, at least three vehicles are known to have been allocated in turn to this service; each with specially adapted gangway connections: *Car Nos. 17* and *19* and *Monaco*.[97]

The new 'Train Ferry' steamers could carry a train of 12 sleeping cars, or, alternatively, 40 loaded goods wagons. For this purpose, four lines of rails over the greater part of the train space had been provided, and at the stern these converged into two tracks by which the trains passed on to the shore across a drawbridge at the end of the dock.

The speed of the vessels that ran in the 'Ferry Service' averaged 15 knots, but were capable of steaming at over 17½ knots when required. On the Newhaven route, a first-class Pullman car service (and at one time briefly by one second-class car) continued to connect with sailings to Dieppe.[98]

The second-class cars allocated to this service, were originally built as third-class cars in 1923 for the London & North Eastern Railway with running *Nos. 51* and *50*. Upon transfer to the Newhaven train they ran briefly as second-class *Nos. 1* and *2* then renumbered again in February 1927 upon withdrawal of second-class facilities to third-class *Nos. 19* and *17* (taking these numbers when two elderly cars previously downgraded and bearing the same numbers were withdrawn). While the Southern Railway had no 'objection to two second-class cars being used', concern was voiced regarding 'so many restrictions upon running of Pullman cars, owing to the many types in existence', and they wanted 'to guard against difficulties in this direction'.[99]

By 1933 the turbine steamer 'Brighton', of 306 feet long and accommodating 1,450 passengers, built for the Southern Railway's Cross-Channel Services, made its debut. The 'Brighton' was the fastest steamer of her size in the world and had an impressive speed of 25 knots.[100]

By comparison, on the London & North Eastern Railway lines, daily Continental services with first- and second-class Pullman accommodation ran on the Royal Mail route via Harwich between London (Liverpool Street) and Hook of Holland, Flushing and Antwerp (and a Summer service only to Zeebrugge) departing 19.42 and 20.30 respectively. (It is anticipated that these services and those from Southampton Docks will feature in *Pullman Profile No. 6.*)

SOUTHERN RAILWAY

GOLDEN ARROW SERVICE.

REDUCTION IN FARE

and revised timings from

MAY 15th, 1931.

LONDON to PARIS £4 12 6

(including reserved Pullman seats from Victoria to Dover and Calais to Paris).

TIMETABLE.

LONDON (Victoria) dep. 11. 0 a.m.	PARIS (Nord) – dep. 12.20 p.m.
PARIS (Nord) – arr. 5.40 p.m.	LONDON (Victoria) arr. 7. 0 p.m.

The T.S.S. "CANTERBURY"

will run in this service.

For tickets (including reserved seats) for this "Limited" service, apply to the

CONTINENTAL ENQUIRY OFFICE,

Southern Railway, Victoria Station, London, S.W.I,

or any Tourist Agency.

Waterloo Station, S.E.1.
April, 1931.

H. A. WALKER,
General Manager.

Ctl. 1301/⁴⁰·⁰⁰⁰/₂₄/₄/₃₁

Printed in England by
McCorquodale & Co. Ltd., London.—282129.

Pullman cars with brake compartments: Aurora, Flora, Juno and Montana, 1923

During July and August 1922, the General Manager of the South Eastern and Chatham Railway (SECR) P.C. Tempest and Davison Dalziel discussed the matter of running an all-Pullman Dover boat train, without the need of using ordinary railway carriages topping and tailing. A standing instruction had been in force for some time that would not allow the massive 12-wheel timber cars introduced almost two years before (as outlined in *Pullman Profile 1*), as well as the 'A-type' Pullmans of 1910-1914, to run next to certain classes of the company's locomotives. It was for this purpose that Dalziel decided to construct four entirely new cars.[101]

Early indications determined that the new vehicles 'should be eight-wheeled brake parlour' cars, so that they would be suitable for running next to the engine on all occasions as required, and both parties agreed that the construction 'shall be carried out under the terms of the Agreement

between the Pullman Company and the Managing Committee of the 31 May 1912'.[102] Built by the Birmingham Railway Carriage & Wagon Company at a cost of £ 5,050 each with timber bodies and a livery of crimson-lake, classically named *Aurora, Flora, Juno* and *Montana* were 34 tonnes each, 65 ft. in length, 8 ft. 7 ins. wide and just over 12 ft. 6 ins. in height. Similar to earlier builds, the vestibule inward opening doors were to an identical oblong windowpane design, but these were the first cars running on the SECR fitted from new with four-section sliding lights; the pioneers were 12-wheel Clayton-built Pullman cars used on Great Eastern Railway services some three years before.

Each vehicle contained a guard's compartment with seat, hand brake, guard's valve and gauge, together with a letter rack and table at one end, with two coupés and two spacious saloons

A builders' photograph of **Montana**, *as new in 1923, showing off its crimson lake livery, 'American-type' four-wheel wooden bogies and white rim wheels. Note the vestibule door with adjustable drop light to the left, gained entry to the guard's compartment.*

accommodating 26 first-class passengers in total. Unusually, slight variations in equipment were apparent upon their delivery, as evidently the case by an exchange of memoranda between Davison Dalziel and his Chief Engineer, Mr Johnson. *Juno* and *Aurora* were fitted with 1 ft. 8 in.-width adjustable buffers, in contrast to those fitted to *Flora* and *Montana* which were 2 ft. 0 ins. in dimension. The reason for these differences are unfortunately obscure, although the subsequent report confirms that all four cars were fitted with standard centre couplings, 'American-type' wooden bogies and adjustable vestibules which were approved by the SECR Chief Engineer prior to their running in service. And while the surviving (amended) specification required the latest 'Type-D' table lamps for this lot, two notably different versions were supplied by the builder upon delivery, *Aurora* and *Juno* receiving wider based ormolu lamps for the coupé compartments only, whereas the remainder were rendered in brass to a wholly different

dimension though featuring similar characteristics. (The reasoning for these anomalies remain unknown, which apart from anything else adds to the mystique and unusual practices governing Pullman management decision-making at the time. In any event, a similar practice was replicated during 1929 when the super-luxe French-built Pullmans for long-distance Côte d'Azur service were constructed by Entreprises Industrielles Charantaises, of Aytré, La Rochelle.)

The interiors were however extravagantly and luxuriantly appointed, providing a range of individual decorative features, with richly figured mahogany panelling throughout, including large oval glass partitions between saloons classically executed. All the armchairs were covered in red dyed Morocco leather with similarly coloured matching carpet. *Flora*, named after the Roman goddess of flowers, fertility and spring flora, was furnished with quartered marquetry

An exterior view of **Flora** *awaiting attention outside Preston Park Works, 13 February, 1952. During renovation and a full body repaint, the body side clips were subsequently removed.*

Above: *An exterior view of Aurora awaiting attention, and still retaining 'Cunarder' roof boards, 29 May 1952. At times during the 1920s,* Aurora *and one of its sisters were used topping and tailing on the popular King's Cross to Newmarket race specials hauled by Ivatt Atlantic locomotives. This train was routed via Hitchin and the operations worked from Battersea until 1930. Thereafter vehicles from Northern allocated services were used.*

Far left: *A mullion panel that once adorned the interior of* Flora. *The garlands of flowers are intricately and finely executed, while the reverse confirms this panel was completed in February 1923.*

Left: *A finely detailed mullion panel that once belonged to* Juno. *See opposite page.*

panels detailing a protrusion of colourful inlaid rose garlands to a unique design, crimpled ribbons and arabesque motifs relieved in satinwood and eucalyptus.

Juno named after the ancient Roman goddess, the protector and counsellor of the state, received finely detailed panels with intricate amphorae (claimed to be in the manner of 19th-century Sèvres-style decorative urns), set within a framework of drapes and wreaths. *Aurora*, the Roman goddess of dawn, was noted for its richness of ribbons, swags and drapes, together with oversized bulkhead marquetry medallions, which offered great eye-appeal. *Montana,* possibly named after a yacht co-owned by Lord Dalziel, was finished with small ribbons, flowers and drapes, relying on similar design elements

A striking interior view of the main saloons of Juno photographed in 1948. At this time, fixed curtain rods are shown, together with examples of 'A-' and 'D-type' table lamps. The armchairs are replacements from c 1934.

to those featured in *Flora*. Catalogued as the Pullman Car Company's 'F-type', all four cars were delivered for traffic during May 1923, and prior to their inaugural public runs points of interest were released by Pullman management, proclaiming that these vehicles 'incorporated improvements of design, construction and equipment, though without departure from the standard Pullman characteristics which had done so much to popularise "luxury travel" at small supplementary charges'.[103] They were pressed into service on the nominally all-Pullman 'Continental Express', and continued to run when numerous new 'K-type' cars were introduced a year later (per *Pullman Profile 2*) topping and tailing in their original colours until 1927/28, when each were progressively repainted in the then standard colours of umber below the waist and cream above, fully lined and decorated. *Juno* and *Montana* occasionally ventured over London & North Eastern Railway metals – on race specials to Newmarket, invariably in the company of remodelled former South Eastern Railway 'Folkestone Car Train' saloons. However, all four cars were generally allocated to the Dover boat train pool, and each were destined at one time or another to form part of the new 'Golden Arrow Limited'. *Aurora* and *Flora* had the distinction of being included in the inaugural run in May 1929.

By 1931, *Aurora* and *Flora* were briefly allocated to the new 'Bournemouth Belle', and later still, transferred momentarily with *Juno* to ocean liner workings in connection with the fixed sailings of the RMS 'Aquitania' intermittently, only to return again to Southampton in 1936 for the special inaugural trip conveying passengers to the RMS 'Queen Mary'. By October 1946, they formed part of

Above: *A glimpse inside* **Flora** *during renovation, showing its bulkhead panelling and exquisite marquetry.*

Left: *A rare view showing* **Car No.154** *(ex* **Flora***) at New Cross Gate, 19 April 1947, sporting 'Golden Arrow' insignia and 'Second-Class' in the decorative cartouche.*

several specials connecting with the maiden post-war voyage of the RMS 'Queen Elizabeth', hauled appropriately by Merchant Navy Class locomotive, No. 21C4, 'Cunard-White Star', driven by Driver G. Hawkins of Nine Elms.[104]

As part of one of a large number of high-profile workings made utilising these vehicles, the State visit of His Majesty the King of the Belgians on 16 November, 1937, for example, *Flora* formed part of a train from Dover Marine to Victoria (with *Pauline*, *Zenobia* and *Lady Dalziel*) accommodating the Marquess of Willingdon, the Marquess of Camden, General Sir Edmund Ironside, Air-Marshall Sir Frederick Bowhill and staff.

Immediately following wartime activities, including spells on the Hurn services, *Flora* was selected for remodelling in 1946, and became a second-class car for the 'Golden Arrow'. As *No. 154* it comprised 23 dining chairs together with two coupé compartments with fixed seating for six, accommodating 35 passengers in total. At one end, the guards' door was fitted with new drop lights, and 1½ in. letters at the bottom of the dado near the doorways identified the vehicle as *No. 154*. The decorative central cartouche simply stated 'Second-Class'.

Throughout Southern Railway and pre-electrification British Railways days, *Aurora*, *Flora* and *Juno* were reclassed (or downgraded) to suit the travelling requirements on the 'Golden Arrow', as referred to, and briefly the seasonal 'Devon Belle'. The *Appendices to the Carriage Working Notices* for September 1952, for instance, records *Aurora* and *Juno* as 'Not classed' and furnished with dining-car chairs, to a similar haphazard interior layout previously set out in *Flora*.[105]

With replacement bogies in most cases (excepting *Montana*) and several refurbishments and minor remodelling during the interim, however, all four finally ended their working careers as first-class cars.

Aurora became *No. 503 Third-Class* in June 1950
Flora became *No. 154 Second-Class* in April 1946
Juno became *No. 502 Third-Class* in June 1950
Montana remained as first-class

Pullman cars with brake compartments: Aurora, Flora, Juno and Montana, 1923

A fine 1950s view of the 'Golden Arrow' at speed hauled by one of the new British Railways standard 4-6-2 Britannia Class locomotives with full regalia.

A plan of the converted interior of **Flora** *into* **SECOND-CLASS** *Car No. 154 (1946). Note: a similar arrangement applied four years later, to both* **Aurora** *and* **Juno** *remodelling them during 1950 to* **THIRD-CLASS** *Cars Nos.* **503** *and* **502**, *respectively.*

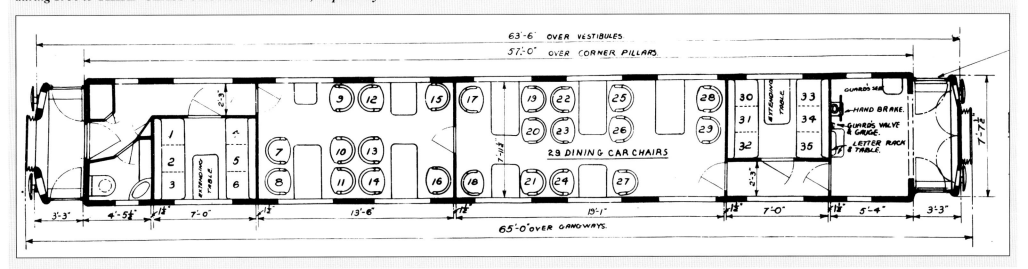

CAR № 503

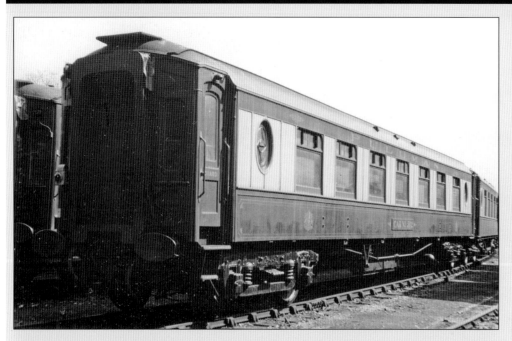

Car No 502 *(ex* **Juno***) at Preston Park, May 1951. Note the running board affixed and covering the original identification. (To the right is an example of a decorated wooden board used briefly from June 1950 for* **Aurora***.)*

In June 1960 *Montana* was withdrawn from service, and swiftly became one of the first of the batch to be converted into a 'camping coach'. It was sold a month later as '*CC 165*' to the Eastern Region for £878 and resided initially at Oulton Broad South, thereafter moving to Heacham in 1962.[106] After the camping coach scheme became obsolete in the late 1960s, the abandoned car was acquired and became a private dwelling at Barnwell Junction, Cambridgeshire.

Aurora, Flora and *Juno* were officially withdrawn by the end of 1962, and following their conversion, cascaded to the Western Region. Although surviving intact for many years latterly at Marazion, Cornwall, as 'camping' or 'holiday coaches' with other Pullman cars *Calais, Alicante* and *Mimosa* until 2001, the ravages of storm weather, vandals and sporadic arson attacks took their toll on these once beautiful vehicles to a state of almost disrepair; at the time of writing, two 'F-type' cars survive in preservation with much of their original lavish marquetry intact.

Flora and *Montana* have been sympathetically restored, complete with lined Pullman livery, and set in a peaceful sylvan haven. Today, they are used as high-quality hotel accommodation (residing with *Alicante* and *Mimosa*) located at the former Petworth railway station, near Chichester, West Sussex.

The decrepit remains of **Aurora***, photographed at Marazion, Cornwall during October 2001. Although an eye-sore, the almost fully exposed timber framing and construction elements are of interest to note, nevertheless. Sadly, by an order of the local council, the vehicle and two others were shortly afterwards broken-up and burnt on site.*

The agreement between the Pullman Car Company Ltd and Compagnie Internationale des Wagons Lits et des Grands Express Européens

A partially completed draft treaty drawn up by the London practice of Ashurst Morris Crisp & Co in December 1924, representing the Pullman Car Company, exists in a private collection. It offers an intriguing insight into the developing working relationship between the Pullman Car and the Wagons Lits companies that has almost been overlooked in studies today.[107]

The agreement and addenda (of which there appears to be at least nine corrections and/or additions over a course of six months or so) highlights some of the important operating aspects that were formally agreed prior to the introduction of the new 'Golden Arrow', and other Continental Pullman services in 1926, the golden jubilee year of the Wagons Lits Company.

Of the 13 articles adhering to this agreement, six are fundamental and formed the basis of the signed agreement three months later in March 1925. These are listed, in order below, and explain how Pullman cars could be run in France, Belgium and elsewhere on the Continent (except Italy). All the corrections and additions were added by Sir (later Lord) Davison Dalziel, in his capacity as Chairman of the Pullman Company and President of the Board of Directors and of the Managing Committee of the Wagons-Lits Company:

'The Pullman Company hereby grants to the Wagons Lits Company the right to use the name of the Pullman Company in connection with the running of buffet and saloon Pullman cars on such railways on the Continent of Europe as the Wagons-Lits shall effectively introduce the use of such cars. It also grants to the Wagons Lits the right to manufacture and use any article the subject of any patent which may for the time being be owned by the Pullman Company.

'The Wagons Lits Company undertakes that in all cases in which it shall decide to put into service within the said area buffet and saloon cars such cars shall, except in the case of force majeure, be of the Pullman type and shall be so described by the Wagons Lits Company. Provided that nothing herein contained shall prevent the Wagons Lits Company from continuing such buffet and saloon car services as are at present in existence such services not to come under the scope of this agreement.

'The Pullman Company shall supply and the Wagons Lits Company shall purchase such number of buffet or saloon Pullman cars up to 200 cars as may be required by the Wagons Lits Company. Such cars shall be in accordance with such specification and shall be supplied upon such terms as to payment and otherwise as may be mutually agreed between the parties hereto. Such a number of the said Pullman cars as shall be agreed shall be constructed within the United Kingdom of Great Britain.

'In consideration of the undertaking of the Pullman Company hereinbefore contained the Wagons Lits Company shall during each year of this agreement pay to the Pullman Company a sum equal to one half of the net profits of each year arising from the exploitation and working within the said area, of all the buffet and saloon Pullman cars of the Wagons Lits Company. The expression "net profits of each year" shall be deemed to mean the revenue derived by the Wagons Lits Company from the working of the said buffet and saloon Pullman cars after deducting (a) all expenses in connection with such working in each year properly chargeable to Revenue account (b) a sum equal to 4 per cent per annum on the capital cost of any buffet or saloon Pullman cars hereafter acquired by the Wagons Lits Company until the whole of the capital cost of such cars shall in such manner have been amortised and (c) a sum equal to 5 per cent on the said capital cost and all capital expenses. Separate accounts of the workings of the said Pullman cars shall be kept.

'All buffet and saloon Pullman cars of the Wagons Lits Company shall be worked as a separate branch of the business of the Wagons Lits Company under the management and control of Direction Générale of the Wagons Lits Company and the Comité d'Administration Générale of that Company. All details in connection with the construction of the first cars intended for use in connection with the first service of cars contemplated by this agreement shall be entrusted to Sir Davison Dalziel together the supervision of all matters connected with the putting of the said first services into operation.

'The Wagons Lits Company shall make up and supply to the Pullman Company during each year of this agreement a detailed account showing the amount payable to the Pullman Company hereunder per individual working, "Golden Arrow", etc, and shall pay to the Pullman Company the amount shown to be due by such account within one month after the completion of such account.'

Trial runs for Calais-Paris service, November 1925

As reported in *The Railway Gazette*, tests were made on the Nord Railway of France in readiness of running the first all-Pullman train between Paris and Calais (and return) consisting of 10 cars. During November 1925, the vehicles that were assembled for this test were apparently two new British-built Wagons-Lits all-steel restaurant cars to a similar profile and masquerading as 'Pullmans', together with two sleeping cars.[108] Although proving to be 'most successful', no meaningful data from the testing was given as to what precisely was involved. However, in an exchange of correspondence with the Director General, Davison Dalziel requested of him that the attendants rostered for the new service should be 'specially selected'. The distance between Paris and Calais of 298 km (187½ miles) was recorded as being made non-stop, in less than three hours.

Probably more than anything, this run simply served to demonstrate not merely the excellent condition of the Nord track, but also the smooth running and other features possessed by the new British-built vehicles that had just been delivered. Monsieur Javary, General Manager of the Nord Railway, and Monsieur Noblemaire, Director General of the Wagons-Lits Company (International Sleeping Car Co), with their respective staff, were duly noted to have accompanied the test train. At this stage, no suggestion of a name for the Pullman service was intimated, but it was widely known that the following year, 1926, was to be an important milestone for the Wagons-Lits Company founded 50 years before in 1876.

Prospective passengers were no doubt more interested to learn from reams of advertisements that meals and refreshments would be served at their seats, as had been the case on the 'Milan-Cannes Pullman' service introduced earlier that year.[109]

The Railway Gazette further advised readers that the timings of these forthcoming Pullman trains had not yet

been definitely fixed at this stage, but the intention at any rate was to run the services non-stop in both directions. There was also a desire, once services were established, to combine a selection of the new Pullmans built in England with a corresponding set built in France when those became available, offering a wide and pleasing selection of internal schemes throughout each train, as it transpired each lot varied considerably in decoration from one builder to another (as illustrated).[110]

In the event, the new services were planned to commence six months later, with an aim to accelerate the timetable where possible once in daily service, by which time all the British-built cars were scheduled for completion.

It was during early September 1926, Le Directeur Général Adjoint, Baron R. Snoy, announced to staff and the press that the new de-luxe Paris-Calais service would be named, in English, the 'Golden Arrow'. Two trains were planned, each of which would comprise 10 Pullman cars offering accommodation for a total 280 passengers, in addition to one or more vans conveying luggage.[111]

While the name had strong connotations to the Company's golden anniversary, it appears that much of the early publicity material released by the Pullman Company and Thomas Cook, the travel agent (for both the English and Continental markets), emphasised rather more tellingly the significant links in the path of the 'Golden Arrow', especially the regal splendours of historical spectacle.

The main promotional focus for this literature detailed the meeting, in June 1520, of King Henry VIII and Francis I at the Field of the Cloth of Gold at Guisnes. This event was shown to good effect in colourful images commissioned by the accomplished illustrator, Christopher Clark, R.I., and how this fine train in 1926 was compared judiciously to the age of pageantry and bejewelled magnificence. In a 'sybaritic age', travel writer, Dell Leigh declares, 'the fastidious traveller delivers himself into the hands of the Pullmanic demigods' during a journey which soon establishes itself as the 'princely path to Paris'.[112]

Business facilities aboard the 'Golden Arrow'. An artists' impression.

The reader was reminded, too, of the importance of Calais, which at one time or another was known as 'the brightest jewel in the English crown' – remaining in English hands for more than 200 years. Rodin immortalised the town in modern eyes by his famous sculpture of 'The Burghers of Calais', depicting that memorable scene in 1346-7 after the Battle of Crécy, when King Edward III starved the inhabitants into surrender after an 11 months' siege.

En route, the towns of Boulogne, Etaples, Abbeville, Amiens, Clermont, Chantilly and St. Denis each became well-versed topics of historical importance and of notable attraction – as the most elegant, comfortable and soon-to-be regular inter-capital train in the world, the 'Golden Arrow', took its flight to and from Paris linking with the Southern Railway's Pullman 'Continental Express'.

The Pullman supplements above the first-class rail ticket were fixed at French francs 92.25 (plus tax of Frs 18) between Paris and Calais or vice versa (with no reductions for children at this time), while set luncheon and dinner on board were fixed at Frs 35. A strong selling point which was invariably laboured in almost all Pullman and Wagons-Lits publicity material explained that the French Customs would examine hand baggage *en-route*.[113]

The inaugural service timetable was the following:

Departure:	12 h	Paris (Gare du Nord) – *Le train 79*
Arrival:	15 h 10	Calais Maritime

(Arrival at London Victoria 19 h 15)

(Departure from London Victoria 10 h 45)

Departure	14 h 30	Calais Maritime – *Le train 78*
Arrival	17 h 40	Paris (Gare du Nord)

French customs official examining hand luggage and travel permits aboard the French 'Golden Arrow'.

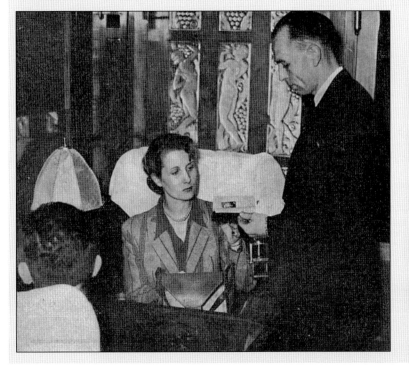

Parlour Car No. 4024 at Calais in the late 1920s. Note that the legend 'Pullman Car', in English, of this Metropolitan-Cammell built vehicle is positioned to the right (and the French equivalent to the extreme left). By contrast, the kitchen cars constructed by the Birmingham Railway Carriage & Wagon Co reversed this feature with the legend 'Voiture Salon Pullman', in French to the right and English to the left. See page 81.

The Birmingham-built 'Flèche d'Or-type' cars, 1926

The Birmingham Railway Carriage & Wagon Co. Ltd.,
Smethwick, Birmingham
Car Nos. 4001–4015 Pullman with kitchen (Wagon-Pullman cuisine)
Car Nos. 4081–4085 Pullman with kitchen (Wagon-Pullman cuisine)

Metropolitan-Cammell Carriage & Wagon Co. Ltd.,
Saltley, Birmingham
Car Nos. 4016–4030 Pullman parlour (Wagon-Pullman)
Car Nos. 4086–4090 Pullman parlour (Wagon-Pullman)

Floor plan of the (1926) kitchen and parlour cars. A 'couplage' arrangement offered in total 56 seats across four saloons, three coupé compartments, two lavatories and fully equipped kitchen.

WAGONS-PULLMAN et WAGONS-PULLMAN-CUISINE
TYPE " GOLDEN-ARROW "
COUPLAGE PULLMAN 1re CLASSE, à 56 PLACES

PULLMAN CARS WITH AND WITHOUT KITCHEN
" GOLDEN ARROW " TYPE
1st CLASS PULLMAN COUPLAGE WITH 56 SEATS

CONSTRUCTION MÉTALLIQUE (Diagramme 55)   STEEL CONSTRUCTION (Diagram 55)

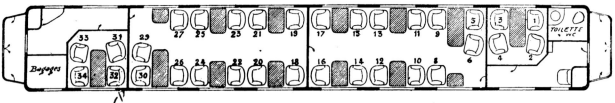

Wagon-Salon-Pullman à 32 places, sans cuisine :
2 Grands Salons de 12 places,
2 Petits Salons de 4 places,
Cabine à bagages.

Pullman Car without kitchen with 32 seats :
2 large Saloons with 12 seats,
2 Coupés with 4 seats,
Luggage room.

CONSTRUCTION MÉTALLIQUE (Diagramme 54)   STEEL CONSTRUCTION (Diagram 54)

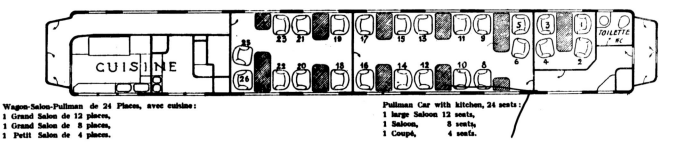

Wagon-Salon-Pullman de 24 Places, avec cuisine :
1 Grand Salon de 12 places,
1 Grand Salon de 8 places,
1 Petit Salon de 4 places.

Pullman Car with kitchen, 24 seats :
1 large Saloon 12 seats,
1 Saloon,   8 seats,
1 Coupé,   4 seats.

Through the intermediary and direct negotiating of Davison Dalziel orders for a total of 90 Pullman cars conforming to Continental railway requirements were placed in Britain and France for the Compagnie Internationale des Wagons Lits et des Grands Express Européens (CIWL) with four rolling stock builders, namely the Birmingham Railway Carriage & Wagon Co. Ltd; the Metropolitan Carriage, Wagon & Finance Co Ltd, Birmingham; the Leeds Forge Co. Ltd; and a subsidiary of CIWL, La Compagnie Générale des Constructions (CGC), France.

The cars resembled in their general outlines and certain other particulars the latest Pullmans then running on British railways, the main differences being in respect of the greater proportions employed and some of the details specific to running on Continental railways. While the scheme of decorations differed considerably from that previously adopted in the same class of vehicles in England, the familiar trademarks and branding that distinguished Pullman travel were all there: the table lamps, oval lavatory windows, elliptical vestibule doors, decoration and livery, marquetry and deep cushioned armchairs.[114]

The Birmingham-built 'Flèche d'Or-type' cars, 1926

The 20 cars built by the Birmingham Railway Carriage & Wagon Company all included kitchens and pantries, and were released in stages between 21 July 1926 and 14 April 1927, as were the 20 parlour cars supplied by the Metropolitan Carriage, Wagon & Finance Company adhering to a similar timetable.

Unlike Pullmans running on the Southern Railway, the underframes of these new vehicles featured a heavy longitudinal centre steel girder built up of plates and angles, while the buffing and draw gear was of the standard 'Chevalier and Rey' system, used on the Continent, as illustrated. The brakes were of combined Westinghouse automatic and 'moderable' type (sic) with a screw pattern hand brake operated from the vestibule at one end of each vehicle – all

three types actuating independently the blocks on all wheels. In conjunction with the Westinghouse apparatus, an internal passenger alarm was fitted with call boxes and handle in each saloon, corridor and coupé.

The body shell of these new cars was constructed entirely of steel for greater strength and durability which included the press-steel pillars, window frames and roof bracing. The sliding lights (detailed below) were formed of light-steel pressings and finished-off in brass, and all joints in the panelling were covered with rolled steel round-edge mouldings. The ends constructed in a similar manner to the sides were also coated inside with thick 'Celotex' asbestos for insulation, while the roofing was lagged inside with heavy canvas.

Above: *A builders' photograph of* **Kitchen Car No. 4005,** *as new, shows its incredibly solid and robust construction and livery with elaborate lining. Clearly seen are the fluid clean lines, white rimmed wheels and roof, decorative arrows and general window arrangement which characterised this type of Pullman car.*

In a contrasting view of **Parlour Car No. 4016,** *as new, although decorated externally to the same specification as the Birmingham RCW vehicles, a subtle difference to the Metropolitan cars was the shape of the elliptical sliding windows of the vestibule doors. Note the door to the left with partially opened window.*

The flooring comprised corrugated galvanised sheets riveted direct to the underframes. The depressions formed by the corrugation was filled with a bitumen compound. On top of this steel floor slabs of compressed cork were placed, which in turn was held down by rubber linoleum followed by thick pile Axminster carpet. The floors in the vestibules and corridors were fitted with Docker Brothers 'Induroleum' fireproof material covered with black-and-white interlocking rubber tiles, familiarly used in most Pullman cars built during the 1920s.

The kitchen cars featured one large and one small saloon, accommodating 20 passengers, together with a coupé compartment seating four, totalling 24, lavatory, office (or pantry) and kitchen. The parlour cars, by comparison, consisted of two large saloons flanked at either end by two coupé compartments with overall seating for 32 passengers.

The saloons and coupé compartments were finished in veneered plywood with 'tasteful marqueterie decoration'. No more than three of the cars in each order had the same interior design although seat moquette differed extensively, so that 15 vehicles ordered from each of the Birmingham firms were divided into five distinctly different schemes. In some cases, for instance, the mullion panels and partitions were of inlaid quartered and figured mahogany, while others were finished in pearwood, and others again with maple burr.

As described in other *Pullman Profiles*, details of special or particular interest are also noted: the ceilings of these vehicles were similar in fact to those cars running in British service during the 1920s, that is, of plywood covered with Tynecastle linen, with simple decorative mouldings of three different 'leaf' or 'floral' patterns and finished-off matt white. Double-face brass encased clocks with 24-hour Arabic numbers in black and red, were positioned between saloons.

The immaculate and lavish interior of Car No. 4001, *as new. It is seen here, prior to entering service, showing off the use of various historic and classical elements in an architecturally ingenious fashion which gave compelling directness in the 1920s. Designed and executed by the Bath Cabinet Makers Ltd, the principal veneers were of Cuban figured mahogany and white pearwood. The armchairs were covered in floral moquette of green, yellow and fawn colours.*

The coupé interior of Car No. 4001 *offering accommodation for four passengers. These compartments were a feature of all French (and English) 'Golden Arrow' Pullmans and probably appealed to those passengers seeking more intimacy than the saloons could provide. Besides exclusivity, they often replicated the decorations of the rest of the car. Note to the left, the passenger alarm fitted with call box and handle.*

The fixed windows were large and similar in profile to the latest Pullman type with a top sliding for ventilation of four sections (two of which were fixed) rendered in polished brass, while the vestibule doors with oval panes of plate glass were uniquely split into two parts: the lower part fixed and the top moveable by a small knob handle for ventilation. (An added distinction between the kitchen and parlour cars was the vestibule doors. While similar in form from one to another, the Metropolitan cars featured sharper angles to the flange framing and were initially finished-off with a painted border which emphasised the shape, the differences seen to good effect by comparing photographs of *Car No.4001* with *Car No.4025*).

The tables all had plate glass tops, and in each coupé compartment an extension was available, if desired, which was specially located and stored in a wall-mounted unit along the corridor.

The armchairs with a fluted finish were of a similar profile regardless of builder throughout, covered in various moquette or morocco leather in colours to tone with the woodwork and carpets. Small hassocks (foot stools) were also provided, invariably matching the carpet and trimmed with leather and felt.

Stylish and exuberant. A saloon partition of Metropolitan Cammell Parlour Car, No. 4018, now preserved at Mulhouse, France.

The interior decoration of the cars built by the Birmingham Railway Carriage & Wagon Company was subcontracted to the Bath Cabinet Makers Co Ltd., while those built by the Metropolitan Carriage, Wagon & Finance Company were undertaken by Morison & Co of Edinburgh and Martyn & Company of Cheltenham, both of whom were famed for their ornamental work and high-profile commissions for the Cunard White Star and other shipping lines. (Under the formidable control of William Robert Reid, Morison's were later to secure a revised contract to supply all the marquetry panelling, decorative ceilings and carpets of the Metropolitan cars).

Hot and cold-water supply was provided in the lavatories, and all fittings were either white metal or nickel silver plated. A hot water heater was also provided. The water supply in each vehicle was carried in a copper tank concealed in the roof. At the opposite end of the cars with kitchen and pantry, shelving was provided to accommodate passengers' larger items of luggage, while small hat and parcel racks to a standard British design first introduced two years before were also fitted above each window.

The kitchen interior was constructed entirely in steel and fitted with a large coal-burning range, the corridor partition behind this being well insulated with Celotex asbestos and ventilated. There were two sinks located in the kitchen providing ample water supply, carried in large circulating copper tanks situated in the roof. These tanks could be replenished either from the side of the car or from the roof. A profusion of large and small fitted cupboards with locks were located at the kitchen end of the car for storage, foodstuffs, linen and silver. The flooring was of 'Induroleum' and covered with metal grids, similarly to those featured in Pullmans running on British railways, where high standards of sanitation in the kitchens and wear and tear would be expected. The entrance to the kitchen was fitted with a collapsible Bostwick gate which was lockable.

The pantry or office was finished in polished mahogany and fitted with numerous cupboards for the storage of bone china, silverware and wine. A large ice cupboard with perforated walls designed to accommodate meat and poultry adjoined the pantry. The wine cupboards were well insulated and fitted with ice containers, while racks for the various types of glassware were also provided. Unlike the kitchen flooring, the pantry floor was covered with a wooden grid.

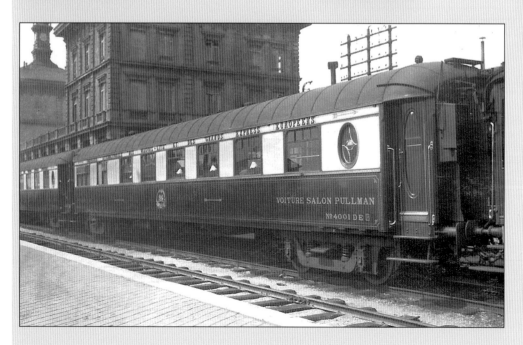

An exterior view of **Car No.4001** *(with kitchen) at Calais station in the late 1920s waiting to depart for Paris. Note the original livery (of umber and cream) with detailed lining and numerous arrows. By 1932, this vehicle was one of eight selected for remodelling to second-class with fixed 2+1 seating which, according to Broncard and Mertens in their detailed analysis in* **Rail Magazine** *(No.23, March 1979, p.16) progressively displaced by 1935 the first-class 'luxe' capacity of the train by 50 per cent.*

Interior view of **Car No. 4017,** *as new, featuring shaded shell motifs with garden nymphs each flanking a vase of flowers. The mullion panels of diamond pattern are of sandalwood and ash; this scheme designed by Martyn & Co was similarly shared with* **Car Nos. 4016** *and* **4021.**

The cars were all fitted throughout with electric lights, fans and bell equipment. The electrical equipment installed by Stone's of Deptford included ceiling and bracket lights finished in polished brass and exquisitely designed. Standard 'Type A' table lamps with silk shade (stencil stamped on the felt base with the number of the car to which the lamp belonged) were located on every table, to a design similar to those featured in Pullmans elsewhere.

An electric 'Imperiston' ventilating fan, supplied by the Stone's company, was fitted in each saloon encased within an attractive brass cover, flanked by pull-down manual ventilators, while the coupé compartments were suitably fitted with small ventilators.

A low-pressure steam heating system carried out by the Laycock Engineering Company, consisted of three longitudinal pipes, which extended from partition to partition in each saloon (and compartment) affixed to the body side near the floor and exposed, although much later, during the late 1940s, some cars were fitted with decorative grills. Heat regulating apparatus was fixed on each partition to allow passengers to regulate where desired the climate from one saloon to another.

All the cars were painted in the standard colours of most English Pullmans, namely umber for the lower and cream for the upper panels and lined out in gold with golden arrow adornments (with the exception of the last 10 cars Nos. 4081-4090 which were despatched just prior to the Leeds built cars, which were the first complete batch in 1927 to appear in the latest Wagons-Lits colour scheme of blue and cream).

The interior of Metropolitan Carriage & Wagon built Parlour Car No 4089. An extraordinary scheme is introduced which relies on a colourful frieze for its main decoration, with figured mullion panels exploring the themes of travel and mythical folklore. This saloon arguably showcases the very best of English craftsmanship and skill. The diverse nature of Pullman car decoration was an important element of their appeal. The panelling was complemented by Morocco leather-covered armchairs, as an alternative to moquette, which found favour on other Pullman trains in the 1920s, particularly those operating in Egypt.

In almost all known communications between the builders and the Wagons-Lits and Pullman Companies, these vehicles were described as the 'Flèche d'Or type' (although the actual service itself was almost always known from the very beginning at least, in English, as the 'Golden Arrow') but it appears many were in fact allocated immediately to newly-introduced Pullman services elsewhere. The inscriptions above the windows on the lateral cantrail consisted of the words 'Compagnie Internationale des Wagons-Lits et des Grands Express Européens' in blackened raised bronze letters to form a contrast to the cream panels. The Wagons-Lits coat-of-arms in the centre of the lower panels was in the form of a polished bronze casting, while the lettering in gold leaf transfers on most of the Birmingham-built vehicles displayed 'Pullman Car' in English at one end, and 'Voiture Salon Pullman' in French at the other. Arrows in gold leaf were also placed on the sides of the first 30 cars to denote that they formed part of what would become the 'Flèche d'Or'/'Golden Arrow' trains, which later plainly inhibited to some extent their deployment to other services, if required[115]

Once inspected and released by the Builders, the vehicles were all conveyed to Belgium by the Harwich-Zeebrugge ferry service, and thereafter by rail to Paris for victualling and service preparation.

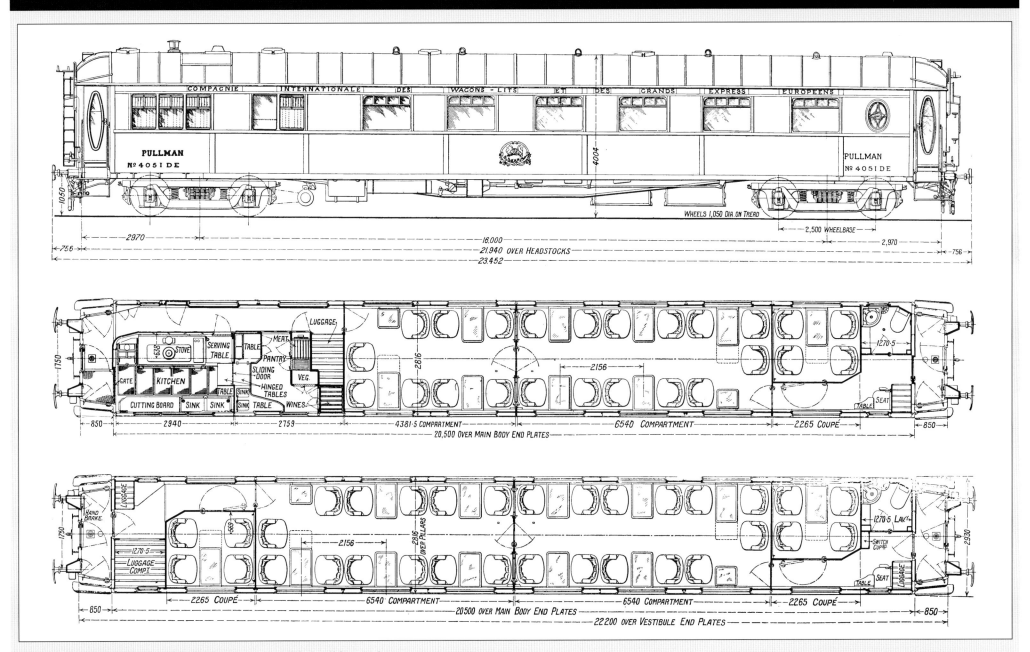

Elevation and plan of the Leeds Forge Company 'Flèche d'Or-type' cars.

The Leeds Forge Co. order, 1926/7

Car Nos. 4051 – 4065 Pullman with kitchen (Wagon-Pullman cuisine)
Car Nos. 4066 – 4080 Pullman parlour (Wagon-Pullman)

Of the 90 all-steel Pullman cars ordered on behalf of the Compagnie Internationale des Wagons-Lits split between various British and French manufacturers, Sir Davison Dalziel awarded 30 cars to be built at the Newlay Works of the Leeds Forge Company Limited, Leeds.

Although this order was scheduled for completion at the end of May 1926, the General Strike in Britain unfortunately prolonged their entry into service by almost seven months, with the last five cars duly released by the Builder on 12 February 1927. While known as the 'Flèche d'Or type', these vehicles were specifically allocated to run in numerous new Pullman routes throughout the Continent, as well as replacements for all wooden-bodied cars previously secured on lease-hire arrangements then currently running in service between Italy and the South of France, as outlined in *Profile 2*. A batch of cars, including *No.4057*, which were destined to run on the Milano-Ancona and Milano-Livorno and other domestic services, ran with the Wagons-Lits branding in Italian: *'Compagnia Internazionale delle Carrozze con Letti e dei Grandi Treni Espressi Europei'*. Invariably, publicity material advertised these services as 'Treni Pullman di Lusso Estivi'.

On Tuesday, 1 February 1927, a small party, consisting of officials of the Leeds Forge Company and representatives of the press and other invited guests, travelled to Leeds by the 10.10 am express from London (King's Cross), a Pullman car being placed at their disposal, courtesy of the Pullman Chairman. The purpose of the visit was to inspect the last five cars remaining which were almost ready for shipment, and to see first-hand the various processes involved in the manufacture of luxury vehicles at both the Armley and Newlay Works. According to *The Railway Gazette*, the tour was conducted by the principal officers and general managers of the Leeds company (and several from Cammell Laird & Co Ltd to which they were now associated), including Mr A.S. Bailey, the Managing Director.[116]

As noted elsewhere, the new cars conformed to the Continental running gauge and to standards of the Belgian, French and Italian railways, but they were in many respects similar internally to almost all the English Pullmans constructed throughout the 1920s. As recorded by *The Railway Gazette*, those cars already running in the 'Golden Arrow', were said to have given the greatest satisfaction at speed. The bogies of these vehicles, similar in every respect to the Birmingham-built cars were of the equalising beam type with nests of bolster springs giving a smooth ride. The wheels, axles and axle-boxes were of the Wagons-Lits standard type as required by the railways over which the cars ran.

However, unlike most of those vehicles provided by the Birmingham builders, these new Leeds-built cars were readily distinguishable by being the first to be painted externally in blue on the lower panels and cream on the upper, rather than in the traditional umber and cream livery. Additionally, on the lower exterior panel of each car, surrounded by fine lining, only the legend 'Pullman' at the extreme ends (and white-coloured running numbers) were used; all letters were finished in raised polished brass (as illustrated).

A Builders' photograph of **Car No. 4061,** *with kitchen, as new. The livery is blue in colour on the lower panels and cream above with the usual Wagons Lits Company branding in French.*

An order of 15 kitchen cars and 15 parlour cars had been constructed, and were ultimately despatched, in phases, from Leeds to France (Paris St. Denis CIWL works) via Temple Mills and the Harwich-Zeebrugge freight train ferry service. Conforming in dimensions and general amenity to the cars allocated to the new flagship service only three months before, the 'Leeds-built' cars, differed only in the finish and interior design executed exclusively by Waring & Gillow, the noted English furniture manufacturer. In all, there were a staggering 15 different schemes, including two almost exact reproductions of the 'Argus' car – as built by the Midland Railway Carriage and Wagon Co, in 1924 – replicating the enormous bulkhead bracket lights with ornamental flame, tinted mirrors, intricate fluted floral motif beading and quartered panelling, which according to *The Locomotive* correspondent [the 'Argus' car] 'aroused so much admiration at the Wembley Exhibition' that year.[117]

As with all Wagons-Lits Company Pullman cars (Nos. 4001-4090), each parlour car offered accommodation for 32 passengers and each kitchen car 24 passengers. The parlour cars each weighed 46 tons 12 cwt. (47.4 tonnes), and the kitchen cars 50 tons 4 cwt. 3 qrs. 25 lb. (51 tonnes).

In addition to the usual interior mahogany, maple and ash panelling, with floral and geometric inlays of diverse and numerous patterns, exotic veneers were also featured in some of the 'Leeds-built' cars, including highly detailed Chinese lacquer work of landscape scenes, animals and birds, a decorative medium which was much in vogue throughout the 1920s.[118]

An official interior view of what is believed to be Pullman kitchen car No 4053 showing one of the 15 diverse interior designs; in this case floral motifs rendered in marquetry inlays and repeat seat moquette.

A Builders' photograph of a parlour car for comparison. **Car No. 4076, as new.**

An attractive interior photograph of Car No. 4057 featuring a decorative scheme of white doves within a surround of flowers recorded in colours of yellow and red. Note the armchairs, hat racks, bracket lights, table lamps and the corridor door (in the background) conform almost exactly to furnishings used time and again in British Pullman cars built from the mid-1920s.

An interior view of one of the coupé compartments of Car No. 4067. *The decorative scheme relies on a repeat floral design, mirrors and skilfully matched quarter veneers.*

For comparison, an interior view of another Waring & Gillow designed vehicle showing a modern floral interpretation on a raised pediment.

T4956

An interior view of Car No. 4052 repeating an almost identical marquetry scheme as used previously in the Pullman car Pauline of 1924 (per Pullman Profile No. 2). An abundance of colourful flora, a Grecian muse and Morocco leather covered chairs in place of moquette offer a sumptuous and comfortable environment for the long-distance traveller.

Above: *A vibrantly coloured marquetry panel of maple, burr wood, mahogany and dyed veneers from C.G.C. Kitchen car No. 4040.*

Interior view of Car No. 4066, as new, featuring typical floral marquetry and armchair moquette, but introducing a stylistic modern alternative to the traditional pleated lamp shade. Note to the right the unusually sized arm and head rests of the chairs flanking the walls. These features were experimental for the added comfort of passengers, but in the event they were destined to be short-lived.

The C.G.C. order, 1927/8

Car Nos. 4031-4040 Pullman with kitchen (Wagon-Pullman cuisine)
Car Nos. 4041-4050 Pullman parlour (Wagon-Pullman)

These French-built cars, totalling 20 in number and constructed at the St. Denis workshops of the Compagnie Générale des Constructions (C.G.C.), a subsidiary of CIWL, were released in batches between September 1927 and January 1928.

Although barely distinguishable externally, only their simplified flush lavatory window surrounds and vestibule entrance doors betrayed their C.G.C. origins. Often praised by many observers in the popular press as some of the finest Pullmans then running in Continental service, their distinct and brightly coloured interior decorative schemes, in the emerging style that became 'Art Deco', were considered avant-garde. A new design of hat rack and several different types of table lamp gave the interiors unique flair and style, that was bold, elegant and undeniably French.

An artist's impression of the saloon interior of a Continental Pullman car. Similar in both overall dimensions and outward appearance to the British-built cars, they formed the last batch of vehicles released of the 'Flèche d'Or-type'.

A mullion panel with a modern and brightly-coloured interpretation of a vase of flowers.

INT. WAGONS-LITS CY.

London – Paris by the GOLDEN ARROW

An All Pullman train

Promoted by striking artwork by W.S. Bylitipolos and, later, the Baynard Press, the advertised Wagons-Lits 'Golden Arrow' service was inaugurated on 11 September 1926. It took place just 13 days after the first fare-paying passenger run of the long-haul 'Sud Express Pullman' from Paris to the coastal resort of Biarritz and the Spanish frontier, noted as the first train composed entirely of Pullman cars to run in France.

Among the distinguished guests on this glittering of trains were Sir Davison Dalziel; M Despret, President of the International Sleeping Car Company; Comte de Segur Lamoignon, Vice-President of the Board of Directors; Mr F.H. Houlder; Baron Snoy, General Manager; M Neef, Manager of the Administrative services; M Van Dievoet, Secretary General, and M Margot, Traffic Manager (the International Sleeping Car Company); M de Waru, Vice-President of the Board of Directors; Mr H.M. Snow, MVO., Agent-General, London; M Javary, Traffic Manager; M Moyrand, Operating Superintendent; M Girard, Secretary-General (the French Northern Railway Company); Mr C.C. Verrinder, Manager of the Paris office of the Southern Railway; M Plytas, Chief of the secretarial staff of the French Ministry of Public Works; MM Rivet and Maison, Directors at the Ministry of Public Works; M Margot, General Manager of the PLM Railway; M Bonnet, General Manager of the Suez Canal Co; M Baudry de Saunier of the Touring Club of France; the Aga Khan; M Vincent, Mayor of Calais; M Farjon, Mayor of Boulogne; Dr Baukeley Gavin; Messrs O. Hoare, R. Guinness, T. Powell, E.A. Ashton, W.S. Sedcole, Baron Emilie Erlanger, Hon. H.E. Fitzalan Howard; Messrs H.A. Sire, CBE., Chief Commercial Manager; E.C. Cox, CBE., Chief Operating Superintendent; F.A. Brant, Continental Assistant (Southern Railway); and Mr F.H. Spiller (T. Cook & Son).[120]

According to Monsieur Roger Commault, a large number of visitors took a keen interest in the proceedings by reportedly flocking to the Paris station to catch a glimpse of the train, while other well-wishers were peppered along the lineside. As the result of trial non-stop runs made on the Nord Railway between Paris and Calais the previous year, when a train composed of two new Wagons-Lits all-steel restaurant cars masquerading as Pullmans (with two sleeping cars in tow) covered the distance of 185 miles in less than 3 hours, it was decided that the new all-Pullman car trains should be accelerated once the pattern of service was established. However, the recorded running times for the two inaugural journeys were slightly slower, as follows:

Depart Paris (Nord) 10.25am

Arrive Calais (Maritime) 1.30pm

Depart Calais (Maritime) 2.30pm

Arrive Paris (Nord) 5.40pm

At the invitation of the Nord Railway Company and the Wagons Lits Company, the 'Golden Arrow' consisted of a large number of railway officials and newspaper representatives who travelled from Paris to Calais and back. The train was hauled by a 4-6-2 type locomotive (No. 3.1205) and composed of 10 Pullman cars (five vehicles from each Birmingham firm) and a baggage car, the total weight being just over 500 tons or 510,980 kg.[1v]

Opposite: *An atmospheric scene showing passengers at the Gare du Nord boarding the 'Flèche d'Or' bound for Calais.*

The long train drew out sharply at 10.25 a.m. from the Gare du Nord on to the multi-track approach roads, and apparently 'reached a high speed sustained for long periods', as outlined by *The Railway Magazine* correspondent.[121]

Both luncheon and tea on the return trip were served to passengers *en route* using specially commissioned white and gold-coloured fine bone china, supplied by Elkington & Co Ltd, England, to a new pattern shared between the Wagons-Lits and Pullman Car Companies, but badged with their respective coat of arms. While the epicurean experience varied considerably over the years from the elaborate five courses or more, to light meals and refreshments, the inaugural luncheon was a typically lavish affair:

Hors d'Œuvre

Homard Thermador

Timbale de Ris d'Agneau

Perdreaux Rôtis

Salade

Soufflé au Marasquin

Desserts

Calais Maritime was reached just before 1.30pm, the distance having been covered at an average speed exceeding 60 miles per hour. On the return journey five minutes extra were allowed, and as the Gare du Nord was duly reached on schedule time at 5.40pm, the speed averaged just under 58 miles per hour. In the course of an interview, Sir Davison Dalziel, who had already received enthusiastic congratulations at Calais, said to reporters:

'The event probably marks the most important innovation in travel between England and France since the Nord Railway first opened international traffic, and proves that the Pullman habit will now take a firm hold of the leading French and other Continental railways. There is already talk of a wide extension of these services in the near future. It is not without interest that the Pullman Company is a partner with the Wagons-Lits in the financial results of the development of Pullman services on the Continent – an arrangement which is likely to prove of the highest value to the Pullman Company in coming years.'[122]

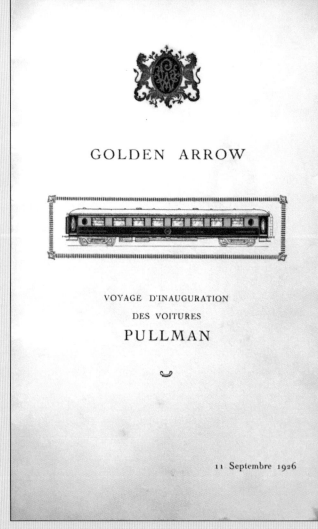

GOLDEN ARROW

VOYAGE D'INAUGURATION

DES VOITURES

PULLMAN

11 Septembre 1926

Based on the timetabled services, the 'Golden Arrow' as it was termed in all official papers initially – rather than its later, more familiar French incarnation as 'La Flèche d'Or' – offered an improvement of at least 35 minutes ahead of the best available time by express trains previously maintaining a service. A major selling point for the passenger was also that hand baggage examination took place on the train, rather than at the Customs Hall at Calais Maritime. A further facility which became possible by 1929, was the handling of heavy trunks and luggage. By the signing of a form, and providing address particulars and keys to the special Railway representative, passengers were relieved for a small fee of all worry and queuing at the Customs. This luggage would be examined at Victoria station under the care of the Southern Railway, and delivered to the destination by motor the same evening in the London delivery area, and the next day in other districts. The initiative later proved so popular, that corresponding arrangements were also made for delivery in Paris.

The initial Pullman supplementary fare booked at London Victoria station, Thos. Cook & son or other appointed travel agencies was approximately 13 shillings and 8 pence., this being exclusive of the usual 3 shillings and 6 pence supplement on the corresponding cars of the 'Pullman Continental Express' run between London and Dover (and vice versa) in connecting with the French 'Golden Arrow'. The introduction of these notable improvements in travel comfort was 'largely due to the efforts made by Sir Davison Dalziel, who, as Chairman of the Board of Administration of the International Sleeping Car Company and Chairman of the Pullman Car Company, had for years advocated and developed the more extended use of Pullman cars'. Both to him, the personnel of the railway companies and all concerned in the production of the luxurious vehicles placed in service, an extended congratulatory note was made by *The Railway Magazine* correspondent expressing 'the hope that the enterprise of the companies will receive its due reward'.[123]

The ordinary General Meeting of the members of the Pullman Car Co Ltd, held later in December, 1926, at Winchester House, Old Broad Street, London, makes for interesting reading, for the Chairman outlined the management's ongoing interest in foreign developments. In addition to the 'princely path to Paris' service, Dalziel named three new limited Pullman trains which would be inaugurated on 15 May the following year: Paris to Brussels and Amsterdam,

Calais to Vichy and Calais to Brussels, all with direct connections to/from London.

Dalziel concluded: 'As you are aware, we are joint partners with the Compagnie des Wagons-Lits in all the Pullman services on the Continent, and it is not unreasonable to think that we may eventually benefit by them … your enterprise is popular with the public and is well patronised, and I am still more glad to be able to say that it holds the goodwill of the railway companies with which it is in direct contact. I think I am right in saying that no train in the world carries daily so many first-class passengers as the Pullman 10.45 am from London to Dover, and, after that, no other train in Europe so many as are to be found, on an average, in the "Golden Arrow" from Calais to Paris.'[124]

The new Pullman service proved to be an encouraging success, with its seamless and matching connection with the Southern Railway's all-Pullman 'Continental Express', which train was exclusively composed of first-class Pullman cars of both eight- and twelve-wheel varieties. These arrangements remained in place until May 1929, when the English counterpart was at last renamed the 'Golden Arrow' coinciding with the introduction of a specially built steamer, the 'Canterbury', for the exclusive use of Pullman passengers only.

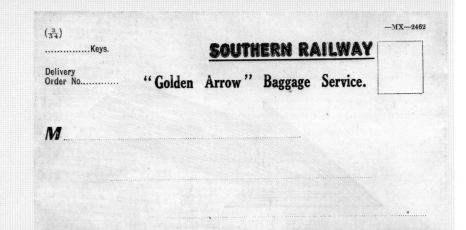

*Right and above right: **Special baggage delivery service notification and pressure-resistant envelope for keys, 1929 and 1934 respectively.***

*Far right: **La Flèche d'Or advertisement promoted by the Wagons Lits Company.***

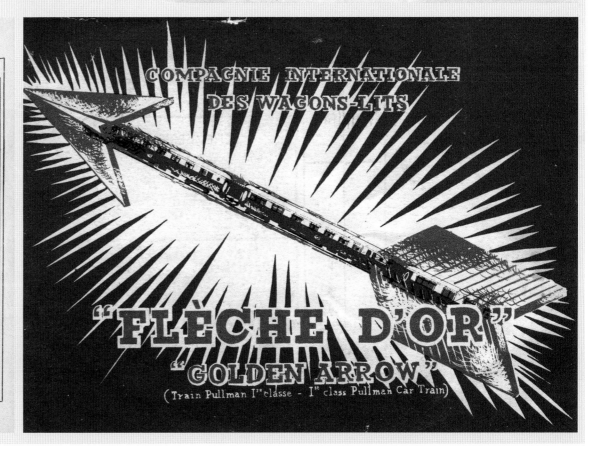

The inauguration of the accelerated 'Golden Arrow', 1929

The renaming of the 'Continental Express' to the 'Golden Arrow' was said to be due no less to the marketing acumen of Sir Herbert Walker of the Southern Railway, who reorganised and enhanced the London-Paris service in close collaboration with the Pullman Chairman. To show a common identity – nowadays known as corporate image-building – the intention was to cover the three sections of the service as a continuous luxury brand from Victoria to Dover (78 miles); Dover to Calais (25 miles); Calais to Paris (184 miles) and vice versa. In his detailed article celebrating 40 years of the service in 1969, Alec Hasenson argues that 'there was more to it than mere name-changing, however. The "Arrow" was given its own steamer, the *Canterbury*, specially built, so that there was no danger of contamination with other passengers … and, by agreement with customs at Dover, arrangements were made for "Golden Arrow" passengers to be passed through on to the ship as quickly as possible'.[125]

'This magnificent service', Frank Harding, the General Manager of the Pullman Car Company insisted, 'recognises to the full the great importance of first impressions received by visitors to this country, and was considered one of the most widely-known services in the world. Many efforts have been made to copy the title of this train and various "Arrows" had at one time or another been introduced into Continental services, but no name had ever been devised and no other service introduced which could equal that of the "Golden Arrow Limited"'.[126]

By the beginning of 1929, the English cars allocated to the 'Dover Pullman Continental Express', or 'White Pullman' service as it was sometimes called, were generally some of the best in the Southern pool – many of which were built during the 1924/7 period including *Argus, Aurelia, Medusa* and *Zenobia*. Occasionally, too, the massive all-timber 12-wheelers of 1921 often seen in the mixed composite

Continental boat trains – *Calais, Portia* and *Neptune* to name but a few – were added to strengthen the formation, topped and tailed by several 'F-Type' cars with guard and brake accommodation, as earlier outlined. At this time, there were two distinctly different liveries still in use on the Eastern Section: the crimson lake of the SECR and the 'old standard' – which ran together simultaneously for a short time, before almost all the vehicles were repainted by late 1930 in a livery of umber above and below the windows and cream in the middle.

The 'new service de-luxe', as it was dubbed in countless Southern Railway publicity brochures and glossy posters, made its grand entrance with a host of invited guests, including HM Government officials and a broad representation of British, French and American press for the inaugural run. Within days it seems that everyone who was anyone travelling to or from Paris appeared to travel on this train, which was quickly heralded as one of the luxuries and wonders of the age – as was once the *Concorde*, the joint British-French supersonic passenger airplane that operated until 2003.

One of a series of brochures and posters, in English, promoting the 'Golden Arrow' service from 15 May 1929.

The special timings of the inauguration of 'the new and accelerated train' took place on Wednesday 15 May and Thursday, 16 May, 1929, as follows:

		a.m.	p.m.
London (Victoria)	depart		10.51
Dover Marine	arrive		12.30
	depart		12.55 SS 'Canterbury'
Calais Maritime	arrive		2.10
	depart		2.25
Paris (Nord)	arrive		5.35

The 10.51am train left from Platform 1 at Victoria and, for the record, was composed as follows:

Engine

Corridor First Brake

Pullman Parlour Car *Glencoe*

Pullman Kitchen Car *Marjorie* (Kitchen leading)

Pullman Kitchen Car *Argus* (Kitchen trailing)

Pullman Parlour Car *Leona*

Corridor First Brake

Note: The new 'Golden Arrow Limited' departed from Platform 2 at 11.0am and was composed of the following vehicles:

Engine

Pullman Brake Car *Aurora*

Pullman Kitchen Car *Pauline* (Kitchen trailing)

Pullman Kitchen Car *Chloria* (Kitchen leading)

Pullman Parlour Car *Rosemary*

Pullman Parlour Car *Minerva*

Pullman Kitchen Car *Zenobia* (Kitchen trailing)

Pullman Kitchen Car *Cecilia* (Kitchen leading)

Pullman Parlour Car *Niobe*

Pullman Kitchen Car *Geraldine* (Kitchen trailing)

Pullman Brake Car *Flora*

1 Baggage Box Truck

1 Van

Thursday, 16 May:

		noon	p.m.
Paris (Nord)	depart		12.0
Calais Maritime	arrive		3.10
	depart		3.25
Dover Marine	arrive		4.40
	depart		5.5 *Golden Arrow Limited*
London (Victoria)	arrive		6.48

A special ticket was issued to each of the invited guests authorising travel for the named holder from London to Paris, and return, by the special Pullman train in advance of the 'Golden Arrow Limited' outward.

Special card ticket for the inaugural trip, 15/16 May 1929, issued to the General Manager of the Southern Railway, Major G.S. Szlumper.

MINISTRY OF THE INTERIOR

Passport Control Ticket

This ticket to be given up at the Passport Control Office at Calais

(VOIR AU DOS)

Golden Arrow

SPECIAL TICKET
FOR
INAUGURATION
OF THE NEW
"GOLDEN ARROW
LIMITED"
•
LONDON (Victoria)
AND
PARIS (Nord)
May 15-16, 1929

Passport Control ticket for the inaugural trip; all subsequent 'Golden Arrow' tickets had the arrow printed in the opposite direction!

Light refreshments were served *en route* to Dover and luncheon on board the 'Flèche d'Or'.

On the return journey the following day, the invited guests received luncheon on the train to Calais, and afternoon tea was later offered on the 'Golden Arrow Limited' upon departure from Dover Marine.

The special ticket, also known as a 'Visa of Administrations' and accepted by the British and French authorities in lieu of a passport, was validated by the General Managers of the Nord Railway; the Pullman Car Company; the Southern Railway and the Wagons-Lits Company.

A large presentation envelope was specially printed for the occasion with material supplied jointly by the Southern Railway and Pullman Company which included a programme, various brochures, customs regulatory requirements, notice of 'an automobile drive and sightseeing around Paris', together with details of the overnight accommodation at either the Hôtel Ambassador or Hôtel Commodore, both of which were in close proximity to the Gare du Nord. The accompanying examples of ephemera, reproduced in this Profile, were presented to Major G.S. Szlumper, General Manager of the Southern Railway.

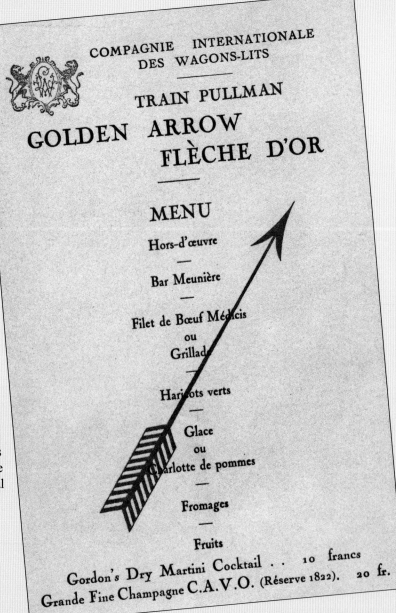

Brightly coloured printed pocket timetable of the new service as issued by the Southern Railway.

A Golden Arrow poster, in French, advertising the new service.

Composition of the Special Party

Brig. Gen. The Hon. Everard Baring, CVO, CBE., Chairman of the Southern Railway

Rt. Hon. Viscount Churchill GCVO., Chairman of the Great Western Railway

Rt. Hon. Viscount Inchcape, GCSI, GCMG, KCIE., Director of the Great Western Railway

Southern Railway

Major G.S. Szlumper, General Manager

J.B. Elliot, Esq, Assistant to General Manager (Public Relations and Advertising. A position invented for, and held by Elliot from 1925)

H.A Sire, Esq., CBE, Chief Commercial Manager

F.A. Brant, Esq., OBE, Continental Traffic Assistant

C. Cooper, Esq, Deputy Continental Traffic Assistant

C.C. Verrinder, Esq, Paris Agent

E.C. Cox, Esq., CBE., MVO, Chief Operating Superintendent

H.E.O. Wheeler, Esq., OBE, Assistant Operating Superintendent (Train Services.)

G.R. Newcombe, Esq., Docks and Marine Manager

R.P. Biddle, Esq, Assistant Marine Manager

Capt. J.T. Blake, RN., CBE, Divisional Marine Manager

Northern Railway of France

Monsieur Javary, Directeur-General

Monsieur Motrand, Chef de l'Exploitation

Monsieur Rieter, London Correspondent

International Sleeping Car Company (Compagnie International des Wagons-Lits)

Monsieur le Baron Snoy, Directeur-General, Administrateur

Monsieur Loth, Directeur de l'Exploitation Generale

Monsieur Bugniet, Directeur de la Direction Regionale de Paris

Monsieur Garcey, Directeur du Service Commercial

H.M. Snow, Esq., MVO, Agent-General, London

Major O.V. Thomas, Chef d'Agence, London

Pullman Car Company

G.H. Griffiths, Esq., CBE, General Manager

London & North Eastern Railway

C. Dandridge, Esq, Advertising Manager

J.R. Hind, Esq, Information Agent

HM Government

Sir William Haldane-Porter, CB, Chief Inspector, Aliens Branch, Home Office

A.J. Dyke, Esq., CB., CBE, Deputy Chairman, HM Customs

N. Thompson, Esq., ISO., OBE, Inspector General of the Waterguard

W. Young, Esq., CB, Senior Commissioner, Customs and Excise

Republic of France

Monsieur Billecocq, Deputy Consul-General, London

Monsieur Maurice Vignon, Director, Office Francais du Tourisme, London

Thos. Cook & Sons, Ltd

Stanley Adams, Esq, Director; London Correspondent (International Sleeping Car Company)

E. Huskisson, Esq, General Representative

Wm. Denny & Bros., Ltd – Builders of T.S.S. 'Canterbury'

Sir Archibald Denny, Bart Director

Jack Denny, Esq Director

THE PRESS (BRITISH)

Newspapers or Agency

Daily Mail, P Bewscher, Esq

Daily Mail (Continental Edition), W.L. Warden, Esq (*Directeur-General, Paris*)

Daily News, F.H. Champion, Esq (*News Editor*)

Daily Sketch, A. Courtoyse, Esq (*Editor*)

Daily Telegraph, J.E. Sewell, Esq

Morning Post, A. David, Esq (*News Editor*)

The Times, Percy Watson, Esq (*Advertisement Manager*)

The Star, P.W. Johnson, Esq

Financial Times, J.V. Turner, Esq

Sunday Times, E. Munton, Esq (*News Editor*)

The Observer, J.M. Blanch, Esq (*News Editor*)

Press Association, H. Martin, Esq (*Editor-in-Chief*)

Central News, R.F. Church, Esq (*News Editor*)

Exchange Telegraph Company, C. Nicholls, Esq

Reuter's Agency, J. Pigg, Esq

British United Press, H. Bailey, Esq (*Managing Editor*)

London Feature Service, David L. Blumenfeld, Esq (*Director*)

Topical Press Agency, J. Helsby, Esq (*Proprietor*)

Pathe Gazette, A.N. Sanders, Esq (*Editor*)

The Tatler, Colonel H.G. Morphett (*Advertisement Manager*)

The Bystander, Comyns Beaumont, Esq (*Editor*)

The Bystander, Miss Helen McKie

Piccadilly, A.S. Allberry, Esq (*Editor*)

Vogue, Mrs Towers Settle (*Editor*)

The Boulevardier (Paris), Richard Viner, Esq (*London Correspondent*)

Railway Gazette, J.A. Kay, Esq (*Editor and Managing Director*)

Modern Transport, F.C. Coleman, Esq (*Editor and Managing Director*)

Newcastle Journal, H. Watson, Esq (*London Editor*)

Yorkshire Observer, S. Oddy, Esq (*London Editor*)

Liverpool Post, R. Keir, Esq

Yorkshire Post, J. Jobson, Esq (*London Editor*)

Starmer Group, F.M. Inwood, Esq (*London News Editor*)

Allied Newspaper Group, N.H. Booth, Esq

Kentish Express, Sir Charles Igglesden (*Editor and Proprietor; Past Pres. Inst. of Journalists*)

Kent Messenger, H.R.P. Boorman, Esq (*Editor and Proprietor*)

Surrey Comet, F. Newling Jones, Esq (*Editor*)

Dover Standard, E.W. Betts, Esq (*Editor*)

Leytonstone Express, J.G. Lockes, Esq (*Editor and Proprietor*)

THE PRESS (FRENCH)

Le Temps, Monsieur R.L. Cru (*London Correspondent*)

THE PRESS (AMERICAN)

New York Times, C.A. Selden, Esq (*London Correspondent*)

New York World, A.S. Mann, Esq (*Staff Correspondent*)

New York American, R.W. Ritchie, Esq (*London Correspondent*)

New York Herald-Tribune, Neil Fraser, Esq (*Business Representative*)

New York Sun, J.W. Grigg, Esq (*London Correspondent*)

Chicago Tribune, J.S. Steele, Esq (*London Correspondent*)

Baltimore Sun, W.A.S Douglas, Esq (*London Correspondent*)

Associated Press, Wade Weiner, Esq (*Staff Correspondent*)

United Press Associations of America, R McLellan, Esq (*Staff Correspondent*)

International News Service, T.C. Watson, Esq (*Staff Correspondent*)

Harry Lotery, Esq

E.P. Leigh-Bennett, Esq

F.M. Lambert, Esq, Managing Director, The Photochrom Co

J.W. Davenport, Esq, Press Information Bureau, Southern Rly

Aesthetically pleasing. A marquetry frieze of a repeat pattern that once adorned a space between a passenger window and hat rack of **Car No.4037.**

SS 'Canterbury'

ailing in connection with the new 'Golden Arrow Limited' London-Paris and London-Brussels Pullman services, a new luxury Cross-Channel steamer christened the 'Canterbury' – unofficially known as the 'Pullman steamer' and by then the largest Cross-Channel ship ever constructed – was introduced on Wednesday, 15 May 1929.

The most striking feature of the revised service was the arrangement by which the steamer would be reserved exclusively to this service, and would leave the ports just over 15 minutes or so upon the arrival of the train, instead of waiting hitherto for the following second portion. In this way, time was saved, and greater comfort would be available on the ship, as the numbers were initially limited to the capacity of the train.

The Railway Gazette reported that the previous overcrowding and discomfort during 'the journey to France are now entirely avoided, as the numbers of passengers travelling are restricted to about 250-300'.[127] And as far as possible, the 'Canterbury' would remain in 'Golden Arrow' service, but during short periods when undergoing overhauls, etc., the older 'Isle of Thanet' and 'Maid of Kent' would take up the service and so maintain the special ship arrangements.

With an overall length of 335 ft., extreme breadth of 48 ft., and a moulded depth of 17 ft, the oil-burning 'Canterbury' weighed 2,912 tons (later increasing to 3,100 tons). She was ordered in March 1928 and built by Wm. Denny & Brothers, of Dumbarton, Scotland, and among her special features included a greater number of private *de-luxe* cabins, screened-off alcoves, in addition to a palm court, a restaurant, a buffet and a glass-sheltered awning deck. As on the earlier Cross-Channel vessels, including the 'Isle of Thanet' and 'Maid of Kent', ample seating accommodation was a notable consideration throughout the vessel, with larger and more comfortable armchairs of an 'improved design' which were spaced out and affixed evenly in rows of two, three or four.[128]

The SS 'Canterbury'.

The boat deck was unobstructed by the lifeboats which were hung from over-frame davits. At the forward end of the deck was a 'deck house' containing the main entrance, panelled in contrasting light and dark mahogany panels, while an observation room contained upholstered settees and a smattering of cane furniture.

A glimpse inside the garden lounge located on the awning deck, with cane furniture and potted palms so redolent of large hotels and London clubs, together with armchair comfort found in the lounges and general rooms throughout the vessel.

Two *cabines-de-luxe* were located at the after end of the entrance hall, and advertised at a charge of 84 shillings each, per crossing, which according to contemporary brochures could be transformed into one large suite, if desired.

A long open vista with seat recesses at the ship's side was divided from each other by mahogany pillars with a low-panelled dado rail, together with racks above for hand baggage. The armchairs on this deck were separated back-to-back and deeply upholstered with high backs and head rests. At the after end was situated a lounge with a small buffet restaurant and travel enquiry office.

What was described in the press releases and the in-house Pullman magazine *The Golden Way* as 'an unusual room' was arranged at the after end of the awning deck, in the form of a palm court or garden lounge (and, later, during the mid-1930s styled as a verandah café). The walls were designed to give the impression of jointed cream-coloured stone, with arched windows surrounded by treillage motifs in contrasting green. Carved baskets of flowers were located on the walls, while cane furniture, brightly coloured cushions and potted palms offered an attractive space to the passenger.[129]

From the central part of the awning deck lounge, a wide staircase with mahogany newel posts and open wrought-iron decorative balustrading gave access to the main deck. On this deck was the main dining room which could accommodate 100 passengers in pleasant surroundings. A cashiers' desk noted for its elaborate brass grill work, and mahogany panelling, was located near to the entrance and cloakroom. On the starboard side was the smoke room, decorated in half-timbered oak straps with plaster panels in an Old English style, while screened seat recesses, complete with turned open balustrading, and substantial square posts, were also attractive features nearby. From this entrance access was possible to a number of private cabins with lavatories (each available at 42 shillings), and the separate ladies' and gentlemen's saloons on the lower deck.

GOLDEN ARROW
T.S. Canterbury

Spirits, Beers and Soft Drinks

Spirits & Wines

			s. d.	Fr. Frs.
Cocktails Various	...	...	2 6	60
Whisky		nip	1 9	42
Gin	...	,,	1 9	42
Gin and Angostura	...	glass	1 10	44
Gin and Votrix	...	,,	2 6	60
Votrix, Sweet or Dry	...	,,	1 6	36
Sherry	...	,,	3 0	72
Port	...	,,	3 0	72
Brandy	...	,,	3 0	72

Beers & Cyder

			s. d.	Fr. Frs.
Bass's Pale Ale		bottle	1 6	36
Worthington's Pale Ale		,,	1 6	36
Guinness' Stout		,,	1 6	36
Light or Brown Ale		,,	1 4	32
Graham's Lager		,,	1 6	36
Mackeson's Stout		,,	1 6	36
Whiteway's "Whimple" Cyder		,,	1 0	24

Soft Drinks

			s. d.	Fr. Frs.
Lemonade		Split bottle	6	12
Soda Water	...	,,	6	12
Dry Ginger Ale		,,	8	16
Ginger Beer	...	,,	8	16
Lime Juice Cordial	...	glass	6	12
Lemon or Orange Squash		,,	6	12

Cigarettes

	50's		25's	
	s. d.	Fr. Frs.	s. d.	Fr. Frs.
Abdulla No. 7	6 8	160		
do. No. 11	10 0	240		
State Express 555	6 8	160	3 4	80
Player's "Medium"	5 10	140	2 11	70
Senior Service	5 10	140	2 11	70
Capstan "Medium"	5 10	140	2 11	70
Churchman's No. 1	6 3	150		
Woodbines	4 5	106		

Tobacco

		s. d.	Fr. Frs.
Bell's "Three Nuns"	2 oz.	5 9	138
Players Medium Navy Cut	,,	5 8	136
Ogden's "St. Julien"	,,	5 2	124
Scots Cake Flake	4 oz.	10 10	260

The vessel was propelled by twin screws driven by two sets of 'Parsons-type' turbines, through single-reduction gearing, which at full speed propeller revolutions were about 260. The four Babcock & Wilcox water-tube boilers were arranged to burn oil fuel under air pressure, while the latest electrical plant was provided for lighting, heating and cooking. A special Thermo-tank supply and inductor exhaust system gave adequate heating, and regulated forced air ventilation in the passenger accommodation. An ingenious system of electrically illuminated signs for the guidance of passengers was fitted in all passenger saloons and corridors, and an installation of modern foam fire extinguishers was located throughout the vessel for immediate use if required.[130]

Offering improved travelling facilities by the Short Sea Route, the 'Canterbury', with its special provision to store sealed containers in its hold for registered baggage, formed an important part of the widely advertised accelerated timings of 6 hours 35 minutes from London to Paris, and went into regular service following the inauguration of the 'Golden Arrow Limited'.

A special, highly-promoted first-class fare from London to Paris covering reserved Pullman car seats in the English and French Pullman trains, and the passage from Dover to Calais by the 'Canterbury', was initially advertised at a rate of £5. (Due to the worldwide slump taking hold and with passenger receipts drastically falling, the fare was reduced on 15 May 1931 in an attempt to entice prospective travellers to £4 12s 6d, the date coinciding with the admittance of ordinary passengers from other trains.)

Passengers who had booked first-class, via Dover and Calais, holding single tickets to destinations beyond Paris, or return tickets to Paris and beyond, could travel by the 'Golden Arrow' service on payment of a special Pullman supplement of 28 shillings and 11 pence between London and Paris in each direction.

Unloading luggage following arrival at Calais.

While new travelling arrangements were made easier in London by 1929, *The Golden Way* magazine began to regularly advertise a special omnibus service operating to/from King's Cross Station to connect with the long-distance Pullman trains serving the North. It was therefore possible to travel by the 'Queen of Scots Pullman' from Edinburgh (and later Glasgow) with connecting Continental services from Victoria to Paris, Brussels, Cologne, Basle and beyond.[131]

On deck and taking the fresh sea air. Pullman Conductor Mr Walter Badger is in the background ensuring that passengers' travel requirements have been addressed.

Just prior to the outbreak of World War 2, the 'Canterbury' sailed on her last passenger service on 3 September 1939, and was commandeered for war service in the Channel shortly thereafter. Remarkably, she was one of the vessels used in the Dunkirk evacuation, in northern waters bringing the first American troops to Northern Ireland, later taking soldiers over to the Normandy beaches on D-Day and ending the war bringing huge volumes of troops back on leave.[132]

Pullman Democrats

In a November 1929 edition of *The Standard* the following was reported:

'I met yesterday a man who has probably made more trips to Paris than any other man living. His name is Walter Badger, and he has been in charge of the Pullmans of the famous 11 o'clock service from Victoria to Paris ever since Pullmans were introduced on the service almost twenty years ago.

'Great places have taken place in the attitude of the public towards the service. "People are more democratic now", he explained. "They carry less baggage, and those who make the journey often always look out for us at the beginning of the trip. They do not like new faces, and I have to be very careful in making changes in my staff …"

'"I think I know nearly 75 per cent. of our regular travellers by name," he went on. "It gives them pleasure to be recognised, and I receive scores of invitations to visit them at home afterwards. Sir William Orpen is one of the most frequent passengers to Paris, and I have often been invited to his home. He takes great pleasure in hearing about all the curious things that happen on a journey between London and Paris."

Seat 13

"You have no idea of the number of passengers who refuse Seat 13 although it is the most comfortable in the car. Others will not sit in any other. One famous man won a small fortune in Paris after travelling on this seat. On his return he said to me: "That seat 13 brought me luck. I will never sit in any other seat".'

The Standard, 4 November 1929

One of a host of stories told by Mr Badger in 1947 makes for amusing reading:

A gentleman who was only just in time to catch the "Golden Arrow" one morning came to me very distressed and excited, 'What do you think has happened?' he said, 'As I was jumping out of the taxi I felt something snap and find that I have broken my braces, I can't go all the way to Paris with my hands in my pockets to keep my trousers up. Can you help me?' Trying to look sympathetic, without laughing, I promised to do what I could. I never thought a catastrophe like this could happen on the "Golden Arrow". Knowing that one of the attendants wore a belt and braces, I called him to one side and explained the gentleman's dilemma and asked him if he would like to sell his braces, the transfer was soon made, the attendant well recompensed and the trousers were under control…'

Theatrical impresario Sir Johnston Forbes Robertson (1853 – 1937) seen here, was considered to be one of the finest English actors of his time. He is about to board a Pullman train bound for London.

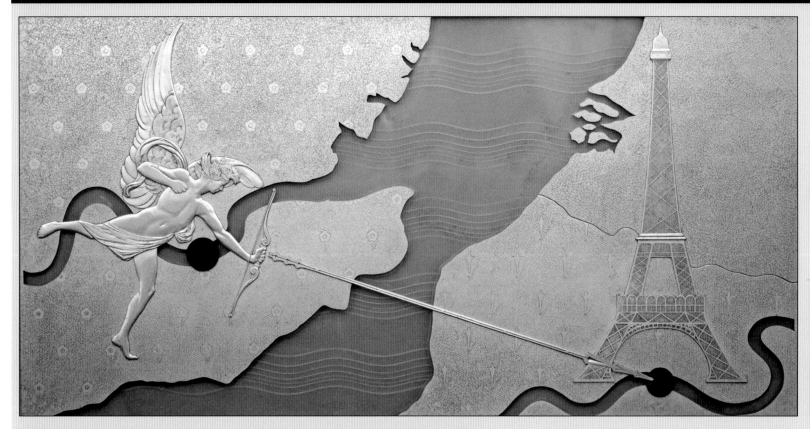

Left: *One of two aluminium plaques specially designed and executed by Messrs J. Starkie Gardner and Co Ltd. of Wandsworth formed part of the decoration in the Trianon Bar Cars.*

Below: *The plaque as shown was installed in the 'Plastics Car', No 5.*

Claimed by Clerke & Hannah in their monthly diary of events for the Pullman passenger, 'This is Europe', 'Paris smiles at you the moment you are introduced, and in a remarkably short time you feel that you have known her all your life. For Paris is an extrovert among cities – she has, to be sure, her hidden depths of personality but she flaunts her charms very openly and is extremely companionable'.[133]

In the June 1927 edition, it was further suggested that a few practical hints may be useful for the first-time 'Golden Arrow' visitor, including making the most of mealtimes. (A 1937 re-print for the Paris International Exhibition again emphasised these points, accompanied by modern colourful graphics by Georges Barbier)

'The apéritif is an essential to the French way of life, and nothing could be more pleasant than sipping one in a leisurely fashion in a café on the Boulevards, in the open air if the weather is at all pleasant. Sherry is usually obtainable, but does not occupy the same place of honour that it does in England, and cocktails are obtainable only in the bars of the more fashionable hotels, notably at the Ritz. Cinzano, Dubonnet, Vermouth and Pernod are the favourites; the last may prove a trap to the unwary.

'Restaurants are obliged to show their menus with prices outside, which is a great boon to those who must budget carefully with their currency allowance ...

'If luxury is everything and money is a secondary consideration, the best restaurants will give you gastronomic delights that cannot be excelled anywhere in the world.'

Conversely, London sights and hotels have an 'equal character and personality', we are told as those in Paris. Visitors coming to these shores for business or pleasure and staying overnight in the Capital 'experience a long and mellow tradition of gracious hospitality behind them. They will surely appreciate the solid sincerity of this tradition ... people come to Britain, and come in ever-increasing numbers, not only to see this country, but to sample the British way of life'[134]

Bournemouth Air Specials

An early post-war view of British statesman Winston Churchill boarding a Pullman car with his wife Clementina, at Victoria, surrounded by press photographers. Although no evidence has come to light that Churchill used the 'Bournemouth Air Special', throughout his life he was a prolific user of Pullman cars.

During much of the interregnum and immediately post war, Pullman special trains were run between London (Victoria) and Bournemouth (West). These specials, called the 'Hush Hush' or 'Ghost Train' were run in connection with the British Overseas Airways Corporation (B.O.A.C.) air services between Poole Harbour and Baltimore, USA, for example, and Hurn aerodrome and the Continent; connection between Poole and Bournemouth West station was by road.

The composition of each train generally comprised at least two Pullmans, together with Southern Railway first-class corridor brakes at each end, four or five vehicles in all. The locomotive was often an ex London & South Western Railway Drummond 'T9' 4-4-0.

The 'Bournemouth Air Specials', as they became to be known, provided the only known non-stop regular services between Bournemouth and Victoria (and vice versa). Initially, at least, the head code was one disc at the chimney, one right side of the boiler, and on centre of the buffet beam, but this arrangement was later altered to the standard Bournemouth code.[135]

According to *The Bournemouth Daily* about 120 passengers bound for all parts of the world would board the train every night. During the war years, the departure of this train was a 'top secret', because Cabinet Ministers, diplomats, Service chiefs and high officials could be seen on it almost every night. Among the passengers were 'foreigners of royal blood, Lord Wavell, Lord Halifax, Lord Alanbrooke, Lord Portal of Hungerford and many others.[136]

According to Pullman Inspector Badger (as he then was), the passengers also included private soldiers and non-commissioned officers who were going on important secret duties overseas and were urgently required there, besides business men and others going abroad on urgent war missions.[137]

Left: *This early post-war photograph shows a typical platform scene with Inspector Badger assisting a passenger.*

Below: *On board the 'Airways Special', Inspector Badger discusses travel arrangements with a lady passenger in car Niobe, January 1946, prior to this car's transfer to the 'Golden Arrow'.*

During the period 1942-1945 more than 30,000 passengers travelled on the train, which was seen as the first stage of a journey that would have taken them anywhere along the 60,000 miles of B.O.A.C. air routes in the land planes from Hurn or the flying-boats from Poole harbour to such places as Calcutta, Cairo, South Africa, Australia and North America.[138]

Dinner was served on the 'down' journey, and upon arrival at Bournemouth West station passengers alighted and spent the 'night stop' in one or other of the large hotels in the locality.[139] While the Pullman cars varied from time to time, many previously saw regular service on the Dover and Folkestone boat trains, including *Flora, Clementina, Cosmo Bonsor, Daphne* and *Hawthorn,* each fitted with specially adapted windows and doors and painted all-over umber to be less conspicuous to enemy aircraft. On almost all trips, Inspector Badger looked after the comfort of passengers.[140]

Departing from a platform at Victoria adjoining the headquarters of the B.O.A.C. in Buckingham Palace Road, the timings of these trains were as follows:

*From London (Victoria) at 7.8 pm (stopping at Christchurch *en route*, if required, for Hurn Airport).

*From Bournemouth (West) nominally at 3 pm.[141] (From Bournemouth West the mainline was followed to Wimbledon, and then onto the Wimbledon-Holborn route to Streatham Common, where the spur was taken to join the mainline from East Croydon to Victoria.)

Inspector Badger also worked on another special train with two cars placed at the disposal of King George VI for his many visits to different parts of the South where the armies were stationed. When this train was wanted, Badger was notified that 'Mr Groves would be travelling to a certain place on such and such a date'. Badger records that 'His Majesty on returning to the train after reviewing the troops was very particular in wiping his shoes before entering the car'.

A rare 1946 exterior view of **Cosmo Bonsor** *painted all-over umber, and faintly showing its specially adapted windows and vestibule doors.*

Pullman cars in N.A.A.F.I service

For the purpose of providing meals in troop and leave trains, the following five 'G-type' (formerly 'A-type') Pullman cars, with kitchen facilities, familiar for many years on the Dover and Folkestone boat trains and other services in Kent, were temporarily transferred to the control of the Navy, Army and Air Force Institute (N.A.A.F.I.) just prior to the end of World War 2. The vehicles were each painted dark green all over, carrying their N.A.A.F.I. numbers in small yellow letters at the bottom of the body sides, near the entrance vestibule doors.

Corunna	N.A.A.F.I. No. 29
Savona	N.A.A.F.I. No. 38
Sapphire	N.A.A.F.I. No. 37
Palermo	N.A.A.F.I. No. 21
Seville	N.A.A.F.I. No. 3

The cars were later restored to their original condition following overhaul at Preston Park Works, Brighton, and by 1947 each are recorded running again with extra-fare accommodation.

(Note: Although some of the above vehicles were originally parlour cars and remodelled during the 1920s, they all featured kitchens – of varying size – at the time of requisition in 1944; further alterations to their accommodation subsequently took place when reassigned to Pullman workings. See drawings per the appendix.)

Sapphire *at Preston Park, one of the five 'G-type' cars converted for N.A.A.F.I. use, and seen here freshly painted and ready for 'extra-fare' service following its overhaul and refurbishment.*

The return of the 'Golden Arrow' and 'Flèche d'Or, 1946

The resumption of the 'Golden Arrow' was seen by many observers as one of the most vigorous signs that the country was getting back to some sort of peace and normality after almost six lean years.[142]

Coinciding with the inaugural passenger service on Monday, 15 April 1947, the BBC Home Service broadcast a Dover-Calais feature live from Dover Castle and the quayside. The programme included the start of the 'Golden Arrow' service, and interviews with a selection of people from Dover and Calais, as detailed later.[143]

Freshly painted and highly glossed, the eight Pullmans assembled together had probably recaptured some of the 'Golden Arrow's' one-time exclusiveness with five first- and, for the first time, two second-class cars, together with a novel bar car, known as 'Trianon'.

On 13 April, the Saturday preceding, from Victoria to Dover and back, the special demonstration run was made to enable press, B.B.C., cinema representatives and other influential people to experience a foretaste of the facilities to come. The platform entrance at Victoria was specially decorated, and a very large crowd, including a 'youthful element', gathered on the departing platform (repeated again with the inaugural run), requiring supervision from police and station staff on both occasions. Sir Eustace Missenden of the Southern Railway, and Mr Frank Harding of the Pullman Car Co, had invited guests to this preview so that the train and ship could be inspected in more leisurely conditions than possible when in service.

Adhering to a daily schedule, the first public run was a colourful affair. Departure times for this 'de-luxe' train and other International European Expresses, including the 'Simplon Orient Express', were now reflected on a new indicator board located on the passenger concourse, crowned 'The Gateway to the Continent' and above this a clock. In addition, boards flanking a 'Golden Gateway' decorating the entrance to platform 8 provided departure times and daily sea conditions.

'Pullman and perfection'. A Pullman car attendant shows off the new all-white monkey jacket in 1946 (prior to the introduction a year later of the more familiar jackets with blue lapels), as he waits for passengers at one of the entrances to car 'F'.

The first public service of the 'Golden Arrow' was seen off at 10 am by Mr Alfred Barnes, Minister of Transport, who is reported to have said that the occasion marked not only a new service on the Southern Railway, but was of 'special significance in the opportunity it gave of renewing contacts with France, of the importance of whose civilisation the war had given us a deeper realisation'.[144]

The inaugural departure of the 'Flèche d'Or' with its locomotive adorned with flags and gleaming Pullmans (Côte d'Azur-type) in tow (together with ordinary carriages and a Wagons-Lits diner) departed from the temporary Calais Maritime station with Capt. H.A.Dannatt, the engine driver, and M. Vachez (sous chef de dépôt, Calais) at the controls.[145] Paris was reached at 6.45 pm.

By 1 July 1947, the volumes of passengers had increased to such an extent that the formation became exclusively 'first-class Pullman only' between Paris and Calais, recorded as the only Pullman service on the Continent (post-World War 2) to be composed of all-Pullman stock.[146] However, by 1950 demand had fluctuated once more, allowing second-class Pullmans to be added again to the formation, as well as, ordinary stock on occasions.

A novel newspaper and magazine trolley is captured in this now timeless scene at the temporary Calais Maritime station in 1947. The Pullman car in the background ('Côte d'Azur-type') with its Rene Prou-designed table lamps and shades forms part of the 'Golden Arrow'/'Flèche d'Or' bound for Paris.

Above: *The sense of speed is emphasised in this stylish and colourful 1946 brochure issued by the Wagons-lits Company to advertise the 'Flèche d'Or'/'Golden Arrow' service.*

Right: *The service indicator at the Gare du Nord (entrance to Platform 4) announces the 'Flèche d'Or' (Express Train, No. 19) to London, via Calais and Dover. Seat reservations were obligatory. Wagons-Lits Pullman ticket holders could identify their car by the pentagonal white plates mounted on the waist-line of the cars, in contrast to the metal plaques fixed to the doorways on most British Pullman cars.*

Opposite: *The spacious concourse at Victoria station for International Continental Expresses, showing to the immediate right, the attractive 'Golden Arrow' archway.*

The BBC Home Service broadcast

Transmission:

Monday, 15 April, 1946 at 6.30-7pm HOME

Overseas:

N. American:	Tuesday/ Wednesday 16/17 April:	0130-0200 GMT
Pacific:	Wednesday 17 April:	0815-0845
African:	Wednesday 17 April:	1700-1730

Rehearsals:

Sunday, 14 April at 3pm Shalimar Hotel, Dover

Monday, 15 April at 2pm Quayside, Dover (Customs House)

                at 3.30pm Effects Rehearsal with London

                at 4.30pm Full Rehearsal London-Dover-Calais

                at 5.30-6pm Final run through to be recorded in London

Quayside: Wynford Vaughan Thomas

                     Lt. Col. Turner

                     Major Strange

                     Miss Scanlon of the Shalimar Hotel

                     Capt. Walker of the ss Canterbury

Castle: Bruce Belfrage

                     The Mayor of Dover

Announcer (London): 'Today, for the first time since September 1939, the "Golden Arrow" Pullman Express took civilian passengers from London to Paris via Dover and Calais. The story of the resumption of the "Golden Arrow" boat train service starts off a two-way exchange programme between the two Channel ports.

'In Dover Wynford Vaughan Thomas, and in Calais Pierre Lefevre, are waiting to introduce the people of the two ports to one another across the 20 miles of Channel that have separated them for so many years. We take you now over to Dover – and then from "DOVER TO CALAIS". Over to Wynford Vaughan Thomas in Dover.

Above: *Almost obliterated: the once stunningly attractive Birmingham Railway Carriage & Wagon built Pullman kitchen car* No. 4005 *photographed as a wreck outside Calais in 1946.*

Left: *'Golden Arrow' attendants smartly dressed with new all-white monkey jackets, ties and specially designed badges receiving final instruction from Inspector Stroud prior to the inaugural trip.*

Wynford: 'I'm standing on the quayside in Dover. It's a glorious day and you can just see the faint line of the French coast, where the Germans for so long manned the guns that shelled Dover. Now over on that coast the French people are waiting to exchange greetings with the British, for the first time since the war. Hello Calais. Hello Calais. This is Dover calling Calais.

Pierre: 'Hello Dover. Hello Dover. We are ready here in Calais. I'm talking to you from the Hotel Metropole – the only hotel left in Calais. From the window, we've a wonderful view of what was once the heart of Calais and is now a bombed, shelled waste land. There's nothing left of the centre of this town that has been a battlefield twice, a target for our bombers many times and the object of German vengeance in their final retreat. Now the old Calais Nord is completely destroyed and from the harbour for a mile or more inland it's all dusty, open ground. And by the way, if you hear any bangs, it will only be mines exploding on the beaches.

All the same, today it's a cheerful scene. Just outside this window the French are working on the railway and all over the town they're toiling feverishly to clear the ruins ready for rebuilding. The spirit of the people of Calais is wonderful and they're all ready to rejoice on this day, when civilian traffic has been started up again between the two ports – so, over to you Dover – to start this programme with the first good news of the "Golden Arrow's" journey from London through to Dover and Calais.

Wynford: 'Well, here's the sound you're waiting for – the "Golden Arrow" starting up on its first journey since 1939.

London recordings: 'Golden Arrow' starts…

> Wynford introducing Mr Walter Badger: 'I think I must have crossed from Dover to Calais about four thousand times – from 1926 when the service started, till 1939. I was Inspector-in-Charge of the "Golden Arrow" all that time.
>
> 'I've always liked the service, because everybody that was anybody used to travel and I got to know 'em all. Kings and dukes and duchesses and cabinet ministers, diplomats and ambassadors. They knew me too. They sometime called me the 'unofficial ambassador'. I had to look after 'em all, you see. I took the Shah of Persia back with me one time, and King Alfonso, and more than I could mention. The Grand Duke Michael of Russia and his two little girls travelled more than anyone. They practically grew up with me, those children.
>
> 'The traffic used to be pretty heavy. In fact, my hair's all gone in front with – "Good morning, madam", "good morning, sir" – with raising my cap, you see. I wasn't on the last trip myself, but Mr Stroud here was the conductor then.
>
> Mr Stroud: 'I was in Paris the day war broke out. I was the last man to work the "Golden Arrow" all the way – and I had to scramble on to a train and come back as a passenger. I stood all the way to Calais I remember. It's grand now to be doing my job again on this first trip.
>
> Wynford: 'And here we are – arriving in Dover!'

(End of London recordings)

'And so the 'Golden Arrow' arrived in Dover where the SS "Canterbury" was ready to take the passengers across to Calais. And here at the quayside, now, just back from the trip across the Straits, is the skipper of the "Canterbury" – Captain Gordon Walker D.S.C.

Capt. Walker: '… over in Calais they were waiting for us with a grand welcome. But that's my old friend Monsieur Corbier's story. M. Corbier has been interpreter on the other side for twenty years and is over in Calais ready to take up the tale. Hello M. Corbier – this is the great moment when you can tell the world about that beloved railway of yours.

Mons. Corbier: 'Hello Captain Walker. I am so glad you got back in time. I wish I had crossed the Channel with you like I do for so many years. It was wonderful for me to be here to see the "Canterbury" come in to Calais to welcome her passenger as they come in like this.

London effects: Arrival of 'Canterbury'. Long whistle of train.

Pierre: 'And that was the "Flèche d'Or" – the French "Golden Arrow" Pullman starting on the last part of the journey to Paris. I know this is a big day for people over there, but it's really wonderful in Calais to see this great luxury train pulling out of what was once the quayside station – the Gare Maritime. It's true that as the train started up, it travelled over something like a battlefield, a great waste land with only a broken shell of a building stocking up here and there, but it *did* travel – the line *was* working again.

Wynford: 'And is the railway really back to anything like normal over there in Calais?

M. Corbier: 'Excuse me, but I am going to say you my inspiration – to tell the people in Dover what I can. I have been back on the railway work for a year now. I live in my office. My wife is not back yet, because like so many Calaisiens we have no home. I work, then I sleep at the station. I go to bed 9 to 10, like a nice little boy. There is no more to do, you see. But all day we work. Already we have nice painted huts where the station was.

'And the trains run as you hear. When Calais was liberated, there was not one mile of railway line – not a single mile. Every bridge, every embankment is shelled, bombed or destroyed by sabotage like I do myself when the Boches are here. The Germans before they left let in the sea through the dykes, they dynamite the quays, they take away or destroy the cranes.

'You see, we have a big job. And the workers here do it this way. They take away rubbish in little carts with horses. They do it just a little bit at a time. They lay down track mile after mile by hand. They have no machines. Only the British Army help with machines when they can.

Pierre: 'And I wonder if the passengers who went through Calais on their way to Paris in the "Flèche d'Or" realised that there is no central signalling and interlocking mechanism? That every point all along the line has to be thrown by hand levers.

M Corbier: 'If you don't mind me saying so … I do not think passengers worry about such things. Why should they? It is very comfortable in the train and we do not wish to bother their

little heads. Although now I think the passengers will be different in peace time. Then it was like Monsieur Badger – I cannot say that name – who speak to us from the 'Golden Arrow' – it was like he says, on the train you meet everybody – princes – everybody… Now it is people who have work to do, only these people take the train.'

Wynford: 'I think that's true of most of the travellers who come to Dover, M. Corbier. They're working hard in Dover to get the town ready for holiday makers. But at the moment the only hotel that's been open for civilians all through the war is still the only place to put up for a night in Dover. The Shalimar Hotel has become famous in England during the war, so we've asked the proprietress Miss Scanlon to talk to Calais.'

Pierre: 'I'm glad Miss Scanlon is there, because we want her to meet Madame Simon, proprietress of the Hotel Metropole where we're speaking from now. The Metropole is the only hotel left in Calais – there aren't even the foundations of the older hotels left standing. Madame Simon, come and speak to Miss Scanlon in Dover.'

Mme. Simon: 'Hallo Miss Scanlon. It is very nice to speak to you. My English is not so good, but I hope you understand.'

Miss Scanlon: 'Hallo Madame Simon. Your English sounds fine. It's nice to be able to hear your voice. I haven't been over to Calais since the war before this last one. And then I went specially to have a look at the Metropole, because you see, I've got a soft spot for the Calais Metropole.'

Pierre: 'I don't think you'd recognise the walls of the restaurant, Miss Scanlon. We're in there now and surrounded by great wall drawings made by the Germans of French prisoners being taken away to slave labour.'

Mme. Simon: 'They are horrible. Anyway, I am glad you cannot see us now. We are not really tidy after all the mess the Germans make. And we have not many staff.'

Miss Scanlon: 'Oh, we have staff troubles in Dover – and what with the lift going wrong and meals to get ready there's work for a dozen pair of hands. Then it's difficult to get sheets and blankets and we like our guests to bring their own towels.'

Mme. Simon: 'Here it is very bad too. Everything was destroyed – blankets, mattresses, chairs, tables. You see in the war the Germans live and sleep here at the Metropole. They leave not one room for us – we sleep downstairs in the cellar. They make terrible noise – they sing and shout. And if my father does not clean for them quickly – quickly – they throw him out of the door.'

Miss Scanlon: 'My guests had to eat in the basement for a month when the shelling was bad over here – but it must have been terrible for you to have to live in the basement of your own hotel. But how did all your furniture get destroyed?'

*Opposite: **The re-inaugurated 'Golden Arrow' storms out of Victoria station up Grosvenor Bank bound for Dover. The locomotive is 'Merchant Navy' class No 21C1 'Channel Packet'.***

Mme. Simon: 'When the fight comes here at the liberation, many of us go outside the town. My father stayed in the hotel and locked the door. The S.S. came back and he does not open. The S.S. go tack-tack, and bullets come through. Then the S.S. come in and take everything. We have a few things now, but no carpet at all.'

Miss Scanlon: 'Do you find that your guests grumble? I find it hard to get used to people's little peacetime worries nowadays.'

Mme. Simon: 'Oh, here they are content if they get a room – it is the only hotel at all, and the rest of Calais Nord is more destroyed.'

Miss Scanlon: 'How do you manage for food? Our rations are strict, but we are lucky because Kent is a vegetable growing county and we're never short of fresh greens.'

Mme. Simon: 'In Calais we do not have them – no potatoes at all. And bread is on tickets you understand? But we have special rations for the travellers who start again now. Sometimes we have real coffee. And we have beer. But sometime there is a British Tommy who will not agree it is beer. Hey, there – isn't that right, soldier?'

Pierre: 'A big part of the story of Dover and Calais at the moment is the Transit camps and the troops going to and fro on leave. But I'm not sure that the British Tommy gets the best possible view of either of the ports.'

[…]

Wynford: 'Now Dover and Calais must think of the future. And to look forward, to talk to you of the future, and of Dover's plans for prosperity and reconstruction – here is the Mayor of Dover to speak to the Mayor of Calais.'

Mayor of Dover: 'Monsieur Le Maire, it is a great privilege to send greetings to you and to the people of Calais from Dover. For five years the Dover-Calais Front was the only one where British and German troops were in permanent contact. The war was very real to the peoples of both towns, and in a way, we had a lot in common. Now we're trying to make the bonds deeper.

'The first step was an exchange of visits between the Mayors of Dover and Calais. Your predecessor, M. Le Maire, came over to see us and my predecessor at Dover returned the visit.

'You see the prosperity of the two ports is, to a certain extent, interdependent. Calais is the obvious route for goods made in Dover and destined for Continental markets. And we are planning new industries in the war-damaged areas here. We've already got one of the largest papermills in the South of England, and other manufacturers are planning to set up factories in bombed and shelled sites.

'We've got a difficult road ahead of us. But we've laid our plans – bold, imaginative plans to rebuild 270 acres of the centre of the town.

'In the meantime, today civilian traffic begins again between Dover and Calais with the re-introduction of the "Golden Arrow" Pullman service, and I feel this is the start of a new life for these two ports.

Mayor of Calais: (speaks in French, but no recording is known to survive)

Pierre: (translating) 'May I, Mr Mayor, return your greetings. Although I have my time taken up, day in, day out, with the innumerable worries of a city recovering from almost complete annihilation, I hope that one day soon, our friends from Dover will be frequently crossing the 20 miles of sea that separate us. Such a link between our two towns, added to those already existing because of the military traffic, and this service restarted today by the "Flèche d'Or", will be a sure sign for us of the speedy return to the days of peacetime prosperity.

Bruce Belfrage: 'Now Dover is full of life, all the people who can find homes are back again, and there is an air of returning prosperity. We rejoice to know that Calais also is getting back to normal, is overcoming the terrible difficulties, and working cheerfully to rebuild the ruins. And we rejoice today in the knowledge that once more the people of our two countries can travel again on the "Golden Arrow" service.

Announcer (London): 'You have been listening to a two-way exchange programme from "Dover to Calais" narrated in Dover by Wynford Vaughan Thomas and Bruce Belfrange, and by Pierre Lefevre in Calais. Arranged by the BBC in co-operation with Radio Diffusion National Francaise and produced by Marjorie Banks and Pierre Lefevre.'

END.

Merchant Navy class locomotives No 21C1 *'Channel Packet' (photographed at Eastleigh), and used on the inaugural trip of the post-war 'Golden Arrow', 13 April 1946.*

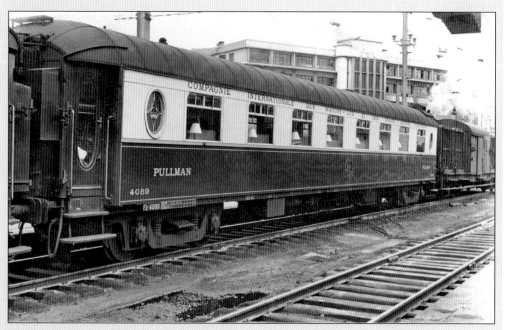

Parlour *Car No 4089 in the 'Golden Arrow' formation at Gare du Nord in 1950.*

Mr Walter Badger – *Chef-du-train*

In May 1946, *The Tatler and Bystander*, in conjunction with the revival of the 'Golden Arrow', published an article about Mr Walter Badger, a personality who was well known by regular passengers on the famous pre-war train, rising in rank to the unique position of Chief Inspector.

He was aboard the inaugural post-war 'Golden Arrow' service and it was the first time that he had been in Paris since September 1939. In that respect, perhaps, he was like many passengers, but there was one difference. That trip was approximately the 4,000[th] time that he travelled between Victoria and the Gare du Nord.

He was Mr Walter James William Badger of Streatham – Badger of the 'Golden Arrow' – who for the 12 years that the service ran up to 1939 was Inspector on the train – the *'Chef-du-train'*, as the French called him.

During February 1946, Mr Badger was officially appointed Chief Inspector on all the Southern Railway Pullman services; but he told *The Tatler and Bystander* that he 'still prefers to travel on his old route when possible'.[147]

For some years before the 'Golden Arrow' arrived, Badger used to accompany the first boat train service all the way from either Charing Cross or Victoria stations to Paris. He thus became a very familiar figure to regular travellers on this route from 1910. All told, Badger calculated, that he must have made just over 4,000 trips to Paris and the same number back. Although he always needed to carry a passport, never once was it asked for or stamped; all the port and police authorities on both sides of the Channel knew him so well.

Badger is reported to have said 'that never once was I bored on those trips; a bit queasy perhaps in a mid-winter Channel gale, but never bored'.[148]

He took too much interest in his many distinguished passengers, of whom he remembered Lord Derby, Viceroy Lord Curzon, Sir William Orpen (who painted the 1914-18 war pictures), the Aga Khan and Admiral Beatty as the most-ready and most amusing conversationalists among his 'regulars'. *The Tatler and Bystander* even suggested that his title of 'Inspector' was really far too ordinary a title for him. In some ways, Badger was the 'Golden Arrow'.

Apart from being a general guide, philosopher and friend, he was usually the counsellor, confidant, entertainer (on occasions, even banker to those returning financially distressed after a few hectic days in Paris), to all who sought his company or his advice on the trip. He was, of necessity, the recipient of many secrets, political and domestic. He often knew about pending

Mr Walter Badger (1939). Note the elaborate lapel and hat inscriptions proudly worn indicating rank. He had the honour to meet many distinguished persons including their Majesties King George VI and Queen Elizabeth when Duke and Duchess of York. The first occasion was part of their honeymoon (1923) and another time when they went to Paris to attend a dinner at the Caledonian Club. On the return journey, Badger recorded that the Duke sent for him and congratulated him for the very pleasant journey.

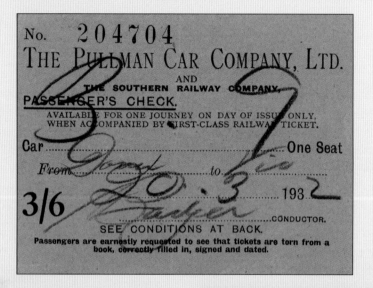

Left: *A 1930s photograph from the Walter Badger collection showing his former colleagues: three attendants, chef, and the 'on-board' cat, named 'Socrates'!*

Government changes, or Society divorces and snap marriages long before they became public. There was something about Mr Badger which probably compelled people with an overburdening secret to take him into their confidence.

Badger proudly claimed that he was the first to popularise the 'new-fangled' Pullman cars when they made their début on the Brighton line, as the 'Southern Belle' in 1908, and had met and looked after most of the world-household names in the course of his cross-Channel journeys. He had been in contact with nearly all the crowned and ex-crowned heads of Europe, the majority of the ruling Prince's of India, the British and international aristocracy (and crookery, too. One well-known financier gaolbird on his first trip after release from prison commented to Badger between puffs at his cigar, 'Golden Arrow, eh, Badger, nice change after the broad arrow'.)[149]

He had known the American millionaires and film stars, headliners in industry, outstanding figures on Europe's political stage in the 1920s and 1930s, and the flock of artistic dilettanti who in those days flitted between London and Paris as easily as one might take a bus from Hyde Park to Piccadilly or the Strand. Badger knew them all, before retiring from Pullman employment in 1951 after 43 years' service.

Several of the free Pullman passes issued to Mr Walter Badger, together with a 1932 supplementary ticket issued by him, in his capacity as Inspector.

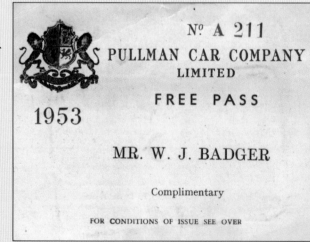

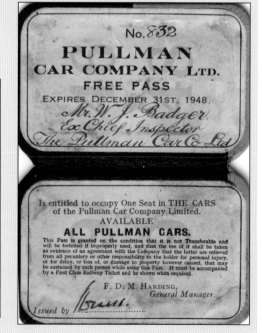

GOLDEN ARROW

The TS 'Invicta'

The Southern Railway's new Cross-Channel boat TS 'Invicta' of 4,178 tons commenced 'Golden arrow' service on Tuesday 15 October 1946, when she relieved the 'Canterbury', which had been operating since the resumption of the world-renowned luxe service between Dover and Calais, six months previously.[150] (The 'Canterbury' was destined to be transferred to Folkestone by 1 December, promoting a completely new service between Folkestone and Calais.)

The Master of the TS 'Invicta', Capt. H.L. Payne O.B.E., R.D., sailed under the flag of the Commodore of the Dover and Folkestone Fleet, to which appointment he had succeeded Capt. Hancock upon retirement.[151]

The vessel was said to be the last word in Cross-Channel luxury, and also noteworthy as the first of the fleet to carry five decks. Although it had only commenced the Dover-Calais run from October 1946, she was by no means a stranger at Dover. Launched at Dumbarton in 1939, at the ship yard of Messrs. William Denny and Bros, Ltd., the 'Invicta' became at that point in time the largest vessel built for the Cross-Channel service to France. Measuring 350ft in length, she boasted a speed of 22.5 knots and could comfortably accommodate almost 1,300 passengers.[152]

Following distinguished war service at Dieppe and Normandy, she arrived at Dover at the end of 1945 still in war-paint to ferry British Army of the Rhine (B.A.O.R) troops to Calais.[153]

Captain H.L. Payne on the deck of the TS 'Invicta'.

Alighting Pullman passengers make their way towards the quay for embarkation. Note the small sign to the immediate right – 'Victoria Boat Train. Golden Arrow service'.

Above: *A timeless mid-1960s scene at Dover Marine with passengers making their way to the gangplanks for boarding TS 'Invicta'.*

Top right: *Entrance to the upper deck general lounge.*

Right: *Promenade deck comfortable armchair accommodation aboard the TS 'Invicta'.*

Compared to the luxurious accommodation offered by the 'Canterbury', the radar-equipped 'Invicta' was also a fine Cross-Channel vessel, but up-to-date in its overall styling, complete with two continuous decks, main and upper, together with a promenade deck extending almost the whole of her length. A large tea lounge with chintz-covered furniture, and private cabins, were located on the promenade deck, whilst a first-class restaurant accommodating 84 persons, a ladies' room, another general lounge and smoke room were on the upper deck. Forward on the main deck was a first-class ladies' lounge, private cabins, and aft, the third-class accommodation, including a restaurant with accommodation for 58 persons, smoke room and several lounges. Supplemental charges were made for both cabins and alcoves; the smaller private cabins and alcoves were advertised from 10 shillings, and the special cabins located on 'B' deck were available at £2.[154]

The navigation of the ship was one of its outstanding features. In addition to being fitted with radar, wing cabs to the bridge, which projected beyond the ship's side, and a bow rudder for

A study of the bow of the **TS Invicta** *just prior to sailing.*

entering harbour stern first, were installed. The design of the bridge, wheel-house, chart room, and the location of the various navigational instruments, had all been arranged to simplify the running of the ship and berthing her under difficult conditions.[155]

Below passenger decks was the most up-to-date machinery, having converted from coal to oil burning, and the main propelling machinery consisted of two independent sets of Parson's latest steam turbines. Steam was supplied by two Yarrow-type oil-fired water tube boilers. The oil fuel installation consisted of two steam pumping and heating units, and the oil was burnt under a closed 'stoke-hold system' of forced draught and six patented air distributors and burners fitted to each boiler.[156] A day before entering 'Golden Arrow' service, the *Dover Express* records a detailed report of the celebratory lunch held on board the ship, presided over by Mr R.P. Biddle C.B.E., the Docks and Marine Manager of the Southern Railway, who entertained a large number of guests.[157]

With the lunch concluded, Mr Biddle proposed the health of the guests and declared that the 'Invicta' under the capable command of Capt. Payne, would 'foster trade and friendship between Great Britain and France, and further the "Entente Cordiale" so necessary for peace and prosperity'.

The Mayor of Dover, replying, said that 'at first he wondered why there was so much luxury for a one-hour trip', but recognised that the town of Dover was the 'Gateway of Britain', and 'no method of entry to such a gateway could be too comfortable or too luxurious'. The Mayor added that he hoped the Southern Railway would soon make the Lord Warden Hotel (at the time still part of a Naval Base, until 30 November 1946, and known as H.M.S. 'Wasp') as luxurious as the 'Invicta'. M. De Croix, President of the Calais Chamber of Commerce replied (sadly, only a few words of his reply has been traced).[158]

However, it was clear the re-inauguration of the 'Golden Arrow' service was seen by all as a welcome return to peace and prosperity. The service had continued to grow in popularity, and maintained 'a remarkable record of punctuality'. For the month of June 1946, for example, over 29,000 passengers in or out were carried, steadily increasing each month thereafter 'to such an extent a third train is now being run'.[159]

During the luncheon, the 'Invicta' cruised down to Dungeness and back.

Transforming Car No. 5 *into the neoteric all-plastic interior (later* Trianon Bar *[II]). Note the original marquetry is still in-situ and just discernible to the right. Contoured Formica sheet panels were simply affixed to batons.*

Workmen add the finishing touches to the new panelling, prior to installation of the electric strip lighting.

The 'Trianon Bar' car

Acknowledging historic Anglo-French relations that have been enjoyed since 1904, culminating with the signing of a series of agreements known as the 'Entente Cordiale', the Pullman Company honoured its French counterpart by naming their new and novel 'Golden Arrow' bar car *Trianon*,[160] whose name is indelibly linked to Queen Marie Antoinette and her court in the late 18th century. Built for her enjoyment, two Neoclassical style pavilions or châteaux in the grounds of the palace of Versailles, west of Paris, bear the name 'Trianon'.

An interior photograph of **Trianon** *(formerly* **Diamond***) in 1946 with a passenger and Pullman staff in view.*

The one-time Buffet *Car No. 5* (1917) which became *Trianon Bar* (II) in 1946, as previously outlined, had an ultra-modern plastic laminate lined interior[161] but on the trial run significant difficulties developed, causing delay in the 'dress rehearsal' arrival at Dover, necessitating bogie repairs.[162] On rare occasions during the late 1940s either of the elderly 12-wheel bar cars *Grosvenor* and *Myrtle* deputised when the *Trianon Bar* was out of service.

As reported in *The Dover Express*, Mrs Bessie Ellinor of Dover, who held the distinction of being the first signalwomen to have worked on the Southern Railway, first observed sparks and hot metal that day as the train swiftly passed by. 'I realised the train could be in danger if it was allowed to continue on its journey at that speed', she reported. 'I [immediately] sent an emergency signal to the signal box in advance of the train to have it stopped'.[163]

Once the train had been halted momentarily, it was discovered the '12-wheel bar car' had a hot axle box.

An exterior view of **Trianon** *(formerly* **Diamond***) sporting large painted arrows and other decoration. Note the Pullman coat of arms are relocated to the far ends of the car.*

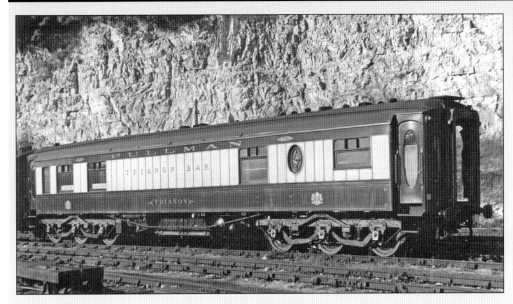

For comparison purposes: **Trianon Bar (II)** *and* **Grosvenor** – *the latter with body mounted clips for 'Golden Arrow' workings; both photographed at Preston Park Works yard in 1950.*

Two bar cars are photographed together momentarily on Dover Pier following the arrival of the 'Trial Trip'. The 'Plastics Car' – later becoming **Trianon Bar (II)** *ex No.5 – is on the left, and* **Trianon** *(ex Diamond) can be seen with 'Golden Arrow' roof board to the right. The former is shortly to be removed from the train due to a hot box. In the background the SS 'Canterbury' can be dimly seen to the extreme right berthed in close proximity to the Marine Station.*

Due to the seriousness of the situation, the vehicle was removed from the train at Dover Marine, and within days returned to the Pullman Company workshops at Preston Park, Brighton, for specialist attention before later returning as a regular feature of the train.

*Kitchen car **Carina** prior to entering service. The stylish and graceful lines of the 'U-type' cars can be clearly seen in this official photograph.*

Following a March 1939 Pullman Car Company Board meeting, approval was finally granted to acquire seven new Pullman cars of 'up-to-date design' earmarked to replace some older cars running on the London & North Eastern Railway (LNER). A draft agreement was prepared by the company secretary, E.J. Morris, with the selected Builder, Birmingham Railway Carriage & Wagon Co. Ltd, to progress the matter and, by the following July, 'the Chairman was in negotiation with the Financier, Dudley Docker, on the details'.[164]

From what can be determined, armchair type and decorations had already been considered by Pullman's Chief Engineer during the initial planning stages a year before, and a quotation had been sought from Waring & Gillow, the English furniture maker. However, the outbreak of World War in September 1939 arrested all work on this project, although records indicate that numerous technical drawings had been completed, and a selection of timbers 'prepared' in advance, quite possibly as samples.

Almost 10 years later, the project was resurrected. At a Board meeting on 5 May 1949, the Pullman Chairman reported that he had had 'satisfactory conversations with Sir Eustace Missenden, Chairman of the new Railway Executive and Sir William Stanier, the company's Technical consultant', and it was agreed to proceed with the purchase of the seven cars from the same Builder.[165] By the following month, work re-commenced when circumstances made it possible, and to which talk of the planned 'Festival of Britain' in 1951 added some incentive to potentially showpiece contemporary inventiveness of British technology by renewing the project.[166]

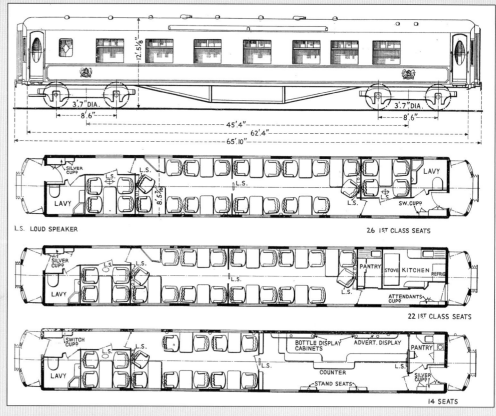

Elevation and plans showing the principal dimensions of the Birmingham-built vehicles.

The Pullman Board considered that their (final) order of new vehicles – which would become their designated 'U-type' and transpiring to be the last 'slab-sided' Pullmans built – would in fact be better placed to form a new Festival 'Golden Arrow' train to promote, and where possible, reshape preconceived ideas of British art, craft and design. Although this decision necessitated considerable design alterations to the original 1930s plans – governed by material restrictions then strictly in force – the use of hard timber framing for their body construction, in place of steel, and a suggestion at this time to finish these cars using a match-boarded finish, were seen by management as a retrograde step.[167] However, these vehicles were intended to contribute to the new image of

Opposite: *Various views of the construction work taking place at Preston Park Works during 1951/2 of 'U-type' cars **Aries** and No. 303 and designated 'K-type' car **Phoenix**.*

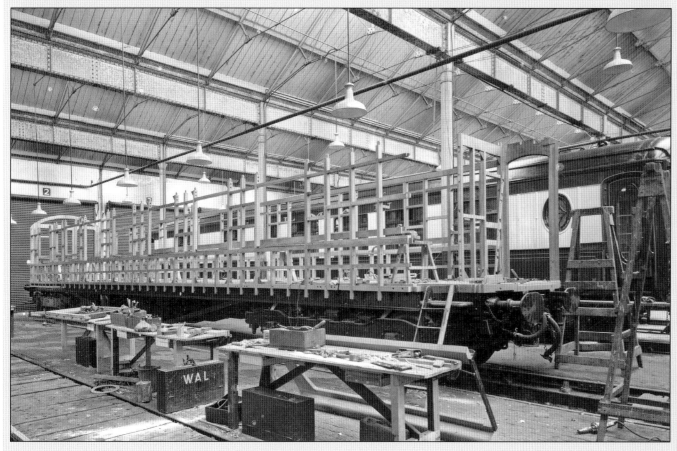

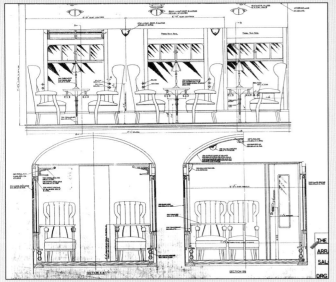

Interior technical drawings of the 'U-type' cars. The seating arrangement is similar to earlier 'K-type' cars (higher density first-class). Special features to note include, parcel/hat racks, lighting, window profiles and lounge door; all to new patterns and designs.

'progressive British technology and design', and possibly nothing could have been more effective in the early post-war period than to counteract the growing competition of air travel between London and Paris. 'If the 1951 summer timings – London (Victoria) dep. 11am., Paris (Gare du Nord) arr. 5.52pm., with a return working at 12.30pm. from Paris, arriving at Victoria 7.30pm – do not compare favourably with those by air, observes *Modern Transport*, at least they cover journeys of some interest and diversity and provide some luxury in these days of austerity'.[168]

The new 'Golden Arrow' train, went into service on Monday, 11 June, 1951 offering accommodation for 184 first- and 78 second-class passengers. The initial formation included three 1920s remodelled and refurbished 'K-type' cars, of five specially allocated* (see images and *Pullman Profile No. 2*), now incorporating lavatory lights of an almost rectangular shape with rounded corners, together with enhanced interior fixtures and fittings, including some new sets of table lamp. Curiously, these older vehicles retained their original vestibule doors with full elliptical oval plate glass, rather than the smaller versions fitted to the 'U-type' cars.[169]

Nevertheless, in keeping with some characteristics of Pullman tradition, the running names of the new cars were derived from mythological characters with Latinized Greek words, and for this set forming the constellation. Builders' photographs of both kitchen cars *Aquila* and *Carina* were habitually used to illustrate the new design elements in the popular press, journals and fashion magazines. The running names are recorded below, together with several specially adapted first- and second-class cars which were allocated to the inaugural service on 11 June 1951 (in order):

Minerva	First-Class Brake Parlour*
Aquila	First-Class Kitchen
Cygnus	First-Class Parlour
Pegasus	First-Class Parlour and Bar Car
Hercules	First-Class Parlour
Orion	First-Class Kitchen
Perseus	First-Class Parlour
Carina	First-Class Kitchen
No. 35	Second-Class Parlour*
No. 208	Second-Class Brake Parlour*

(The 'U-type' first-class parlours accommodated 26 passengers; the kitchen cars 22 and the bar car 14).

The underframes of the new cars were of a 1930s design originally developed by the former LNER, together with their latest heavy-duty type double bolstered bogies with a wheel base of 8 ft. 6 ins. The underframe length was 65 ft. 10 ins. over buffers and 62 ft. 4 ins. over headstocks, and the bogie centres were at 45 ft. 4 ins. The body, which was 63 ft. 1 ins. over vestibules, was constructed of strong timbers, reinforced by diagonal bracing, and the main upright pillars were reinforced with substantial angle iron sections, all galvanised to prevent corrosion. The slab-sided bodies measured 8 ft. 5⅝ ins. across over the panels. In place of match boarding, which

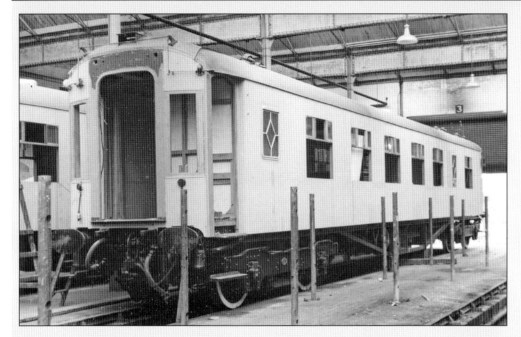 

Almost complete: exterior views of **Aries, Phoenix** *and* **Car No. 303** *prior to painting, lining and varnishing at Preston Park Works.*

appeared in the 1949 revised plans, body sheathing of '14 gauge' mild steel became available a year later. Aluminium was thickly sprayed onto the panels to lessen the risk of corrosion, each of which were joined together by vertical welds.[170]

The roof carlines were of mild steel angle section and the roof panels were welded to carlines. In order to improve insulation and reduction of noise, as well as a fire retardant, the interior of the roof and also the side panels were treated throughout with sprayed-on 'Limpet' blue asbestos ⅜ in. thick. This substance was readily available and popularly used in the industry for its desirable physical properties. Unfortunately, even at this time, it was proving to be an increasingly unpredictable health hazard due to its volatility.[171]

The main windows were double-glazed using the latest Pilkington system of sealed units which, according to Pullman records, had apparently been a resounding success in the observation cars created for the 'Devon Belle' in 1947. This form of glazing had been effective in improving visibility, reducing noise and also providing considerable thermic insulation.[172]

To improve ventilation of the new cars, the depth of the four-pane sliding lights had been increased, too, which marked a stark contrast to Pullmans built during the 1920s and 30s. In

addition to the lights, a special design of Vent-Axis fan had been installed in the roof of each saloon with a capacity of exhausting 270 cubic feet per minute with the train stationary. To provide a free outlet for air being exhausted through the top of the roof, the ventilating unit was equipped on the outside with a novel revolving cowl fitted with vanes. This ensured that it constantly faced the direction of the wind and allowed the air being exhausted from the compartment to have a free passage to the atmosphere through the trailing end of the cowling; the design of which also increased the exhausting capacity of the unit.[173]

As alluded to earlier, one of the significant break-away features of these new cars was the almost rectangular lavatory and pantry lights with rounded corners (contrasting it must be said to the sharp angles of the kitchen and saloon windows). These superseded the smaller oval cathedral lights of American origin, which were a familiar feature of almost all Pullman cars; an exception includes four third-class cars built in 1917 which featured long oblong lights, per *Profile 1*. Engineering tests conducted by the builders' revealed that the rectangular window with a lighter framing and fine diamond centre provided greater light, and the use of green hammered glass appeared to be an improvement, too, as compared with the multi-coloured artic glass usually fitted. The vestibule doors were designed with small oval-shaped elliptical plate glass windows

The seven 'U-Type' cars which departed from standard Pullman 1930s all-steel practice, were originally requested for use on the LNER at the behest of Sir Nigel Gresley during 1938. All received his standard running gear. The idea was to bring Pullman services up to the high speed potential of the 'A4' pacifics, which apparently had to be 'held back' on Pullman workings to a maximum of 90 mph, due to the modest riding qualities of the single bolster standard Pullman steel bogie – which ran best at 75 mph, and less well above this speed. Post-war the Festival of Britain offered a solution to the Pullman Car Company, and the cars were to feature in the 'Golden Arrow' as an improved service from the Continent for visitors. What is surprising is that the SR accepted Gresley's compound bogies which were an unknown quantity to them. Some modifications were possibly made to the springing to reduce throw-over on curves due to Kent Coast restrictions. If this were the case, the riding would have been adversely affected by comparison to the LNER vehicles, and so the object of the original exercise was lost in the process.

fitted with lacquered brass grilles of unique design – rather than the two or three grab rails generally featured – which were flanked by chrome commode rails (as illustrated). This design of vestibule door was fostered, to some limited extent in 1952, during the modernising phase of a small selection of East Coast cars running out of King's Cross, including *Thelma, Car No. 73* and *Car No. 79;* all constructed during 1928, per *Pullman Profile 3* (an exception being the 1927-built car *Niobe* which occasionally ran in 'Golden Arrow' service).[174]

The kitchen water tanks fitted in the car roofs were equipped with Smiths electric water tank indicators. These were of a special design which enabled the travelling Chef to see, at a glance, how much water was carried.

Each car promoted a distinctly different scheme of interior wood panelling, featuring in some cases only a limited amount of costly inlay, and although, noted as 'elegant, fluid and contemporary', were decoratively restrained compared to much of the existing Pullman fleet. However, a greater reliance of bevelled edge peach-tinted mirrors, of various designs, with surrounds in anodised metallic mouldings, were striking and quite unlike the classic pre-war cars relying on complex and sometimes overwhelming marquetry schemes incorporating tendrils, flora, patterns and historical designs. Unlike almost all other Pullman cars in service at one time or another, there were no clocks fitted to these new vehicles, but a white-washed circular-shaped ventilator cover embodying a 'Fleur de Lys' pattern was repeated in each saloon. All the interior schemes, including seat moquette and a small quantity of chairs, were designed and executed by Messrs. Waring & Gillow and, for the first time, moveable curtains – rather than the fixed type commonly seen in many Pullman cars post-1946 – were both lavish in texture and colourful; each of which were partially concealed in a hard board pelmet which gave an added touch of luxury. The seven interior schemes were officially recorded as:

* Quilted Maple with anodised mouldings in old gold – with rust coloured moquette upholstery.

* Weathered Sycamore with anodised mouldings in old gold – with wine coloured moquette with Fleur de Lys pattern.

* Betula with paldao cross banding – with wine coloured moquette with trellis pattern.

* Finely figured Australian Walnut Burr with Australian Walnut cross banding and Sycamore bands – with green coloured seat moquette.

* Straight grained and Burr Mahogany and Cherry Burr – with wine coloured moquette with Fleur de Lys pattern.

* Ucaltu and Sapeli Mahogany – with green coloured moquette.

* Olive Ash and Masur Birch – wine coloured moquette with irregular stripe pattern.

The saloons and passageways were all fully carpeted in the same fawn coloured carpet with a trellis work pattern, laid on heavy-duty rubber underlay. Most of the chairs were made at the Pullman Company's Preston Park Works to a design and profile similar to those previously used in the first-class Southern Electric cars of 1932, although all were completed with a head roll finish, rather than the usual full fluting favoured pre-war. All the materials were supplied by Messrs J. Holdsworth and Company of Halifax, Yorkshire.[175]

The arresting and attractive interior of parlour car **Cygnus,** *as new, featuring quartered panels of Australian walnut burr. Note the tables have laminated tops and lacquered brass 'type N' moveable lamps. The skilfully matched grained panelling contrasts with the small floral seat moquette, apparently coloured green.*

*The interior of the car **Hercules** with tables laid which show off the silverware and 'Lucerne' pattern crockery of cerulean blue and green leaf in this 1962 view. By this time roof straking had become a common feature in almost all cars to safeguard against damage by luggage. All 'U' type parlour cars were fitted with bevelled mirrors to an identical pattern as shown. The kitchen cars **Aquila, Carina,** and **Orion** (and later **Aries**) by contrast featured tapered examples.*

Unlike traditional 1920s Pullman lavatories with their dark mahogany and beaded panelling, these cars were finished off with modern Warerite laminated plastic panels in various 'New Look' colour schemes, of pastel pink and powder blue, while the floors were all similarly surfaced with 'Terrazzo' Mother of Pearl for easy cleaning set in a black and green coloured matrix.

The interior metal furnishings, such as parcel/hat racks were to a much larger and practical design than hitherto known, while 'type-N' table lamps, door handles and coat hooks were of brass with French old gold finish and stove lacquering, all to a mixture of borrowed design elements from the 1920s and 30s – particularly saloon door handles and table lamps that have appeared briefly in one or two older Pullman cars.[176]

However, the wall mounted and ceiling light fittings were to a completely new design by Messrs. Best and Lloyd Ltd of Smethwick. The train lighting system and equipment for the cars had been supplied by Messrs. J. Stone & Co Ltd., Deptford who had had numerous previous commissions with the Pullman Car Company.

As previously outlined, the post-war 1946 re-introduction of the 'Golden Arrow' featured a cocktail bar, known as the 'Trianon Bar', and in the new train a purpose-built vehicle named *Pegasus* incorporated a bar which would carry the name 'Trianon' and also accommodate plaques and furnishings from the older car it replaced – in addition to supplementary fare first-class armchairs for 14 passengers.

The Preston Park Works-designed interior of 'K-type' kitchen car Phoenix of 1952. Note the unique venetian blinds (for steam-hauled cars), black and white check cut moquette, collage panels and 'type O' table lamps. In keeping with the 'U-type' cars the windows profiles, wall mounted lights and hat racks are all to identical designs.

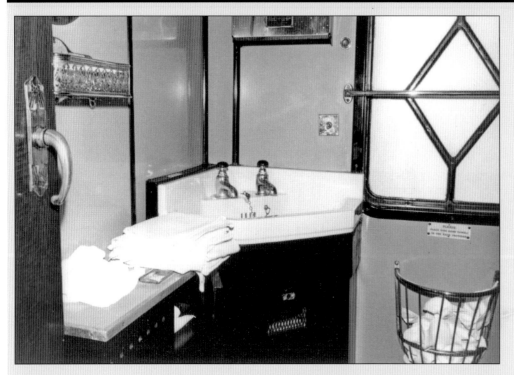

A glimpse inside a lavatory showing the laminated plastic panelled walls, vanity, brush rack and tissue basket.

In conjunction with the Aluminium Development Company, Starkie Gardner & Company of Wandsworth was commissioned to create an aluminium plaque of Eros at Piccadilly Circus, London, shooting an arrow across the Channel to Paris and the Eiffel Tower. It was originally displayed in *Trianon Bar (II)* and subsequently transferred in 1951 to the new 'Trianon' in *Pegasus*.

Here the aim had been to provide that intimate atmosphere which was apparently so necessary for a successful cocktail bar. Individual bar stools were not altogether satisfactory as had been fitted to other bar vehicles, including the veterans *Myrtle* and *Grosvenor* that worked occasionally as temporary replacements in the 'Golden Arrow', but more generally on Newhaven boat trains. Of course, the Pullman management were always concerned that unexpected acceleration and speed reduction of the train could cause accidents to passengers. As an alternative, ingenious 'stand up' seats – similar to those fitted in *Trianon (I)* and, sometime later in *Corunna* – located in close proximity to the bar had been installed. These were about 8 ins. in width and covered in

'Dunlopillo' and moquette to match the armchair upholstery, allowing the passenger the opportunity of taking the 'weight off his or her feet' and having a drink in reasonable comfort, whilst at the same time occupying the minimum of floor space.[177]

Special attention had also been given to the lighting of the bar. That portion of the ceiling which was directly over the bar had been moulded so that recessed subdued lighting provided by Messrs. Wilmot Breedon of Birmingham could be employed, resulting in adequate lighting, but without any glare.

In addition to highly polished walls with simplified geometric cross banding, the principal decorations around the bar area consisted of two attractive aluminium plaques specially designed and executed by Messrs. J. Starkie Gardner and Co Ltd of Wandsworth (famed for their architectural commissions and elaborate metalwork), in collaboration with the Aluminium Development Corporation. Regular travellers on the (post war) 'Golden Arrow' would no doubt have recognised these plaques as having formed part of the decoration of the older *Trianon (I)* installed in the one-time Pullman car *Diamond* and later *Trianon Bar (II)*. From its introduction, the cocktail bar was promoted invariably in publicity material, and as a prominent foot note on all menu cards, offering a pleasant meeting place.[178]

The train was also equipped throughout with a Public-Address system which enabled general information to be given to passengers. This was particularly useful in this train where passengers sought advice as to Customs' examination, embarkation instructions, etc.

A break-through and interesting innovation for 1951 was the use of bottled Calor Gas for cooking, not only on the 'Golden Arrow' but installed in several older cars allocated to boat train duty. Experimenting previously with this medium on other lines, the Pullman Company management considered that it had many advantages for the particular requirements of the 'Golden Arrow' service. The Calor Gas cylinders were lodged in steel boxes mounted beneath the underframes of the kitchen cars, and the valves controlling the emission of gas were mounted adjacent to the cylinders themselves. These were of an electro-magnetic type, operated by a switch from the kitchen which, according to later studies, apparently proved to be economical.[179]

The car exteriors were finished in the standard Pullman colours of cream and umber with gold lettering, white painted roofs and, initially at least, white rimmed wheels.

On Monday, 11 June 1951 at 11 am promptly, the new 'Golden Arrow' departed from Victoria bound for Dover Marine with practically all seats occupied for this trip; a fitting tribute to British craftsmanship and the entrepreneurship of the Pullman Car Company.

On this date, too, the Pullman Company initiated an all-inclusive ticket in coupon form to cover travel, Pullman supplement and basic meal, as on the airways. Sadly, due to lack of interest, this was withdrawn within three months and only re-introduced nine years later with the launch of the 'Blue Pullmans'.[180]

The bar counter was designed with a bay portion. Again, primarily to occupy the minimum floor space, which experience had shown was appreciated by patrons of the cocktail bar, where 'confidential groupings' were possible at the counter. Unlike the other bar cars running in service at this time, Pegasus was not fitted with a kitchen.

By a happy co-incidence, the advent also marked the celebrations in Paris of the 2,000th anniversary of the foundation of that city, thus giving dual significance to a world-famous link between the two capitals.[181]

Four months later, on 11 October, one of the new British Railways standard 4-6-2 Britannia Class locomotives, No.70004 'William Shakespeare' previously exhibited at the 'Festival of Britain' on the South Bank, hauled the train for the first time.

A 1960s interior view of the kitchen range in Car Orion.

The 'Golden Arrow' thunders out of Victoria station on 11 June 1951 formed of ten cars including seven 'U-types', all with white painted roofs and white-rimmed wheels.

Unfortunately, just 10 days later, on 21 October, this locomotive failed at Headcorn with fractured rods working the up train. This caused passengers a great deal of delay, and necessitated the withdrawal of the class from traffic temporarily.

The summer timings of the service were as follows:

Depart London Victoria	11 am
Arrive Paris Gare du Nord	5.52 pm
Depart Paris Gare du Nord	12.30 pm
Arrive London Victoria	7.30 pm

By the following year, 1952, kitchen cars *Aries* and third-class *Car No. 303* (both 'U-type'), as well as parlour car *Phoenix* (conforming to a similar profile and design, but with older underframe, catalogued as 'K-type'), were all constructed at Preston Park Works, Brighton. *Car No. 303* was fitted with brackets for body-mounted carriage boards, similar to those widely used on the 'Golden Arrow' cars at this time. It appears these brackets were rarely, if ever used, however, and quickly removed. As far as can be determined, the vehicle was never officially rostered to the 'Golden Arrow', and generally found service on Southampton Ocean Liner expresses, occasional royal specials (with suites) and 'Bournemouth Belle' duties, although it did feature prominently as a backdrop on more than one occasion for 'Valstar' advertisements for ladies' jackets and coats in the autumn of 1953.

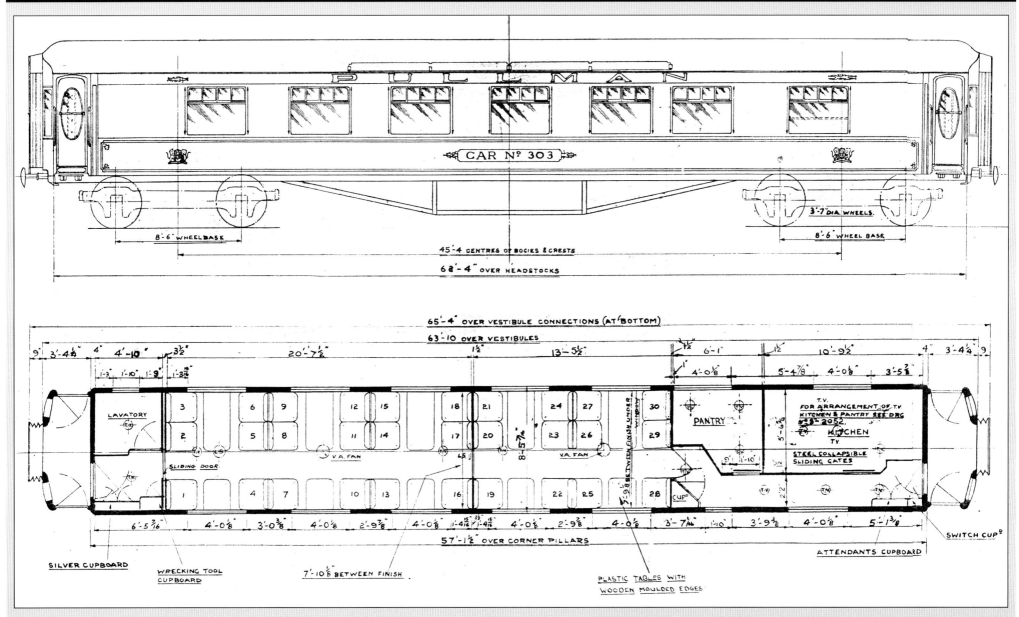

Elevation and plan of 'U-type' Car No. 303.

Brand new **Car No. 303** *is seen outside the yard at Preston Park Works, 1952. Note the body side clips and the vehicle's fluid form and style.*

The following sub-contractors supplied materials for all the 'U-type' cars, including vehicles *Aries, Car No. 303* and 'K-type' car *Phoenix*:

Interior finish:	Waring & Gillow Limited
Exterior paints:	Docker Brothers
	Imperial Chemical Industries Limited
Train lighting:	J. Stone & Co (Deptford)
Light fittings:	Best & Lloyd Limited
Luminator lamps:	Wilmot-Breeden Limited
Upholstery:	John Holdsworth & Co Ltd
Carpets:	James Templeton & Co Ltd
Formica table tops:	Thos. De La Rue (Plastics) Limited
Plastic panels:	Wareite Limited
Metal furniture:	McGeoch & Co Ltd
	Jones & Foster Limited
	Player, Mitchell & Breeden
Locks:	Resilence Lock & Manufacturing Co Ltd
Sliding ventilators:	Henry Hope & Sons Ltd
Public address system:	Broadcast Amplifiers
Window glass:	Pilkington Bros. Ltd
Air extractor fans:	Vent-Axia Limited
Terrazzo flooring:	Scandolo Limited
Lavatory porcelain items:	Shanks & Co Ltd
Brake equipment and steam heating:	Westinghouse Brake & Signal Co Ltd
Metal spraying:	Metallisation Limited
'Limpet' Asbestos:	J.W. Roberts Limited
Cooking stoves:	Radiation (Large Cooking Equipment) Ltd
Fuel systems:	Calor Gas (Distributing) Co Ltd

The arresting simplicity and spaciousness of the interior of **Car No. 303.**

Above and above right: ***Posed interior views of* Car No.35 *and* Hercules *showing so-called* de-luxe *passenger amenities for the different classes.***

Right: ***Painted, varnished and looking strikingly attractive with its white roof and white rimmed wheels,* Aries *is captured on film leaving Preston Park works for the first official time, 15 February 1952.***

The interior of Aries, as new. Subtle decorative features of the 1930s are noted in the mullion panels left and right. The saloon door is complete with brass-finished handles designed in 1932; a pattern as used on 'Southern Electric' cars. The mirrors are similar in size to the Birmingham-built kitchen cars but are differently executed. See p.163 for comparison.

Leading attendant Hawkes photographed inside the main saloon of Cygnus.

The little differences that distinguish the 'Golden Arrow' service

With the introduction of new Pullman cars in 1951, one of a series of brochures was released jointly by the Pullman Car Company and the Southern Region of British Railways, extolling the virtues of travelling upon the 'princely path to Paris'. For the prospective traveller, a great emphasis was placed upon the little differences that distinguished the 'Golden Arrow' service. '… From the moment of stepping aboard a specially decorated Pullman at Victoria to the moment of arrival at the Gare du Nord, there will be no suggestion of haste, no hint of ruffled tempers, and the whole journey will take but six-and-a-half unhurried hours.

'As you stroll down the platform you observe, with amused tolerance, the worried gleam in the eyes of fellow-passengers – the determined set of the jaw that is the heritage of by-gone days of Channel crossing.

'Your Pullman armchair looks inviting. You heave a small contented sigh and subside into its cushioned depths. The train starts almost imperceptibly at 10.45 am, and you find yourself gazing out on the green, sheep-dotted slopes of the Kentish weald, your newspaper lying unopened in your lap.

One hour and 38 minutes later you pull up alongside the quay at Dover Pier. Here again you watch with secret amusement the slightly anxious look on the faces of many of your fellow-passengers. As you follow their gaze you find it directed towards the sea. Will it be rough – will the crossing be a bad one? The atmosphere is reminiscent of a dentist's waiting room. But you know that wind and wave have ceased to be the all-important factors they once were. The Southern Region's luxurious boats are more than capable of coping with unpleasant weather conditions. Built on the lines of ocean steamers, their wide beam, glassed-in decks, and beautifully equipped private cabins cause the journey to resemble a miniature Atlantic 'crossing.

'Special favours attend the travellers on the Golden Arrow Route, and as an honoured guest you need not have your luggage examined in the confusion of the *douane* at Calais. There will be a Customs officer on the Paris train to do it for you and a special ticket allowing you to walk from ship to train without any irritation or hassle.

'At the end of the hour's crossing your porter picks up your luggage and you follow him down the gangway to step into the waiting train, "la Flèche d'Or".

The journey this far has been delightful. The tense expression has faded from the faces of your travelling companions, as they realise that they are experiencing a revolutionised method of London-Paris transportation. And now comes the climax of the occasion, as you are ushered into your blue and cream liveried Pullman. Six cars, interspersed with kitchens, and no two cars upholstered alike, a deep green

A graphic poster commissioned by the Southern Region in conjunction with the Baynard Press. The work was completed by A.N. Wolstenholme, a prolific artist of railway subjects who was well known during the post-war period for his particular and recognisable style. Later still, posters designed by Helen McKie for the Publicity Department of the Southern Region were made available for display in both London and Paris travel agent offices. The basic design was constant, allowing overprinting of appropriate wording, in English or French, as necessary.

One of a broad series of colourful lithographs and artistic posters advertising the service, unmistakably so redolent of the artwork produced throughout much of the 1950s.

A mid-1950s view of the 'Golden Arrow' (with ordinary carriages leading) passing a boat train at speed.

'As you sink comfortably back after the last drop of fragrant coffee, you reach for your book, then hesitate, watching the Picardy landscape slip by. For here history dwells. You hum to yourself the old song:

"Where be the waters to drown regret,

Where is the leaves from Sleep's own tree?

Nowhere else in the world – not yet

In Picardy."

'Picardy's calm, peaceful-looking fields belie the exciting past that is hers. From the moment of disembarking, you are plunged into a land reminiscent of struggle. Calais – bone of contention through centuries of French-English disputes. Queen Mary Tudor was heard to declare that when she died the name "Calais" would be found graven on her heart. How familiar is the story of the six gallant burghers of Calais who, rather than permit the destruction of their beloved town, offered their lives to Edward III. Only the intercession of his Queen, Philippa, saved them from this martyrdom.

'As Calais fades into the distance the outskirts of Boulogne appear. This popular holiday resort has been chosen by various warriors' intent on conquering Britain, as a point from which to sally forth. The first of these were the Romans in the reign of the Emperor Claudius. Again, from 1801-1805 Boulogne was the centre of Napoleon's gigantic preparations – doomed to disappointment as they were – for the invasions of England.

'As you gaze from the windows of your swiftly-moving carriage, you may see the spire of the fine Late-Gothic church of St. Wolfram in Abbeville. This church is one of the world's finest examples of the Flamboyant style. It was from Abbeville that William the Conqueror set sail on a certain fateful Wednesday, September 27, 1066.

leather in one; rich blue moquette for another, royal crimson for a third – inlaid mahogany or molten glass walls, tiled and sparkling lavatories equipped with scented soap and clothes brushes.

'As you pull out of the station, just nineteen minutes after you landed at the pier, a well-trained and efficient attendant places before you the first course of an epicurean lunch – a meal which fully justifies the culinary reputation of France. You have not had to stir from your armchair, for 'Golden Arrow' service does not submit its patrons to the discomfort of staggering through long corridors into a restaurant car, there to sit opposite a total – and perhaps unwelcome – stranger.

'The train is like a club lounge. All meals and refreshments are served to passengers at their seats, and no tedious waiting in Customs at Calais, for this is done *en route* by officials on board.

'Away to the south, perhaps five miles, lies Bailleul en Vimeu, the original home of the Baliol family, which gave two kings to Scotland and its name to Balliol College, Oxford.

'Amiens, the ancient capital of Picardy, was the home of Peter the Hermit, whose exhortations inspired the first of the Crusades. What a wealth of romance this fervour and devotion has given to posterity! The cathedral of Amiens has the distinction of being the largest church in France, and one of the noblest Gothic edifices in Europe.

'You begin to feel the end of the journey approaching as St. Denis rolls into view. Another few minutes and you will be in the heart of Paris, just three hours and ten minutes after leaving Calais. You descend the steps of your lounge on wheels, feeling rested, and ready for the business or pleasure ahead.[182]

Arrival at Paris Gare du Nord by the 'Flèche d'Or' in 1967. A busy platform scene repeated countless times with alighting passengers and station staff assisting with luggage. Pullman car No. 4029 of 1926 waits patiently before the service run-round on 'La Petite Ceinture' (a connection between Paris' railway termini) to its final destination, the magnificent edifice of the Gare de Lyon. This station is located in the XII arrondissement, on the north bank of the river Seine, in the east of Paris and continues today to offer international connections to Germany, Italy, Switzerland and Spain.

Stewardess of the 'Golden Arrow'

From 1946, the 'Golden Arrow' was equipped with public address. Loudspeakers were fitted in each saloon, with an additional loudspeaker in each coupé. The conductor in charge of the train initially made announcements from a prepared script, using a hand microphone and amplifier fitted in one of the vestibules. It quickly became apparent that these announcements should be made in both English and French and, as nothing but perfect language would suffice, special staff, including Ms Elaine Morley who spoke several languages, was recruited for this duty.

With the success of this feature, other all-Pullman trains were fitted with similar apparatus as they came into operation, and those vehicles introduced in 1951 were no exception. By this means, of course, passengers were warned of impending arrival and announcements could be made concerning services available, sea conditions (as applicable) and any emergency.[183]

In July 1954, *Womans' Mirror*, a popular weekly magazine first published in the 1920s, featured an article about Ms Elaine Morley, the only 'stewardess' then on the 'Golden Arrow'.

In an interview conducted by Elizabeth Beresford, Ms Morley explained that it was part of her job to answer passengers' queries, and to make announcements in French and English, before the train departed from London. 'The attendants and I come on board between ten and eleven to get things ready, and between us we may serve one hundred and twenty-eight meals in the swaying rhythm of the speeding train.' During the holiday season, she would sometimes work seven days a week, travelling nearly a thousand miles.

During this period of time, the train would arrive at Folkestone where the passengers alighted for the steamer to France. Lunch was taken by the staff while the train steamed on to Dover to pick up passengers for the return journey. 'If the Channel crossing has been rough', she advised, 'most of them come aboard white and shaky. And what is the first thing they ask for? Pots of tea!'[184]

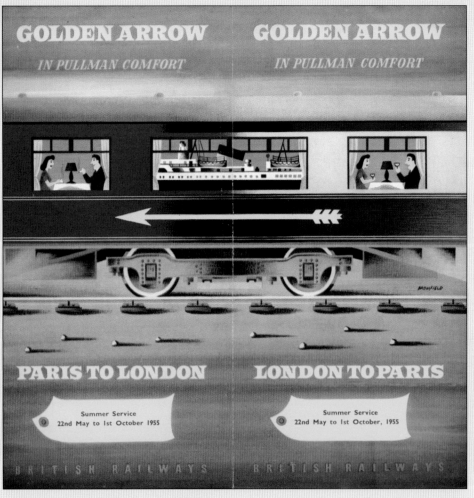

One of a series of colourful 'Golden Arrow' posters by the artist Barber and printed by the Baynard Press, 1955. The difference in travel times for each direction is explained by clock changes between the UK and Europe.

Working on the Pullmans was not without some excitement. During the late winter of 1953, the London-bound 'Golden Arrow' was delayed by fog, and reached Victoria at five o'clock in the morning – ten and a half hours late. 'What a night that was!' exclaimed Ms Morley. 'We served dinner and breakfast as well as tea'. Long after the last passenger had left the train, Ms Morley and the other attendants remained clearing everything away and washing up for the following days' service.

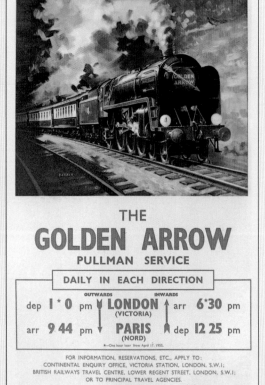

THE
GOLDEN ARROW
PULLMAN SERVICE

DAILY IN EACH DIRECTION			
	OUTWARDS	INWARDS	
dep 1*0 pm	LONDON (VICTORIA)	arr 6*30 pm	
arr 9.44 pm	PARIS (NORD)	dep 12.25 pm	

—One hour later from April 17, 1955.

FOR INFORMATION, RESERVATIONS, ETC., APPLY TO:
CONTINENTAL ENQUIRY OFFICE, VICTORIA STATION, LONDON, S.W.1;
BRITISH RAILWAYS TRAVEL CENTRE, LOWER REGENT STREET, LONDON, S.W.1;
OR TO PRINCIPAL TRAVEL AGENCIES.

BRITISH RAILWAYS

The surviving records of Chief Inspector Walter Badger provide intriguing testimonials from many passengers who expressed their appreciation of the service he and his staff gave on the 'Golden Arrow'. The following are two random examples:

Letter dated 30 September 1948 from H. Shillington, Bank Chambers, High Holborn, London, WC1 addressed to F.D.M. Harding, General Manager of the Pullman Car Company:

'Dear Sir,

'As I was leaving the Bench one day last week, a fellow Magistrate remarked to me, on hearing that I was travelling by the 'Golden Arrow' the next day – "That is the one place where you can still get service".

'I felt sure that you would be pleased to have this unsolicited "testimonial", which only confirms my own experience, which dates back over 40 years, and, as one of the oldest travellers on this route (having crossed the Channel some 2,000 times up to 1939), I can only say that I have always received nothing but the greatest courtesy and the finest service, from the Chief Inspector down through all the staff, including those at ports.

'I well remember the days when our meals, looked after by Mr Badger, were the choice of a Mutton Chop or Sole, and most excellent they were.

Numerous friends of mine, business and personal, including my own family and travellers from abroad have all spoken to me of the "fine arrangements" on the Pullman service, and agree with my contention that the "Golden Arrow" service is the gateway to London.

'... I have always felt that the essence of the success of the Service, was that it was unnecessary to ask for anything; owing to the way the Service was organised, what one wanted was always there. I might add that one of the chief reasons I have never used the "airways" is because I have been so satisfied with the Service given by train and boat ...'

Upon his retirement in December 1951, Mr Badger received a letter from Mary Croft, Personal Assistant to the Duke of Westminster, Brook Street, London. It simply read:

'Dear Mr Badger,

'The Duke of Westminster has asked me to write to you and to send you the enclosed cheque for £20 which he hopes you will accept as a present in recognition of all the help you have given him over many years ...'

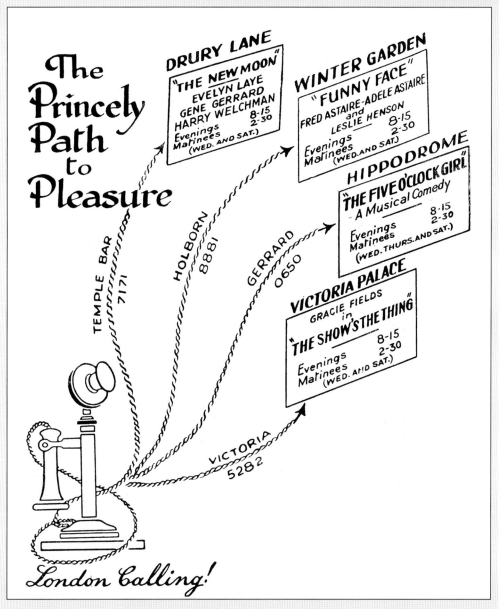

'The princely path to pleasure' – a Pullman Company publication providing visitors with latest theatre plays and dramas in London's West End.

A final farewell as the 'Golden Arrow' is about to depart from London Victoria. The gentleman passenger is standing in the vestibule of car Phoenix adjoining car Niobe, two vehicles used time and again in this prestigious service as well as secondment to numerous royal specials.

Service Timings

As alluded to earlier, in order to meet operating difficulties between Calais and Paris, the outward service in 1952 from London was retimed to leave Victoria at 1pm in the winter and 2pm under the summer timetable. This had been an unpopular move, and although departure times fluctuated over the years, and varied at the London end between 9am, 10am and 10.30am, the outward journey was made, by necessity, via Folkestone to Boulogne. It was hoped that the later timing might have enabled travellers from as far afield as Birmingham and the Midlands to connect without difficulty with this service. In his press announcement, Pullman's General Manager, Frank Harding stated cautiously 'perhaps passengers prefer to reach Paris earlier than they can do on this late timing, and it will be a pity indeed if for any operating reasons the service loses its appeal to Cross-Channel passengers'.[185] Nevertheless, well-known passengers including film personalities among others continued to travel on the train, including Robert Taylor, Diana Dors, Barbara Stanwyck, Kay Kendall, Rex Harrison, Sophia Loren and many, many more. (Eight years later, during May 1960, the departure time reverted back to a morning one.)

The inward journey now being made from Calais to Dover again, the pre-war arrangements had been totally reversed and a great deal of manoeuvring was now required to move the stock from the outward arrival destination of Folkestone Harbour to the inward connecting port of Dover Marine. The heavy train of seven Pullmans and two or more luggage vans required two, and sometimes three, small 0-6-0 tank locomotives to haul it up the short 1-in-30 gradient from the harbour station to the Junction station, which connected with the mainline.

Motive power was always an impressive sight, especially departures from the harbour station. The locomotives allocated to the 'Golden Arrow' were commonly turned out impeccably finished by Stewarts Lane shed. During the 1950s a 'Merchant Navy' or 'Battle of Britain' deputised for the service, although British Rail standard 'Britannia' locomotives – normally No. 70004 'William Shakespeare' or No. 70014 'Iron Duke' – were increasingly used. Later, two Southern Region 1,750 hp diesel electric engines appeared briefly on the service and were followed by sister engine 10203 of 2,000 hp.; each carried a specially made headboard.

By the end of the decade, Calais Maritime station had at long last been rebuilt under challenging conditions. By this time, the journey from London to Paris was generally around 6 hrs. 30 mins, thanks to improved permanent way, in anticipation of electrification in Britain as well as in France. Inevitably, electric traction caught up with the 'Golden Arrow' on 12 June 1961 when a pristine Southern Region electric engine, E5015, with a newly designed simplified headboard, complete with flags and separate cab arrows, inaugurated the service from Victoria to Folkestone and Dover via Sevenoaks, Tonbridge and Ashford. Unfortunately, due to a series of delays on the return up service, arrival at Victoria was 13 minutes late. Notwithstanding, the electric timetable ushered in an accelerated service, with published schedules of 82 minutes to the Marine station and, contrariwise, 85 minutes to Victoria. The last steam-hauled Arrow ran the day before, hauled by 'West Country' class Pacific locomotive 'Appledore'.

'Britannia' class No. 70004 'William Shakespeare' at Stewarts Lane locomotive depot ready for the 'Golden Arrow' service.

The last steam-hauled 'Golden Arrow' departing from Victoria bound for Dover, took place on 11 June 1961 behind No. 34100 'Appledore'. The composition of the train included a General Utility Van, followed by two SR ordinary coaches and Pullman cars Nos: 36 and 34, Carina, Aries, Perseus, Pegasus, Orion and Minerva.

Changes and improvements were already afoot in France, too. Electric traction on the northern region of the S.N.C.F., for instance, was inaugurated between Paris and Lille via Creil, Longueau, Arras and Douai on 7 January 1959.[186] Six months later, the 'Flèche d'Or' ceased to be steam-hauled south of Amiens, and stopped altogether on 11 January 1969, when a 'K-Class' Pacific No.82 brought the last northbound steam-hauled train into Calais Maritime. Diesel engines thereafter provided the usual motive power for the 'Flèche d'Or'.

As outlined previously, in Britain the 'Golden Arrow' was nominally all-Pullman until May 1965, although ordinary second-class coaches were added from time to time. Indeed, albeit briefly, several green-liveried Derby built Mk2 first-class corridor carriages were also included. Thereafter, the one-time world-renowned luxury express became officially part-Pullman only, with no more than four Pullmans included generally in the formation and soon to be subjected to a smattering of experimental liveries and interior remodelling.

Hercules with new elongated Pullman coat of arms at Dover Marine, 1966. A timeless scene, which was so reminiscent of other famous or long-forgotten boat trains. The 'Bombay Express', for example, ran before World War 2 every Thursday from Victoria to Dover en route overland to Marseilles in connection with the P&O service to India which saved two days journey time. Where traffic was justified, a special train formed of Pullman cars was run at 1.50pm but otherwise extra cars were included in the 2.0pm service. The inwards service ran up from Folkestone on Saturdays with either a special train or extra cars in the ordinary service. The Shipping Company paid the Pullman Car Company 3 shillings and 6 pence per passenger.

S307S (ex Carina) *arriving into Victoria Station, January 1970.*

Dover Marine with BR Standard Mk1 coaches, and Pullman cars in varying liveries.

Phoenix *adjoined to* **Car No 208** *(now transformed into S208S and modelling the corporate grey and blue livery at Victoria, 1967).*

BR Institutionalised blue/white and reversed livery cars, and faintly in the distance a Pullman still in umber and cream. Dover Marine, 1969.

A fresh coat of paint it might have, but it's a world away from the glamour of the umber and cream livery with gold lining and running name.

S208S is seen at Dover Marine in the corporate grey and blue livery complete with umber coloured 'arrow' carriage boards. The guard door designation in white standard font is positioned almost at the foot of the entrance.

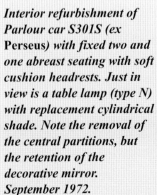

Interior refurbishment of Parlour car S301S (ex Perseus) with fixed two and one abreast seating with soft cushion headrests. Just in view is a table lamp (type N) with replacement cylindrical shade. Note the removal of the central partitions, but the retention of the decorative mirror. September 1972.

The economics of running Pullman cars in France had led to an even more dramatic reduction in their numbers than in England, as observed first-hand by Alec Hasenson. Although the post-war 'Flèche d'Or' had briefly become all-Pullman, first-class only, in July 1947 it was short-lived. As was the case a decade before, second-class Pullmans were, by necessity, reintroduced to the service in October 1949, followed by ordinary carriages of the S.N.C.F. in 1950. By the mid-1950s, Pullman cars continued to dwindle in number, to such an extent that by 1966, only two Pullmans were in service on the 'Flèche d'Or', with meals being provided by the nearby restaurant car. A year later, in December 1967, these 1926-built parlour cars were replaced by just one 20-seat kitchen car built in 1929 serving only light refreshments which, in turn was withdrawn on 1 June 1969 (at the same time as the San Remo sleeper, which was for many years attached to the train).

Meanwhile, British Railways Southern Region continued to run the 'Golden Arrow' until September 1972, at which time changing travelling habits, and the prevailing Inter-City policy, rendered the Pullman brand almost obsolete and surplus to future requirements.

Left: *A September 1968 colour image of the 'Flèche d'Or' near Etaples with Pullman* Car No. 4131 *taking centre stage.*

Below left: *Solitary Pullman Car* No. 4131 *and beyond the San Remo sleeper, at the Gare du Nord, April 1969.*

Below *A contrast in liveries at Dover Marine: BR Corporate blue and grey to the left and Pullman umber and cream to the right.*

Contrasting motive power in the 1960s, Class 73 to the left and Class 71 No E5015 which seems to have been a regular performer on the 'Golden Arrow' to the right.

The final run of the 'Golden Arrow', 30 September 1972

With a prompt departure from Victoria for the very last time, line-side detonators exploded as the train climbed Grosvenor bank, and with it a little bit of railway history. Passengers savoured travelling in style and not-to-be repeated cossetting from well-trained attendants, some marking the occasion with Champagne. Radio and television interviews were conducted *en route* and, later, onboard the 'Maid of Orleans' during the crossing to Calais.

A final glance of passengers settling into their seats of car S302S (ex Phoenix), September 1972.

The train formation was the same for the final 'down' and 'up' trips:

S86731 General Utility Van painted overall blue

S4376 Open Second

S4065 Open Second

S25934 Corridor Second

S25944 Corridor Second

35023 Corridor Brake Second

3773 Open Second

Pullman *S306S* (ex *Orion*)

Pullman *S302S* (ex *Phoenix*)

Pullman *S307S* (ex *Carina*)

Pullman *S308S* (ex *Cygnus*)

Above: *A last glimpse of second-class Pullman accommodation on the 'Golden Arrow', May 1965. This is the interior of Car No. 34. note the removal of the clock sans any plaque replacement.*

Headboard and flags – the Union jack and the Tricolour ready for attachment.

and attached!

160

The inevitable last 'up' journey to London pulled away with *S308S* (ex *Cygnus*) leading behind the engine, coinciding with a brief episode of horn blowing from stationary electric multiple stock as a mark of respect. It was nothing quite like the *cause célèbre*, brashness or sense of public loss felt when the Southern Region's other Pullman train, the 'Brighton Belle', retired five months before. There was neither dancing on the platform, singing or a band playing, nor for that matter a demand to purchase special platform tickets to view the train – behind barriers! The occasion was all rather a solemn and dignified end to a renowned *de-luxe* capital-to-capital service that was once the envy of the world.

The following day, a standard electric multiple-unit train departed from Victoria at the same time as did the 'Golden Arrow' (10.30am), but ran to Folkestone rather than Dover, to connect with British Rail's new cross-Channel ferries 'Hengist' and 'Horsa'.[187]

On 3 October, the last five remaining 'Golden Arrow' cars were hauled together by a Class 73 engine from Clapham carriage sidings to Brighton for storage and disposal.[188] Enquiries about their purchase (and several unsold 'Brighton Belle' cars) were handled by the Sales Controller at the BRB Technical Centre, Derby. *S307S* (ex *Carina*) and *S302S* (ex *Phoenix*) were acquired in 1973 and soon afterwards shipped to France as static restaurants in Lyons. *S306S* (ex *Orion*) went in store at Ashford and *S308S* (ex *Cygnus*) and *S301S* (ex *Perseus*) were eventually purchased by Scottish and Newcastle Breweries, a company founded in 1749.

Within a matter of weeks following the final run, 'Golden Arrow' artefacts ranging from crockery, ephemera, collage panels ex *Phoenix,* and table lamps (at £5 each) were offered for sale at 'Collector's Corner', Euston.

In recent years to commemorate the train's enduring nostalgia, recreations of the 'Golden Arrow' have taken place, all to great excitement and on occasion using some of the original 1951 'U-type' vehicles. One special event from London to Paris which was steam-hauled throughout, commemorated the 75th anniversary of its 1929 inauguration. One of the highlights of this trip included a Wagons-Lits train departing from Calais featuring a 1929-built Pullman parlour car and diner.

A typical working of the modern 'Golden Arrow' photographed in 1970.

S302S *at Victoria prior to the final down service.*

Celebration or commiseration?

The final run of the 'Golden Arrow', 30 September 1972

Right and far right: *Interior view of S307S (ex Carina) and a busy scene at Victoria in anticipation of passengers boarding the last Down train to Dover, 30 September 1972.*

Below: **S302S** *at Brighton awaiting disposal, October 1972*

Below right: **S306S** *at Brighton awaiting disposal, October 1972*

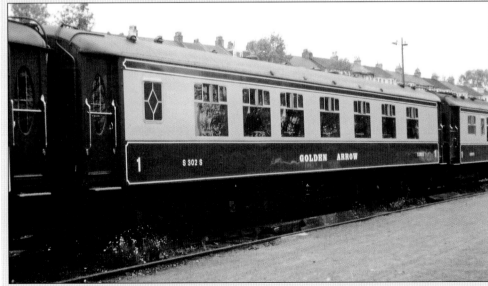

Pullman car design, marquetry and the construction of British identity

The loss of export markets and economic collapse in the late 1920s, the reshaping of empire and Britain's relationship to it, as well as changing class and gender identities, all contributed to a realignment and fragmentation of what constituted 'Britishness' in the early part of the 20th century.[189]

The Pullman Car Company simultaneously evoked tradition and modernity by referencing the metropolitan and the rural to interior design of their fleet. The product of refined taste and connoisseurship, it was an age of a travelling culture of elegant people, of style as represented in *Vogue,* and by the leading artists of the day, including George Barbier, who connected with the glamour of the modern city: London and Paris.

Fine marquetry schemes which were similarly seen in almost all Pullman cars used in Britain and on the Continent. These examples are from one-time 'Flèche d'Or' cars now preserved in Madrid, Spain. For comparison, see earlier Builders' photographs from 1926/7.

In her analysis of Britain immediately prior to the 1920s, Cheryl Buckley argues that design, particularly in terms of 'Englishness', remained important, encapsulating historical revivals and an ongoing concern for the vernacular: Neo-classical and Jacobean styles, for example, which seemingly dominated the furniture catalogues of esteemed manufacturers such as Waring & Gillow and Maple & Company.[190] The deployment of these 'English' traditions proved to have widespread commercial appeal, and as mass cultures they were particularly effective in representing 'Englishness'.

An idealized 'English' past was therefore conjured up by a continual engagement with styles and traditional scenes of rustic life that were intimately tied to the 'English' sense of good taste. All these aspects were captured by Pullman at one time or another in their hallmark marquetry schemes from some of the earliest cars running down to the Kentish ports, while a broad interpretation and interest in design from around the globe overlapped with the enthusiasm also for non-Western arts which were just emerging within modernist circles, including lacquer work. In such a context 'Britishness' was increasingly permeable, providing the ideological setting to a huge consumer potential. If 'Britishness' represented expansionism, then 'Englishness', by contrast, 'stood for the private and intimate, the spiritual and primitive', located in the countryside rather than in the city and town.[191] Change and permanency therefore went hand in hand.

However, the interwar years have been characterised as one long depression, where the economic transformations that occurred during the period had the profoundest effect on design. To some extent, argues Dr Greg Stevenson, with increased consumer expenditure and the growth that followed in industries that responded to textiles and engineering demands, the divisions became blurred between the better-off end of the working class and the middle classes.[192] A cyclic characteristic of the 1920s and '30s was increased consumption and travel and, as several writers commented at the time, it was no longer apparent from looking at a person's clothes to which class they belonged. The Pullman car company carefully nurtured a corporate, 'modernist' identity to its latest vehicles that was at odds with distinctive regional and national identities. It was the aim of the Pullman chairman, Davison Dalziel, to bring visual coherence and unity to its expanding fleet, by the employment of artists and designers to produce posters, vehicle interiors, textiles and typography. But it was not until 1926 that this new corporate identity took on an even wider, recognizable 'international' modern style, with the introduction of the high-profile 'Flèche d'Or'. Conversely, in other forms of competitive transportation, 'Air Union', a French company established in January 1923, advertised their de-luxe 'Pullman Air Car', recognising early the public awareness of the Pullman brand in Britain and America which was associated generally with luxury accommodation.[193]

Between 1910 and 1929 Pullman management became increasingly influenced by manufacturers and designers, stimulated by the development of new scholarship. The taste for new crockery and patterned bone china, for instance, was both a reaction to and a contribution of the growing appreciation of modernist art and design – and again a recurring reassessment of 'English' design.

Pullman car design, marquetry and the construction of British identity

The editor of the *Burlington Magazine*, Roger Fry, widely published articles about changing public taste, recognising that there was an absence of European art and design in railway catering, which were beginning to be favoured by the large steamship companies.[194]

A concern for specific periods of history and particular representations of the 'English' past also characterized the activities of a number of manufacturers, notably the furniture producers Waring & Gillow, and Maple & Co. In part, this was in response to market changes, but it again also connected with the interests in English traditions that came to the fore with the introduction of classicism during the 1910-1925 period, a discernible shift towards 18th-century origins as it attempted to establish new markets, which Pullman eagerly embraced. The original Pullman cars with their Victorian features and fussy dark furnishings were later all replaced by new vehicles whose interior marquetry designs captured the spirit of 18th-century decoration, while the moveable armchairs featured a smattering of revived patterns, including 'Vine', 'Oak leaf' and 'Crimped Ribbon and Wreath', usually associated with the Georgian and Regency periods. (Similar moquette materials were sold through mainstream stockists such as Harrod's, Selfridges and Heal's.) Pullman car interiors were beginning to be noted for their relatively simple lines, uncluttered luxurious fittings and good proportions of its typical furnishings, providing a design language not that dissimilar in some respects to Continental modernism, but with broader appeal as a result of its connection with 'English' traditions. Continuing into the 1930s, aspects of pre-19th-century English design were researched assiduously and from the outset, such publications, as *Country Life* contributed to the growing taste for certain historical styles. The contribution of this popular magazine to notions of good taste was probably significant, as it exposed an increasing preoccupation with simplicity, which invariably overlapped with modernism.

Affirming its commitment to modernist tendencies, furniture manufacturer Waring & Gillow continued to trade on authenticity and continuity, combining modern methods, and the resources of modern machinery. Receiving large-scale commercial projects for Pullman for many years, the company also provided a guide for the discerning customer in identifying and selecting different 'English' styles. For the British Empire Exhibition in 1924 and 1925, for example, a brochure produced to celebrate Waring & Gillow's contribution drew attention to a number of specifically 'British' and 'English' traits, but significantly the terms were used interchangeably. Titled *Past and Present*, this brochure underlined tradition and continuity, craftsmanship and artistic training. After describing the company's exhibits at Wembley, the focus turned to their involvement with the furnishings of two Pullman cars namely *Argus* and *Cynthia*, whose detailed interiors were thus described as 'a modern tendency in decoration, dependent upon simplicity, straight lines, and simple masses, as well as beauty and richness of material used …'[195]

From left to right: ***partition panels that once adorned the 1923-built cars* Montana, Flora, Aurora *and* Juno.**

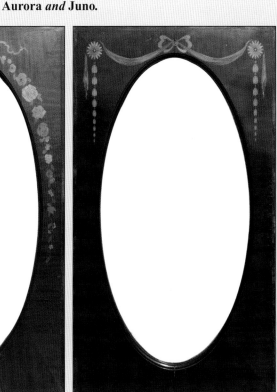

Appendix 1. Extra-fare Pullman car services, 1910-1939

Extra-fare Pullman car services 1910-1939

(London-Folkestone/Dover/Newhaven – to Paris or vice versa)

1910-1921

London (Charing Cross) and (Victoria) – Dover or Folkestone

First-Class supplement – Single: 2 shillings and 6 pence

1922-1923

London (Charing Cross) and (Victoria) – Folkestone or Dover Pier

First-Class supplement – Single: 3 shillings

1924-1928

London (Victoria) to Folkestone or Dover

First-Class supplement – Single: 3 shillings

1926-1927

London (Victoria) to Newhaven
First-Class supplement – Single: 3 shillings

Second-Class supplement – Single: 2 shillings

London (Charing Cross) to Deal, Sandwich, Walmer, Dover Priory, etc
First-Class supplement – Single: 2 shillings

1929 'Golden Arrow'

London (Victoria) to Paris (Gare du Nord)

First-Class – Single: £5 all-inclusive rail/Pullman fare

Note: The Pullman supplementary fare only from London-Paris or vice versa: 28 shillings and 11 pence

Accommodation booked in France from Calais-Paris only or vice versa: 64 Frs. Fr, reducing to 40 Frs. Fr in 1935.

The all-inclusive £5 fare was reduced to £4 12s 6d from 15 May 1931.

From May 1932 Second-Class Pullman cars were introduced to the 'Flèche d'Or'. Accommodation booked in France from Calais-Paris or vice versa: 45 Frs. Fr, reducing to 35 Frs. Fr in 1935.

1935-1939

London (Victoria) – Ashford, Folkestone Central, Sandwich or Dover Priory, etc

First-Class supplement – Single:3 shillings and 6 pence

Third-Class supplement – Single: 1 shilling*

(*Not* Boat Express).

*increasing to 1/6 c.1937.

Extra-fare Pullman car services, 1946

May 1946 'Golden Arrow'

London (Victoria) to Paris (Gare du Nord)

First-Class – Single: £6 and 10 shillings*

Second-Class – Single: £4 and 10 shillings

First-Class fare covered reservation of First-Class Pullman seat on both sides of the Channel. Second-Class fare covered reservation of Second-Class Pullman seat, London to Dover, First-Class steamer and travel in Second-Class ordinary carriage, Calais to Paris.

Passengers holding First-Class tickets via Dover-Calais to or from destinations beyond Paris could travel between London and Paris by the 'Golden Arrow' service on payment of a special Pullman supplement of £1.

Passengers holding Second-Class tickets via Dover-Calais to or from destinations beyond Paris could travel by the 'Golden Arrow' between London and Dover on payment of a special Pullman supplement of 3 shillings.

*(increased to £6 and 15 shillings, by November 1946)

Pullman supplements (per seat and journey made):

November 1946-1951

London (Victoria) to Folkestone Harbour – 5 shillings First-Class

Ostend Boat train – London (Victoria) to Dover – 5 shillings First-Class

Dieppe boat train – London (Victoria) to Newhaven – 4 shillings First-Class

'Golden Arrow' – London (Victoria) to Dover – 5 shillings First-Class

3 shillings Second-Class

Special all-inclusive fare London to Paris (single)

May to October 1949 – £6 First-Class

October 1949

First-Class – Single: £7 and 5 shillings

Second-Class – Single   : £5 13 6

Supplement for Pullman reservations on *both* sides of the Channel:

First-Class – Single: £1 1 2

Second-Class – Single: 13 shillings 6 pence

October 1951 to May 1952 all-inclusive fare

First-Class – Single: £7 17 11

Second-Class – Single: £6 and 6 shillings

Supplement for Pullman accommodation on both sides of the Channel:

First-Class – Single: £1 4 8

Second-Class – Single: 17 shillings

May 1952 to October 1952 all-inclusive fare

First-Class – Single: £8 and 11 shillings

Second-Class – Single: £6 18 6

October 1952 to May 1953 all-inclusive fare

First-Class – Single: £8 and 10 shillings

Second-Class – Single: £6 18 3

May 1953 to October 1953 all-inclusive fare

First-Class – Single: £8 and 10 shillings

Second-Class – Single: £6 17 6

October 1953 to May 1954 all-inclusive fare

First-Class – Single: £9 and 3 shillings

Second-Class – Single: £7 and 7 shillings

May 1954 to October 1955

First-Class (available 1 month) – Single: £7 and 6 shillings

(available 2 months) – Return: £14 and 2 shillings

Second-Class (and First-Class steamer) – Single: £6 4. 6

Return: £12

Supplement for Pullman accommodation on both sides of the Channel:

First-Class – Single: £1 7 2

Second-Class – Single: 18 shillings 8 pence

June to September 1956

First-Class (available 2 months) – Single: £6 and 15 shillings

(available 2 months) – Return: £13 and 10 shillings

Supplement for Pullman accommodation on both sides of the Channel:

First-Class advertised only – Single: £1 and 11 shillings

28 September 1958 to May 1959

London to Paris (including supplement for reservation of Pullman seats on both sides of the Channel).

First-Class advertised only – Single: £8 and 7 shillings

Return: £16 and 14 shillings

May to October 1959

London to Paris (including supplement for reservation of Pullman seats on both sides of the Channel.

First-Class (available 2 months) – Single: £ 8 and 4 shillings

Return: £16 and 8 shillings

'Meal tickets' – Pullman tickets, including the cost of meals in Pullman Cars on both sides of the Channel, also dining car gratuities, could be obtained at the time of booking.

Note: A complete new booklet format was introduced for British Railways printed Pullman tickets at this time (eventually replaced by new stock on 1 December 1962).

Adult and child blank to blank 'Edmondson-type' tickets for First- and Second-Class 'Golden Arrow' continued to be issued as before at the booking office.

A standing instruction gave the new type of ticket a high series number which was required on sales slips and quoted when ordering.[196]

From October 1960 to May 1961

London to Paris (including supplement for reservation of Pullman seats on both sides of the Channel.

First-Class (available 2 months) – Single: £8 6 6

Return: £16 and 13 shillings

Note: First-Class accommodation advertised only, although second-class cars continued to run.

From May to September 1961

London to Paris (including supplement for reservation of Pullman seats on both sides of the Channel).

First-Class (available 2 months) – Single: £8 7 6

Return: £16 and 15 shillings

Note: First-Class accommodation advertised only.

From 27 May 1962 to 1965

London to Paris (including supplement for reservation of Pullman seats on both sides of the Channel).

First-Class (available 2 months) – Single: £8 13 6

Return: £17 and 7 shillings

Note: Southern Region brochures generally only referred to First-Class fares, notwithstanding that Second-Class Pullman accommodation was available on the 'Golden Arrow' until May 1965.

The down 'Golden Arrow' after arrival at Dover Marine, 6 October 1966. In the foreground is Pullman car **Perseus.**

Appendix 1. Extra-fare Pullman car services, 1946-1972

Pullman supplements (per seat and journey made):

London to Dover – 4s 0d Second-Class

6s 0d First-Class

London to Paris (Nord) – 37s 6d First-Class

London to Paris (Lyon) – 39s 0d First-Class

Calais to Paris (Nord) – 31s 6d First-Class

Calais to Paris (Lyon) – 33s 0d First-Class

Note: Ordinary seat reservations:

From London to English ports: 2s (First- and Second-Class)

From French ports: 3s 6d (First- and Second-Class)

From 1 June 1966

London to Dover: 8s 0d First-Class

London to Paris (Nord): 39s 6d First-Class

London to Paris (Lyon): 42s 0d First-Class

Calais to Paris (Nord): 34s 0d First-Class

Calais to Paris (Lyon): 36s 6d First-Class

From 1 June 1970

London to Dover: 8s 0d First-Class

From 1 June 1971 to September 1972

London to Dover: 40 pence First-Class*

*The United Kingdom and the Republic of Ireland decimalised their currencies on 15 February 1971. 'Golden Arrow' Pullman car tickets printed both the old currency and its equivalent since 1969, but by January 1972 featured new pence only.

One of the original Flèche d'Or parlour cars No 4089 built by the Metropolitan-Cammel Carriage & Wagon Co in 1926 – seen here at Gare du Nord in June 1967. Note simplified livery, replacement post-war lamp shade just visible inside, and 'Golden Arrow' running board clipped to the bodyside.

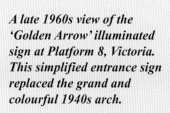

A late 1960s view of the 'Golden Arrow' illuminated sign at Platform 8, Victoria. This simplified entrance sign replaced the grand and colourful 1940s arch.

Appendix 1a. Pullman car supplementary tickets

Pullman car supplementary tickets could be obtained at principal booking offices, travel bureaux or, subject to availability, on-board train. From 1910, tickets issued in advance of travel were 'Edmondson' card-type in various printed colours indicating in small print the railway company, conditions of travel, seat and car number/letter as well as the fee payable. If accommodation was available just prior to departure, the Conductor or Attendant-in-Charge were permitted to issue supplementary tickets and collect monies upon production of a railway ticket to cover the journey and class of travel undertaken. Torn from pre-printed booklets, some of the earliest tickets were allocated to the vehicle in which the passenger travelled – i.e. *Corunna*, *Daphne* and *Valencia*. Later, economies of scale dictated the use of standard paper tickets for either 'Up' or 'Down' services, allowing the Conductor greater freedom to handwrite the car name and other particulars. By 1926, dedicated 'Golden Arrow' and 'Flèche d'Or' type tickets were issued in both Britain and France by the Southern Railway, Wagons-Lits Company or agencies of Thomas Cook & Son. For passport control on the inaugural 1929 'Golden Arrow' trip from Victoria, a special ticket was also issued per passenger which was handed to officials (these were printed with an arrow from right to left, as illustrated; thereafter all other tickets featured arrows from left to right!). Pullman Car tickets for Ocean and Channel Services, where applicable, were issued for First- and Second-Class passengers, coloured either blue, red, yellow, green or white.

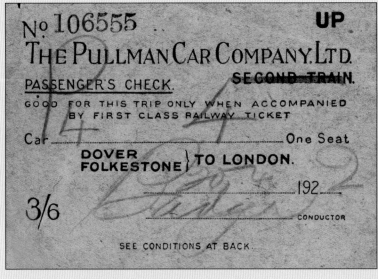

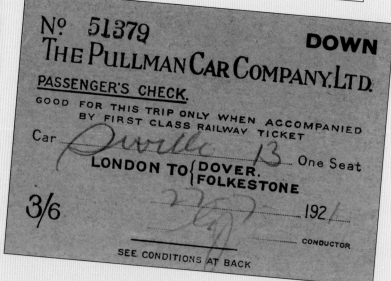

The following represent a random variety of supplementary tickets issued from 1910-1972.

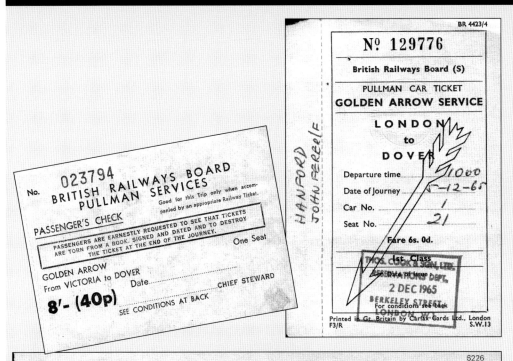

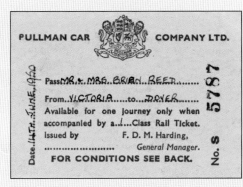

Special free passes and colourful inaugural tickets were issued and/or countersigned by the Chairman and General Manager of the Pullman Car Company. For the inaugural 1929 'Golden Arrow' the tickets were each countersigned by Pullman, Wagons-Lits, Southern Railway and Nord Railway representatives.

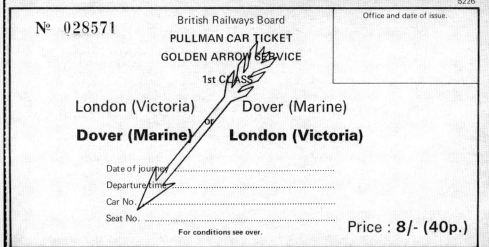

The SS 'Canterbury' running in the Dover-Calais service featured well-furnished restaurants where refreshments and meals could be obtained.

Table d'hôte luncheon 5 shillings

Afternoon Tea 2 shillings

Meals could also be obtained on the steamers between Newhaven and Dieppe at the following prices:

Breakfast: 3 shillings

Luncheon: 5 shillings

Tea (plain): 1 shilling and 6 pence

Supper: 3 shillings and 6 pence

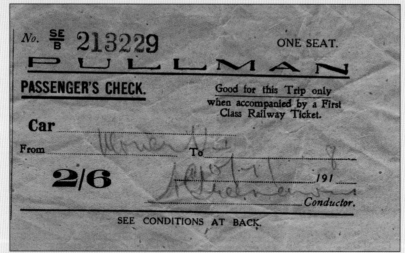

Note: Customs arrangements for new Continental Services in connection with incoming sailings, stipulated that HM Customs, from November 1946, were in place for both hand-baggage and registered baggage examination upon arrival at the Customs examination enclosure on Platform 8, Victoria Station. (Those passengers not travelling to London were examined by Immigration and Health Authorities before clearing Customs at Folkestone or Dover). Pullman staff were reminded that 'they must on no account accept dutiable goods from passengers, either for safe custody or by way of a gift or by purchase'. (Ref: Pullman Company circular No.57)

On the French side, the Customs or *Douane* examined the hand baggage on the way to Paris, and bags not labelled were apt to get mixed when carried by the same porter. Inspector Badger recalled the story in his diary when a lady being asked to open her bag for examination, found to her astonishment and surprise, that it contained a pair of gentlemen's pyjamas, socks, underwear and other men's attire. 'The French Customs got all hot and bothered and all were talking at the same time', Badger noted. He later found the gentleman on the train, and the mistake was put right. 'I advised them to label their baggage in future'.

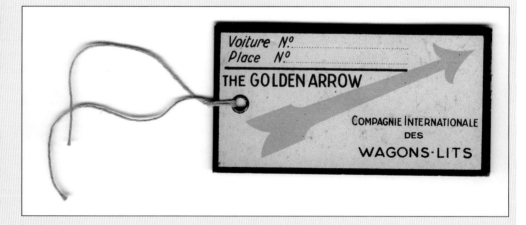

In addition, the sale of wines and spirits in unopened bottles was prohibited. Sales were only made of wines and spirits for consumption on the journey.

(A balanced stock account of wines, spirits and tobacco were carried on each train, and were available for inspection by HM Customs Officers.)

Appendix 3. Compagnie Internationale des Wagons-Lits *'Train Pullman tarif'*

Pullman (First-Class) (1926-1937) *Déjeuner* (Luncheon) Fr. 30

Pullman (First-Class) (1926-1937) *Diner* (Dinner) Fr.30

Pullman (First-Class) (1948) *Déjeuner* (Luncheon) or *Diner* (Dinner) Fr.400*

Pullman (Second-Class) (1954) *Petit déjeuner* (breakfast) Fr. 180

Pullman (Second-Class) (1953) *Déjeuner* (Luncheon) or *Diner* (Dinner) Fr.1000

Note: significant price variations between 1937-1954. The purchasing power of the French Franc was reduced by 70 per cent. during the First-World War to c.1920 and by a further 43 per cent. between 1922 and 1926. By 1959 the Franc was worth less than 2.5 per cent. of its 1933 value.

*subject to ration ticket allowance and other restrictions.

COMPAGNIE INTERNATIONALE DES WAGONS-LITS

TRAIN PULLMAN
GOLDEN ARROW
FLÈCHE D'OR
TARIF

Déjeuner ou Dîner	3o »
Café noir	2 »
Café au lait, Thé ou Chocolat	4 »
Café, Thé ou Chocolat avec lait, pain, beurre, confiture ou miel	8 »
Afternoon tea	12 »
Déjeuner à la fourchette	15 »
Couvert	3 »
Beurre	2 25
Potage	2 50
Hors-d'œuvre avec beurre	5 50
Œuf à la coque (la pièce)	2 50
Œufs plat ou omelette (2 œufs)	6 »
Œufs au bacon ou jambon (2 œufs)	6 50
Poisson	10 »
Viande chaude	11 »
Viande froide	9 »
Poulet (la portion)	15 »
Légumes	3 50
Fromage	3 »
Cake	2 50
Entremets	4 »
Biscuits Palmers	3 »
Fruits	
Confiture	3 »
Miel	3 50
Sandwich	4 »
Citron ou Orange pressé	3 50
Lait	2 50
Tisanes	3 »
Grog	5 50

27-1-37 (Voir la carte des vins au verso. — Wines as per list on other side).

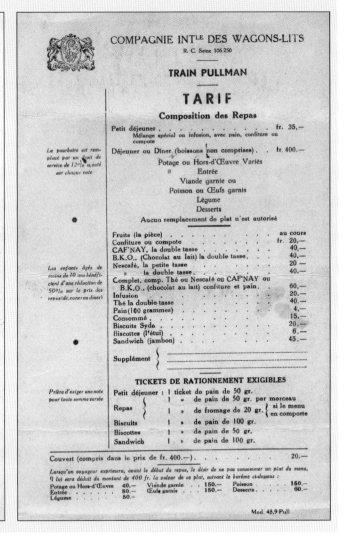

Appendix 4. Bill of Fare – a selection: Pullman Car Company/British Rail Catering, 1920-1972

Pullman *Diner* (1920-1927): 4 shillings

Pullman *Diner* (1928): 4 shillings and 6 pence

'On the "Golden Arrow" passengers will be served in the Pullman fauteuils thus obviating the necessity of any reservation beyond that of the Pullman places themselves'. (*The Golden Way*, Continental Section, September 1926)

Pullman Luncheon/*Déjeuner* (to 1939): 4 shillings and 6 pence

Pullman Christmas Dinner (1937): 5 shillings

Pullman A la Carte: (1946-1949)

Afternoon tea: 2 shillings and 6 pence

Note: By an Order of the Ministry of Food from 1946 to 1950, no meal could consist of more than three courses or exceed 5 shillings in price. All tariffs were subject to day to day availability of supplies.

Pullman car Table d'hôte (1950-1952)

Luncheon: 10 shillings

Dinner: 10 shillings

Light Afternoon tea: 3 shillings

Full Afternoon tea: 3 shillings and 6 pence

Pullman car Table d'hôte (1952-1957)

Luncheon: 12 shillings

Light Afternoon tea: 3 shillings

Pullman Car Table d'hôte (1959-1960)

Luncheon: 12 shillings and 6 pence

Full Afternoon tea: 3 shillings and 6 pence

Dinner: 12 shillings and 6 pence

Pullman Christmas Menu (1961)

Luncheon: 12 shillings

Pullman A la Carte (1962)

Afternoon tea: 4 shillings

Pullman a la Carte (1965-1967)

Afternoon tea: 4 shillings and 6 pence

Pullman Tariff (1968)

Morning Coffee and biscuits service: 3 shillings

Pullman Tariff (1969-1970)

Afternoon tea: 5 shillings and 6 pence

Pullman Tariff (1971-1972)

Coffee and biscuits service: 20 new pence

Afternoon tea: 30 new pence*

(*increasing to 35 new pence, January 1972)

Pullman Tariff (September 1972)

Afternoon tea: 35p

Cold ham and ox-tongue with mixed dressed salad: 60p

Sandwiches (full round): Chicken 26p

Ham and other centres 16p

Coffee per pot per person: 15p

Tea per pot per person: 9p

Pullman car menus and tariffs

All Pullman Car Company menus and tariffs were prepared by the catering superintendent, Mr Claude James, until 1946 (thereafter by Mr Julian Morel). The bill of fare on Ocean and Channel Services was changed every two or three weeks dependant on the season. Almost all menu cards featured the company coat of arms coloured either grey, red or green located at the top of the menu or at the foot, with most later emblazoned with a large arrow at an angle and the train name 'Golden Arrow' in bold letters, while gold-lettered versions were printed for Heads of State, royalty or special occasions. Throughout the 1920s and 1930s, menus were often seen held in a weighted silver-plated holder as part of the place setting, and located at all times close to the table lamp and cruet set. Christmas menus of thick card were almost always free-standing

and depicted a colourful festive scene. By the late 1940s, menu covers with transparent sleeves, for the insertion of menu cards of a 'standard dimension', were increasingly used reflecting Table d'hôte or à la carte one side; afternoon tea and beverages on the reverse. The menu cover itself discreetly advertised the leading cigarette brands or alcoholic drinks, for which listing fees were charged by Pullman.[197]

Until 1939, almost all menus for luncheon or dinner on the 'Golden Arrow' service particularly, were written in French offering either a fixed Table d'hôte or, dependant on the time of day, high tea service. From 1946 a combination of English and French was generally the rule, and à la carte progressively became the preferred choice.

The following examples of English menus date from 1921-1970.

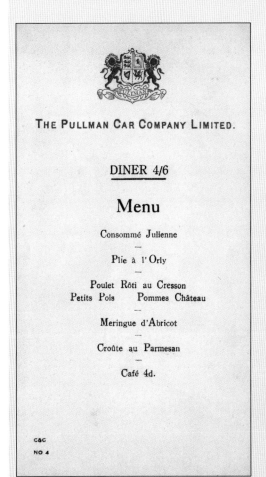

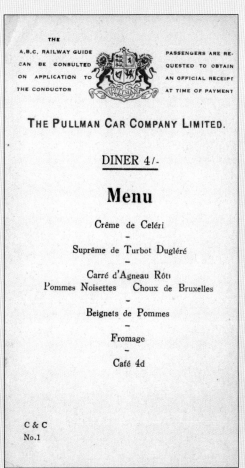

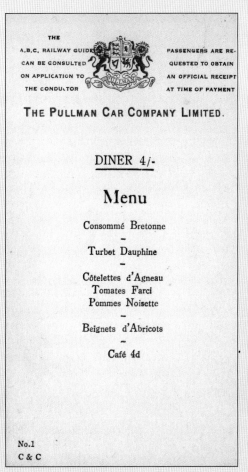

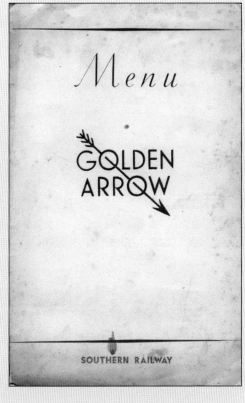

BEVERAGES

Indian Tea	9d.
Café au Lait	9d.
Chocolate	9d.

A LA CARTE

Cut Bread and Butter	6d.
Buttered Toast	6d.
Toasted Crumpets	6d.
Sweet Biscuits	6d.
Fruit Cake	6d.
Gateau Maison	9d.
Jam or Honey	6d.

SANDWICHES

A selection of: Chicken, Smoked Salmon, Ham, Cheese & Tomato, Salad & Pressed Beef.

Plain 3/-   Toasted 3/6

PLATS DU JOUR

Pan Fried Fillets with Sauté Potatoes	2/6
Supreme of Haddock Monte Carlo	2/6
Grilled Cambridge Sausages with Whipped Potatoes	2/6
Welsh Rarebit with Grilled Tomatoes	2/6
Scrambled Egg on Buttered Toast	2/6
Mixed Grill: Sausage, Tomato, Mushrooms and Sauté Potatoes	2/6
Cold Chicken and Mixed Salad	3/-
Salad Panache	1/6

SWEETS

Ice Cream	9d.
Golden Way Trifle	9d.

By an Order of the Ministry of Food, no meal may consist of more than three courses or exceed 5/- in price.

This tariff is subject to day to day availability of supplies.

In case of difficulty or lack of service will passengers please communicate with The General Manager, The Pullman Car Co., Ltd., Victoria Station, London, S.W.1.

PLEASE ASK FOR A BILL

WINE LIST P.T.O.

THE PULLMAN CAR COMPANY LIMITED

"GOLDEN ARROW"

GOLDEN GRILL   4/6

WITH

HOT ROLLS

TOAST   PRESERVES   CAKE

POT OF TEA

OR

ENGLISH TEA   2/-

CRUMPETS OR SCONES

PRESERVES   CAKE

CUT BREAD & BUTTER

POT OF TEA

SANDWICHES PLAIN OR TOASTED CUT TO ORDER

CHICKEN OR SMOKED SALMON 3/-

OTHER CENTRES 1/-

Will Passengers please draw the Conductor's attention to any errors or lack of service. If satisfaction is not obtained write to:

The General Manager, The Pullman Car Company Limited, Victoria Station, London, S.W.1

GOLDEN ARROW   FLÈCHE D'OR

TABLE D'HOTE SERVICE

LUNCHEON 10/-

LIGHT AFTERNOON TEA 3/-   FULL AFTERNOON TEA 3/6

A LA CARTE SERVICE

Soup du Jour	1/6
Smoked Salmon and "Hovis" and Butter	4/6
Grilled Dover Sole and Lemon Wedge	4/6
Omelette	3/6
Assiette Anglaise	4/6
Golden Grill	5/6
Sauté Potatoes 9d. Seasonable Vegetables	...
Cheese Course 2/6 Dessert	2/6

SANDWICHES

Smoked Salmon	3/-
Ham and Other Centres	2/-

SUNDRIES

Cut "Hovis" and White Bread and Butter	9d.
Oven Crisp Rolls and Curled Butter	9d.
Buttered Toast	9d.
Scones, Crumpets	9d.
Fruit Cake	9d.
Individual Preserves—Jam, Honey, Marmalade	9d.

BEVERAGES

Indian Tea, China Tea	1/-
Café au Lait	1/-

ICED WATER IS AVAILABLE ON REQUEST

Passengers are respectively reminded that all items listed on this tariff are subject to availability and that when a "table d'hôte" meal is being served only individual courses from that menu are available "a la carte."

When butter is not available only the best margarine will be served.

The A.B.C. Railway Guide can be consulted on application to the Conductor.

In any difficulty will passengers please send for the CONDUCTOR. Failing satisfaction please write to the GENERAL MANAGER, PULLMAN CAR COMPANY LIMITED, VICTORIA STATION, LONDON, S.W.1 enclosing your receipted bill.

GA/6/54

WINE LIST P.T.O

GOLDEN ARROW   FLÈCHE D'OR

TABLE D'HÔTE SERVICE 12/6

Chilled Fruit Juices

Soup of the day with Golden Croutons

Choice of :   The Chefs Cold Collation

Omelette to choice

From the Grill :   Lamb Chop   Dover Sole   Minute Steak

Two Styles of Potatoes   and   Second Vegetable Tray

Sweet du Jour

Cheese Board

Coffee 1/-

The TRIANON BAR in this train offers a pleasant meeting place.

In any difficulty will passengers please send for the CONDUCTOR. Failing satisfaction, please write to the MANAGING DIRECTOR, PULLMAN CAR CO., LIMITED, VICTORIA STATION, LONDON, S.W.1, enclosing your receipted bill.

Winter

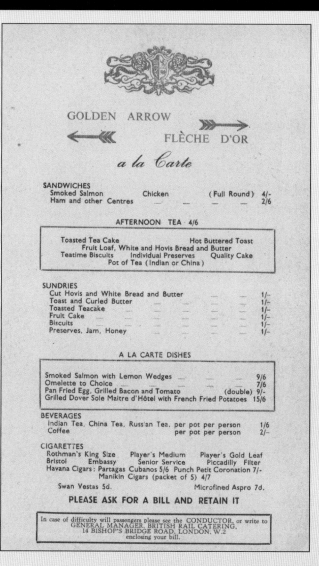

Wine List

as available

		½ Bottle	¼ Bottle
CHAMPAGNE	G.H. Mumm	£1·50	76p
	Cordon Rouge N.V.		
BORDEAUX RED	Médoc	86p	45p
	Chateau Meyney	£1·07	—
BORDEAUX WHITE	Graves	86p	45p
BURGUNDY RED	Mâcon	86p	45p
	Beaune	95p	—
ROSÉ	Beaujolais Rosé	76p	39p
	Rosé D'Anjou	82p	—
BURGUNDY WHITE	Pouilly Fuissé	86p	45p
HOCK & MOSELLE	Liebfraumilch	£1·07	55p
	Zeltinger Riesling	95p	—
ALSATIAN	Riesling	95p	—

SHERRY				
Amontillado No. 4	Miniature 23p	Tio Pepe	Miniature 24p
Walnut Brown	,, 23p	Bristol Cream	,, 24p

APERITIFS
Dubonnet _____ Miniature 23p
Martini Vermouth, Sweet, Dry, Bianco ,, 12p

PORT
Fine Old Ruby _____ Miniature 24p

SPIRITS AND LIQUEURS				
Whisky 'Royal Scot'	Miniature 38p	Cognac V.S.O.P.	Miniature 38p
Whisky	,, 38p	Cognac	,, 33p
Gin London Square	,, 37p	Bénédictine	,, 38p
Gin	,, 37p	Cointreau	,, 38p
Vodka	,, 37p	Drambuie	,, 36p
Rum	,, 37p	Kümmel	,, 36p
Bacardi Rum	,, 37p	Crème de Menthe	,, 36p

Whisky, Gin, Rum and Vodka are offered prepacked
in a securely closed container.

BEERS				
Bass & Worthington	16p	Mackeson Stout	16p
Double Diamond	16p	Whitbread's Ales	16p
McEwans Export	16p	British Lager	16p
Guinness	16p	Danish Lager	17p
		Shandy	12½p

CIDER			
Bulmer's	12½p	Whiteway's	12½p

MINERALS			
Schweppes:			
Ginger Beer	8½p	Tonic Water, Bitter Lemon	7½p
Ginger Ale, Lemonade	7½p	Sparkling Orange	7½p & 10½p
Soda Water	7½p	Pepsi-Cola	10½p
Vichy Célestins	14p	Lime Juice Cordial	7p
Orange Squash	7p	Fruit Juices (Assorted)	8½p

PLEASE ASK FOR A BILL AND RETAIN IT

Appendix 5. Restricted working of Pullman cars

It was a standing instruction that all Pullman cars were restricted from working between Tonbridge and Winchelsea via Hastings, between Canterbury West and Whitstable Harbour, and into Birchington Dock Road.

The 1910/1912/1914 built 'Type A' cars (later designated 'Type G') were restricted from working over the following sections:

Purley and Caterham

Ash and Aldershot Town

Blackheath Junction and Slades Green (via Charlton)

Dartford and Rochester Junction (except in case of emergency only)

North Kent East Junction and Charlton (via Greenwich)

Strood and Maidstone West

Hoo Junction and Port Victoria

Holborn (Low Level) Sidings and Ludgate Hill

Note: The couplers and gangways of 'Type A' cars and 1920/21 built 12-wheel cars were interchangeable, and could be connected to ordinary stock by means of a special adapter.[198]

Mimosa *at Preston Park works, 19 May 1950 with new vestibule doors.*

Battered and bruised – Instruction **Car No 101** *(ex Emerald) outside Preston Park works during 1963 awaiting conversion to a camping coach.*

Left and far left: **Alicante** *and* **Sorrento** *at Preston Park yard on 4 July 1957.*

Appendix 6. The 'Golden Arrow' and Continental boat trains, 1959

On 18 June, 1959, the following 88 'steam-hauled' cars - including 12-wheelers and standard 'K-types' covered in earlier Profiles - were recorded (in order) as available to work on Southern Region boat trains to Dover/Folkestone/Newhaven and Southampton Docks, in addition to specials and 'Bournemouth Belle' workings:

Timber bogie four-wheel 'F-type'

Aurora, Montana, Juno, Flora

**Timber bogie four-wheel 'G-type'
(formerly 'A-type')**

Corunna, Valencia, Rainbow, Mimosa, Sorrento, Florence, Alicante, Daphne, Savona, Regina, Seville, Topaz, Sapphire, Clementina, Ruby, Palermo, Leghorn, Hawthorn

Timber bogie six-wheel 'H-type'

Orpheus, Rosalind, Neptune, Hibernia, Palmyra, Sunbeam, Scotia, Malaga, Nos. 45, 47, 96, 97, 98, 99, Portia, Monaco, Nos. 294, 17, 41, 95.

All Steel bogie. Pullman Standard 'K-type'

Phoenix, Medusa, Aurelia, Cassandra, Penelope, Zena, Cecilia, Chloria, Zenobia, Argus, Minerva, Nos. 27, 54, 55, 169, Ibis, Isle of Thanet, Latona, Nos. 61, 171, 249, 34, Adrian, Diamond, Nos. 35, 36, Nos. 183, 180, 184, Nos. 182, 185, 208.

Timber bogie six-wheel 'S-type'

Grosvenor, Myrtle, Nos. 5, 6, 8.

A tranquil 1966 scene at Dover Marine with three 'U-type' Pullmans and ordinary carriages in view.

Steel bogie N.E. Double Bolster four-wheel 'U-type'

Aquila, Carina, Orion, Pegasus, Cygnus, Hercules, Perseus, Aries, No. 303.

(Pullman Car Company inter-office memo RS.14/JLG/DMG)

Appendix 7. Bookstall service on the 'Golden Arrow', 1948

In co-operation with Messrs W.H. Smith & Son and the Pullman Car Company a new bookstall service available to travellers that fell appropriately in the centenary year of Smith's bookstalls began on 30 August 1948, initially on the 'Thanet Belle' Pullman to Ramsgate, Margate and Broadstairs. The occasion was celebrated by Master Fred Edwards, dressed as a newsboy of 1848, handing supplies of newspapers to the attendants on the train. By the following month, the 'Golden Arrow' benefited from this service, too, offering passengers a selection of novels and fashion magazines on board.[199]

The bookstall service became available again when the 'U-type' cars made their debut in 1951. A selection of books and magazines featured in the bar area of Pegasus.

Appendix 8. The 'Golden Arrow' Pullman lapel badge

All members of the train crews from 1946 were equipped with two lapel badges, a 'Golden Arrow' pattern and a standard pattern. These badges were costly to produce and carried Purchase Tax, and while the initial issue had been made to members of staff without charge, replacements of any lost were charged for at 15 shillings for the 'Golden Arrow' badges and 12 shillings and 6 pence for each of the standard type.

The Pullman Company General Manager, Frank Harding, explained in a company circular of August 1946, that all staff must take 'every care' of these badges and cautions that the cost of replacement in small numbers would probably be much more than the price quoted.[200]

By 1951, a smaller souvenir version of the 'Golden Arrow' badge became available to passengers, retailing at 5 shillings each.

A fitting tribute. Pullman Car Company staff from Preston Park Works record the proud occasion when **Phoenix** *is released for traffic (1952).*

Appendix 9. Pullmans used as 'Supply cars'

During 1932, the question of rental charges due by the Pullman Company to the Southern Railway came under scrutiny when a number of elderly 'supply cars' were subject to revision. The Pullman Company management requested that a special charge should be considered for these vehicles as they were described as 'permanent supply cars providing storage and offering additional kitchen facilities to adjoining vehicles, particularly for large excursion parties' and crucially offered no accommodation for passengers. Per the contractual agreements with the Pullman Car Company, the Southern Railway received almost £10 per Pullman car running annually in service on their lines, although concessions were allowed when overhauls were due or long-term inactivity was reported, for example.

By May 1933, the Southern Railway's Traffic Manager's Office noted that the Pullman Car Company were, by necessity, increasing their supply cars for excursion trains. Some of the original Dover/Folkestone cars – *Sorrento, Sapphire, Palermo* and *Savona* – had been duly converted and stripped of certain interior fittings, during which time they could not be used for the conveyance of passengers. (Indeed, during December 1936, remodelled *Sapphire* was noted as far north as the Midlands, passing Stafford on a football charter – Charlton Athletic vs Bolton Wanderers – consisting of Southern Railway carriages.)

It was agreed that the rent normally charged for these vehicles of approximately 16 shillings and 8 pence per month, would be reduced to 4 shillings and 2 pence per month whilst being used as 'supply cars'.[201]

An exterior view of Palermo *languishing in sidings almost at the end of its working life. This car was once the pride of the Dover line, finally ending its career as a well-equipped 'Holiday Coach' on the Southern Region upon withdrawal in 1962. Sadly it was broken up on-site in 1971.*

Appendix 10. Pullman cars ('F/G-types') converted into 'Holiday' and 'Camping' coaches (with disposal data)

Pullman	Camping Coach No.	Released to BR	Allocated
London Midland Region ('Camp Coach') *Emerald* [202]	*021803*	1 Feb 1964	Betws-y-Coed, North Wales, 1964-1970 Preserved on site.
Scottish Region ('Pullman Camping Coach') *Savona*	*SC44*	29 April 1961	Corpach, 1961-1964
Leghorn	*SC46*	19 May 1961	North Berwick, 1961-1965
Eastern Region ('Camp Coach') *Montana*	*CC165*	11 July 1960	Oulton Broad South, 1960-1961. Heacham, 1962-1965 Preserved at Petworth, West Sussex.
Clementina	*CC166*	11 Nov 1960	Oulton Broad South, 1960-1965
Southern Region ('Holiday Coach') *Ruby*	*P45*	2 March 1961	Lyndhurst Road, 1961-1967
Rainbow[203]	*P49*	10 May 1961	Wrafton, 1961-1964. Yalding, 1965-1967
Sapphire	*P51*	19 April 1961	Bosham, 1961-1964. Sandling, 1965-1967 (on site until 1972) Preserved.
Florence	*P53*	16 May 1961	Exton, 1961-1964
Valencia	*P54*	31 Oct 1961	Amberley, 1962-1967
Regina	*P55*	31 Oct 1961	Amberley, 1962-1967
Hawthorn	*P58*	8 Feb 1962	Littleham, 1962-1964
Daphne	*P60*	1 March 1962	Sway, 1962-1967
Seville	*P61*	8 Feb 1962	Sway, 1962-1967
Corunna	*P62*	30 March 1962	Martin Mill, 1962-1967. On site until late 1971
Sorrento	*P63*	30 March 1962	Martin Mill, 1962-1967. On site until late 1971
Palermo	*P64*	30 March 1962	Martin Mill, 1962-1967. On site until late 1971
Western Region *Mimosa*	*W9869*	8 Oct 1962	Marazion, 1963-1964, thereafter Staff Association until 1981 On site until 2000. Preserved at Petworth, West Sussex.
Flora	*W9871*	30 Nov 1962	Marazion, 1963-1964, thereafter Staff Association until 1981 On site until 1997. Preserved at Petworth, West Sussex.
Juno[204]	*W9872*	30 Nov 1962	Marazion, 1963-1964, thereafter Staff Association until 1981 On site until 2003.

Pullman	Camping Coach No.	Released to BR	Allocated
Aurora[205]	*W9873*	4 February 1963	Fowey, 1963. Marazion, 1964, thereafter Staff Association until 1981 On site until 2003.
Alicante	*W9874*	4 February 1963	Fowey, 1963. Marazion, 1964, thereafter Staff Association until 1981 On site until 2000. Preserved at Petworth, West Sussex.

Note: Interior stripping and conversion work took place at both Preston Park Works, Brighton and Lancing Carriage Works.

Parlour car *Topaz* was withdrawn from service in November 1960, and purchased by Mr Henry Maxwell for preservation. It was initially displayed at Clapham Museum and now resides at the National Railway Museum, York.

During June 1980, *Topaz* (with *Perseus* in the guise of '*Anne*') were used at York station for the filming of 'Chariots of Fire' (directed by Hugh Hudson).

Left: *A quiet interlude. 'F/G-type' cars in the process of conversion at Preston Park Works.*

Opposite: *Onward bound. Two converted vehicles being shunted out of Preston Park yard with the assistance of 'K' class 2-6-0 No. 32340.*

Seville *awaiting camping coach conversion at Preston Park yard, February 1962.*
Note the removal of at least one gangway connection.

Opposite: *The former* **Florence***, converted into 'Pullman Holiday*
Coach' closing P53 and ready for its new life at Exton (1961-1964).

A bird's eye view of 'Holiday Coaches' P54 and P55 at Amberley, 1966.

Below: **Regina** *(P55) is photographed adjacent to* **Valencia** *(P54) at Amberley during 1963. Note that the vehicles have revised (1960) Pullman coat of arms.*

Appendix 10. Pullman cars ('F/G-types') converted into 'Holiday' and 'Camping' coaches (with disposal data)

Above and above right: *Beds, wardrobes, set of drawers and linoleum replace the armchair comfort of the one time coupé compartments. The windows to the left open outwards caravan-style, whilst the washing sinks are not connected to any running water.*

Exterior view of one-time **Juno** *at Marazion, 1997.*

The former Alicante, Aurora and Juno at Marazion, 1997.

Exterior view of one-time Alicante at Marazion, 1997.

The exquisite marquetry panelling of Aurora, 1995.

Appendix 11. Pullman cars in N.A.A.F.I service

The following six Pullman cars with kitchen facilities, at one time familiar on the London-Dover/Folkestone route, were temporarily transferred to the control of the Navy, Army and Air Force Institute at the end of World War 2, for the service of meals in troop and leave trains. Each were painted dark green all over, and carried their N.A.A.F.I. numbers in small yellow letters at the bottom of the body sides, near an entrance vestibule door. The cars were later restored to their original condition (some as late as 1950), and were again put into 'extra fare' Pullman service.

Corunna	N.A.A.F.I. No. 29+
Savona	N.A.A.F.I. No. 38*
Sapphire	N.A.A.F.I. No. 37*
Palermo	N.A.A.F.I. No. 21*
Seville	N.A.A.F.I. No. 3
Rosalind	N.A.A.F.I. No. 18 (12-wheel car)

*Supply cars since June 1933 (*Sapphire* Oct 1935) at which time the buffet rent due to the Southern Railway was reduced from 16 shillings and 8 pence per month to 4 shillings and 2 pence per month. (Letter from Pullman General Manager G.H. Griffiths to Sir Herbert Walker, 7 June 1933. GHG/H/C6138.)

+ During 1938 *Corunna* was fitted with a bar counter.

Note: Following remodelling in the 1920s, the above cars all featured kitchens at the time of requisition in 1944; further adjustments to the interiors took place subsequently.

The partially fire-damaged state of **Emerald** *outside Preston Park works, 29 September 1955. Almost gutted completely but later repaired and used for training purposes, the Pullman Car Company received a recovery from their insurance provider for the full value of the vehicle.*

Appendix 12. Valuation of 'F- and G-type' Pullman cars by Mr W.A. Agnew, 30 September 1937

Each car of the Pullman fleet was examined during the first half of 1937 to determine a reasonable length of life.

In arriving at the initial theoretical value, i.e., the price at which an equivalent vehicle could be purchased, the prices adopted had closely followed those used in a previous valuation for insurance purposes (at April 1934), with some modifications, because of structural alterations and change in use, since that date.

In each case, £50 representing scrap value was taken from the initial value of the car, the money remaining was divided into 30 or 33 parts according to the normal length of life of each car, and the value was arrived at by multiplying a 30th (or 33rd) portion by the probable life in years, and adding £50 to the resulting amount.

The value of the vehicles had been arrived at on the basis of rolling stock prices obtained apparently in 1934, and did not reflect current estimates from the existing carriage builders. The valuation of the Pullman fleet was estimated at £641,067.

Mr W.A. Agnew, who was formerly the Chief Mechanical Engineer of the London Passenger Transport Board, was asked to undertake a valuation of the Company's rolling stock at a fee of £200, by Sir Follett Holt, Chairman of the Pullman Car Company Ltd. The following information was extracted from the official report, now in a private collection:

A glimpse inside **Emerald** *in 1979. Although fire damaged in 1955, several panels remain intact.*

Car	Rebuilt	Type	Valuation	Note
Corunna	1924	First-Class Kitchen	£525	1
Emerald	1924	First-Class Kitchen	£525	1
Sorrento	6/1933	Supply Car	£1,475	2
Savona	6/1933	Supply Car	£1,475	2
Sapphire	10/1935	Supply Car	£1,475	2
Palermo	6/1933	Supply Car	£1,475	2
Valencia	5/1933	Composite	£1,475	2
Florence	6/1933	Composite	£1,475	2
Regina	7/1933	Composite	£1,475	2
Clementina	5/1933	Composite	£1,475	2
Leghorn	7/1933	Composite without kitchen	£840	3*
Cosmo Bonsor	6/1933	Composite	£1,475	2
Alicante	5/1935	Composite	£1,475	2
Seville	5/1933	Composite	£1,475	2
Ruby	7/1933	Composite	£1,158	4
Hawthorn	6/1933	Composite	£1,158	4
Mimosa	7/1935	Composite	£1,475	2
Daphne	5/1933	Composite	£1,158	4
Topaz		First-Class Parlour	£1,158	4
Aurora		First-Class Guard Parlour	£2,690	5
Flora		First-Class Guard Parlour	£2,690	5
Juno		First-Class Guard Parlour	£2,690	5
Montana		First-Class Guard Parlour	£2,690	5

Note 1.	Future life expectancy 3 years i.e. to 1940
2.	Future life expectancy 9 years i.e. to 1946
3.	Future life expectancy 5 years i.e. to 1942
4.	Future life expectancy 7 years i.e. to 1944
5.	Future life expectancy 16 years i.e. to 1953

*Lists of data compiled by J.T. Howard Turner since the 1940s suggest that *Leghorn* was *not* remodelled or rebuilt at any time during its service life. However, Mr Agnew's tabulation and other Pullman records confirm that it was altered, albeit only briefly, to a 'composite' without kitchen facilities (although always running in conjunction with another car on Kent Coast services). During the early 1950s, the vehicle received, for example, new vestibule ends and replacement bogies.

A glimpse of the bar area inside 12-wheel Pullman car **Myrtle** *of 1911 (See* **Pullman Profile No.1**). *On several occasions, including 28 March 1950, this vehicle, as well as the veteran* **Grosvenor**, *deputised at short notice for the* **Trianon Bar** *in the 'Golden Arrow' service. Note: with the exception of* **Leghorn** *and* **Topaz**, *all other parlour cars, as originally built, were remodelled with kitchen and pantry during 1924. (*Alicante, Leghorn *and* Mimosa *later became composite cars rebuilt between 1933-1935.)*

Special Workings

The President of the French Republic and Suite (Private Special Train)

Dover Marine to Victoria, Monday, 16 May 1927

Engine

Flora

Camilla

Pomona (reserved for the President)

Montana

Bogie van No. *2018*

Prince Albert of the Belgians and the Grand Duchess Charlotte and Prince Felix of Luxembourg

Victoria to Dover Marine, Saturday, 16 February 1952
Engine ('Schools' class No. 30919)

Juno

Penelope

Cygnus

Malaga

Montana

Bogie van No. *2341*

HM Queen and Duke of Edinburgh travelled to Winchfield Station in *Aries* en route to RAF Odiham for RAF Coronation Review, 15 July 1953

The inaugural sailing of SS *Caesarea*, 16 November 1960

(Waterloo-Weymouth Quay)

Juno

Daphne

Alicante

Cassandra

Niobe

Visit of Soviet Prime Minister Alexei Kosygin

Gatwick to Victoria, 6 February 1967

Engine

Phoenix

Carina

Aquila

Perseus

Isle of Thanet

(Note: Numerous Pullman cars were specially allocated for Royal and V.I.P. Specials over the years, often drawn from the pool of 'Golden Arrow' cars, particularly those constructed in 1951/2. By 1963, *Aquila, Aries, Cygnus, Phoenix, Minerva* and *Niobe* were listed officially and used as required. Special allocations for other specials, including Lindfield Race Trains involved: *Car No.208, Rosemary, Zenobia* and *Philomel* all regular vehicles at one time on the 'Golden Arrow'.)

16 July, 1956. State visit of King Faisal II of Iraq and Suite having just arrived by special working at Platform 2, Victoria Station. HRH Queen Elizabeth II and Prince Philip and others members of the Royal Family receive their guests

'Golden Arrow Limited'

15 May 1929	3 August 1929	April 1946	18 October 1949
Aurora	*Flora*	*S.C. 154*	*Flora*
Pauline	*Zenobia*	*S.C. 193*	*Sappho*
Chloria	*Rosemary*	*Trianon*	*Cecilia*
Rosemary	*Minerva*	*Onyx*	*Topaz*
Minerva	*Pauline*	*Cecilia*	*Trianon*
Zenobia	*Cecilia*	*Niobe*	*Zenobia*
Cecilia	*Niobe*	*Adrian*	*Onyx*
Niobe	*Fingall*	*Lady Dalziel*	*Malaga*
Geraldine	*Leona*		*T.C.294 as 'second-class'*
Flora	*Chloria*		*T.C.99 as 'second-class'*
Montana			

July 1930	2 August 1930	5 August 1950	1 June 1951
Princess Elizabeth	*Montana*	*T.C. 99 as 'second-class'*	*Car No. 36*
Onyx	*Cecilia*	*T.C. 294 as 'second-class'*	*Car No. 35*
Diamond	*Chloria*	*Malaga*	*Carina*
Pearl	*Minerva (III)*	*Trianon*	*Perseus*
Adrian	*Leona (II)*	*Cecilia*	*Orion*
Ibis	*Pearl*	*Onyx*	*Hercules*
Lydia	*Diamond*	*Zenobia*	*Pegasus*
Glencoe	*Niobe (II)*	*Flora*	*Cygnus*
Adrian	*Lady Dalziel*		*Aquila*
Orpheus			*Minerva*
Lady Dalziel			

11 June 1951	**4 August 1951**
Minerva	*Minerva*
Aquila	*Aquila*
Cygnus	*Cygnus*
Pegasus	*Pegasus*
Hercules	*Hercules*
Orion	*Orion*
Perseus	*Perseus*
Carina	*Carina*
Car No. 35	*Car No. 35*
Car No. 208	*Car No. 36*

September 1952	**4 October 1959**
Car No. 208	*Car No. 36*
Car No. 34	*Car No. 34*
Aries	*Orion*
Cygnus	*Argus*
Carina	*Pegasus*
Pegasus	*Phoenix*
Zena	*Aries*
Orion	*Minerva*
Phoenix	
Niobe	

June 1964	**May 1968**
Isle of Thanet	*S208 (ex Car 208)*
Orion	in BR Corporate livery
Hercules	*Carina*
Aquila	*Perseus*
Perseus	*Orion*
Carina	
Car No. 75	
Car No. 208	

May 1969

S307 (ex Carina) in BR Corporate Livery

S308 (ex Cygnus) in BR Corporate Livery

Orion

S301S (ex Perseus) in new BR (Southern) Pullman livery (blue lower panels and pale grey upper panels. Lettered 'Golden Arrow' in white below the waistline).

June 1972	**30 September 1972**
S301 (ex Perseus)	*S302S*
S302 (ex Phoenix)	*S306S*
S306 (ex Orion)	*S307S*
S307 (ex Carina)	*S308S*
S308 (ex Cygnus)	

'F-Type'

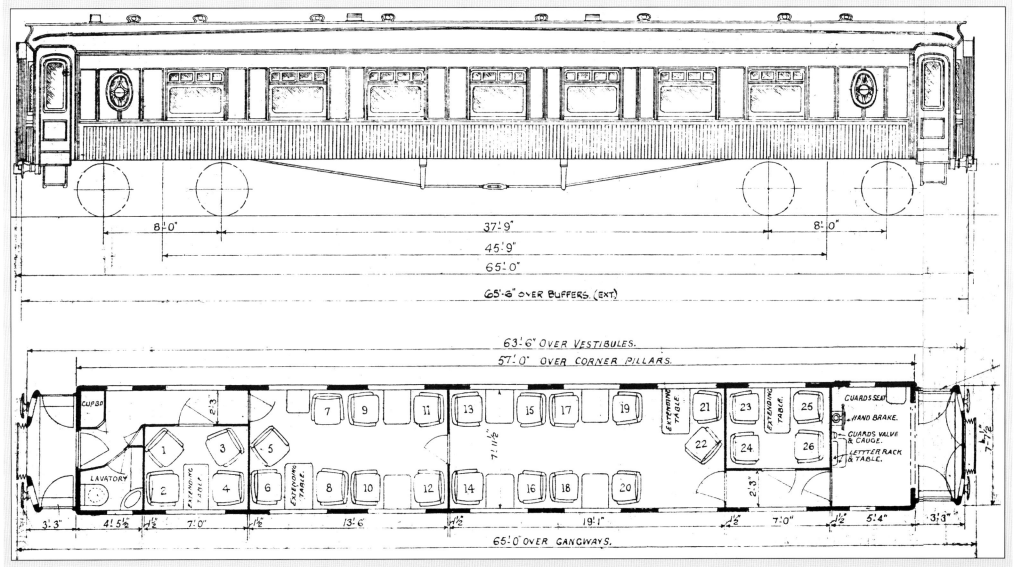

Elevation and floor plan of Birmingham C&W built guard parlour cars **Aurora, Flora, Juno** *and* **Montana,** *as new.*

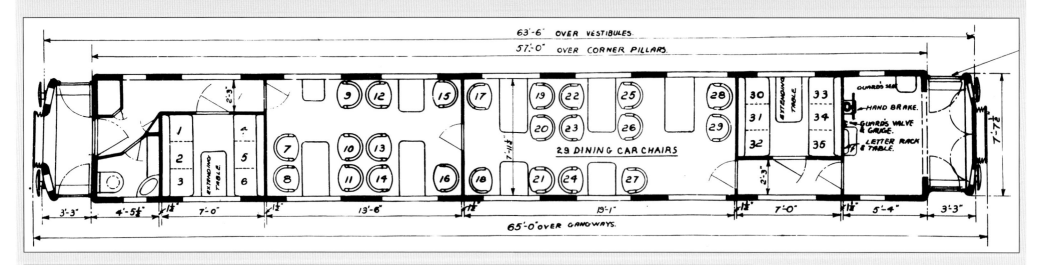

Above: *Remodelled interior plan with dining car chairs in the two saloons and fixed seating in the coupé compartments.* **Flora** *became briefly* **Second-Class Car 154;** *Aurora,* **Third-Class Car 503** *and Juno,* **Third-Class Car 502.** *All were later reconverted to First-Class.*

Exterior view of **Montana** *awaiting attention at Preston Park Yard with Ocean Liner Express roof board, 2 May 1955.*

'(A) G-Type'

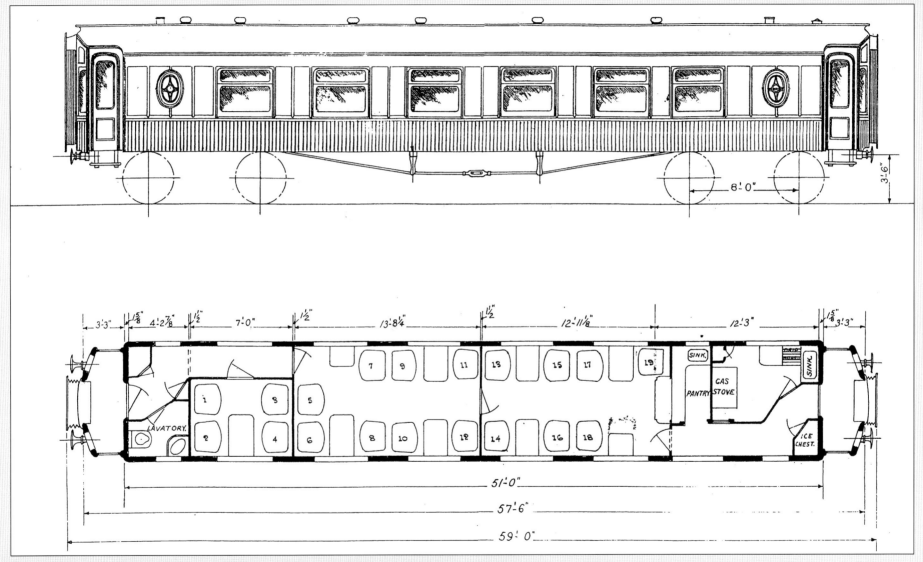

Elevation and floor plan of kitchen cars Regina *and* Florence, *following remodelling in 1918.*

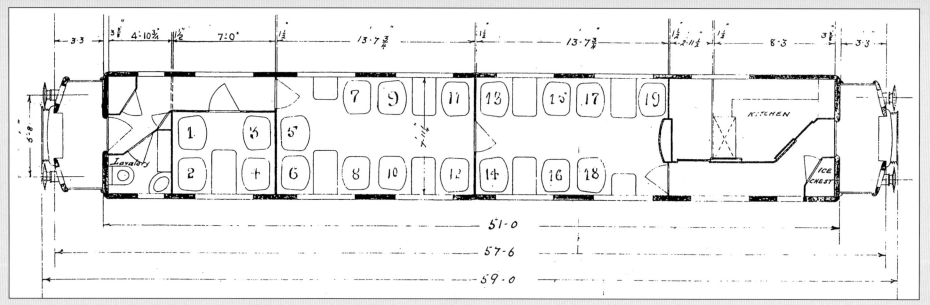

Floor plan showing general arrangement with kitchen and pantry of Cravens-built cars Seville *and* Cosmo Bonsor. *Note the kitchen window was subsequently repositioned when remodelled to a composite, while the pantry became windowless.*

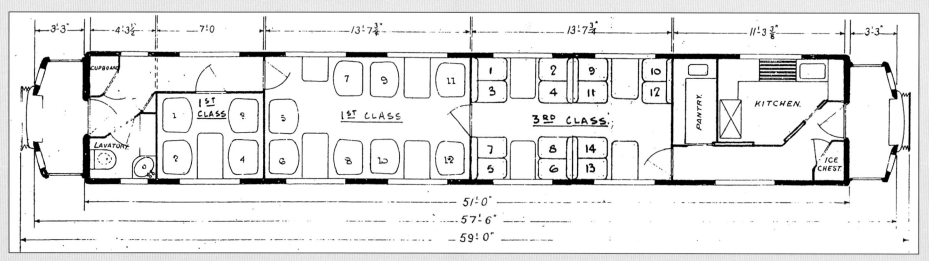

Floor plan of Cravens-built kitchen car Cosmo Bonsor *remodelled as a composite during June 1933, with 12 First- and 14 Third-Class seats. This vehicle was rebuilt to first-class and renamed* Rainbow *in May 1948.*

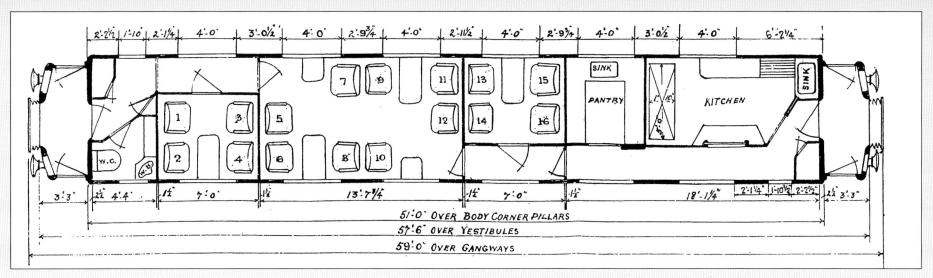

Floor plan of Birmingham C&W kitchen car Savona *(originally constructed as a parlour), and rebuilt and remodelled to include a central coupé compartment and kitchen in January 1924.*

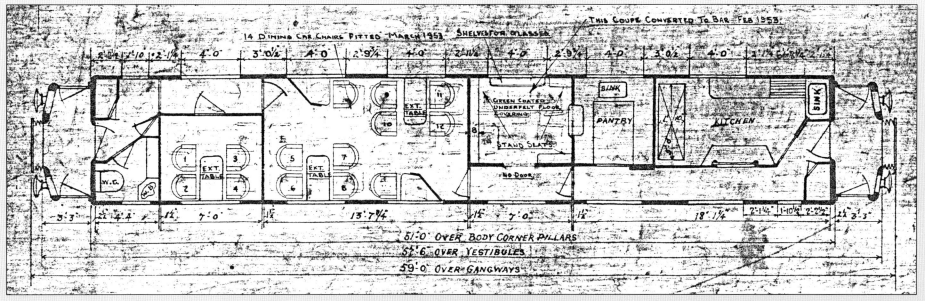

Floor plan of Corunna *with its central coupé converted into a bar. Note, too, the dining car chairs.*

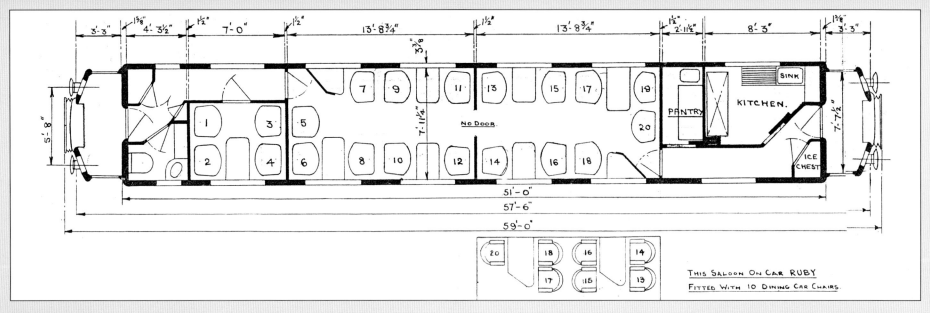

THIS SALOON ON CAR RUBY
FITTED WITH 10 DINING CAR CHAIRS.

Above: *Plan of Birmingham C&W kitchen cars* Daphne *and* Ruby.
Note: These cars had no pantry window, unlike the remodelled 1910-1912 cars and increased their seating capacity following the removal of the saloon glass cabinets. By September 1955 the remaining composite 'G-type' cars serving the Channel Islands, Le Havre and St Malo were converted back to first-class, although Ruby *retained its 10 dining car chairs in one saloon.*

Exterior view of Rainbow *(ex Cosmo Bonsor) at Preston Park Yard awaiting attention, 1952.*

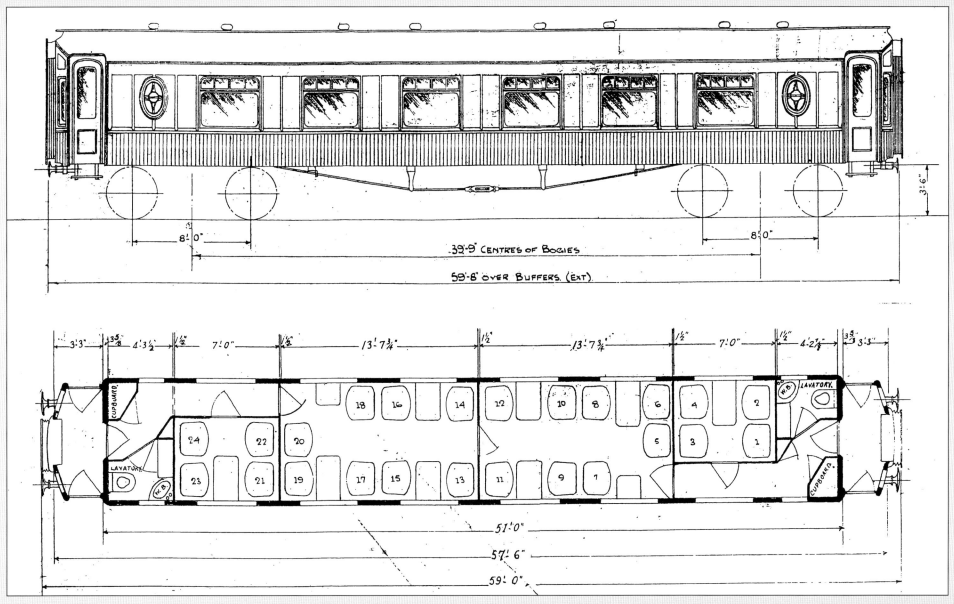

Elevation and floor plan of parlour cars **Alicante** *and* **Leghorn** *(similar to* **Mimosa** *and* **Topaz** *with new sliding lights). Note* **Alicante** *and* **Mimosa** *were remodelled with kitchen and pantry facilities at Longhedge Works in 1924, and both were later converted to composite cars.*

A 1954 photograph of parlour car **Topaz** *at Preston Park Works. Note the original American style equalised 4-wheel timber bogies.*

Withdrawn parlour car 'S308S' formerly 'Cygnus' at Carnforth, Lancashire in April 1978. Note particularly the LNE pattern bogies, lavatory window and body decoration.

Name/Number	BR Southern Number	Withdrawn	Disposal
Perseus	S301S	9/1972	Formed part of Sir Winston Churchill's Funeral Train in January 1965. Prior to repainting in BR blue and grey livery, *Perseus* retained its original coat-of-arms and full lining. Used for special workings on trains conveying the Sovereign, visiting Heads of State and members of the Royal Family. In 1956 Marsal Nikolai Bulganin and Premier Nikita Kruschev of the Soviet Union travelled to London in a seven-car train from Portsmouth. The principals travelled in *Perseus*. Following withdrawal from service and purchase, *Perseus* moved to the North Yorkshire Moors Railway during Oct 1972. By 1977, to 'Steamtown', Carnforth, Lancashire for restoration. Part of the VSOE/ 'British Pullman' operations since 1982.
Phoenix	S302S ('K-type')	9/1972	Under management of the Southern Region Pullman 'Division' (1964) *Phoenix* was allocated for V.I.P. special workings (and throughout much of the 1950s used in Royal trains). Upon withdrawal, all collage panels and table lamps were removed and sold at 'Collectors Corner', Euston. *Phoenix* was acquired and briefly resided at Longmoor Steam Railway. By 1973, transported to Lyon, France and opened as a static restaurant with S307S ex *Carina*. One coupé compartment converted into a bar (retaining as a backdrop, an original mirror with decorative etching). To 'Steamtown', Carnforth, Lancashire for restoration, 1980 for Venice Simplon-Orient Express. New saloon panelling features floral marquetry to an original 1920s 'Flèche d'Or' design. Part of the VSOE operations since 1982. After a short absence following its latest periodic overhaul, it returned from France to the 'British Pullman' during 2018.

Almost forgotten and once the pride of the Southern Region royal trains, 'S302S' waits patiently for any business in its penultimate guise as a roadside diner / bar at Lyon in France. This car was subsequently acquired by VSOE for full restoration and now runs regularly on the British Pullman.

Name/Number	BR Southern Number	Withdrawn	Disposal
Car No 303	7/1967		Upon withdrawal stored at Micheldever with ordinary rolling stock awaiting disposal and withdrawn 'Bournemouth Belle' stock. Sold to scrap merchants, Bird Group, Long Marston, Worcester, October 1968 and dismantled the following year.
Aries	1969		During the summer of 1964, *Aries* was on loan to the North East Region. Upon withdrawal, it is believed the vehicle was used as temporary accommodation during the early 1970s for workers constructing the M62, a 107-mile long west-east trans-Pennine motorway in Northern England. Located at the Yew Tree Inn, Rochdale, Lancashire for many years, before passing through a series of owners who wanted to save the car from demolition. *Aries* is now at the Kent & East Sussex Railway, Tenterden awaiting full restoration.
Aquila	7/1967		Under management of the Southern Region Pullman 'Division' (1963) *Aquila* was reserved for Royal Train duty (as required) and V.I.P. specials, before transfer to the 'Bournemouth Belle' and subsequent withdrawal in 1967. Purchased from British Railways in 1968, with four other Pullman cars by Bulmers Cider of Hereford for exhibition purposes. Sold to Venice Simplon-Orient Express Ltd. Now restored in Pullman-style livery and located at the Colne Valley Railway, Halstead, Essex.

Name/Number	BR Southern Number	Withdrawn	Disposal
Orion	S306S	9/1972	During 1953, *Orion* was used by visiting overseas royalty attending the Coronation of HM Queen Elizabeth II, and generally for special workings on trains conveying the Sovereign, visiting Heads of State and members of the Royal Family. Stored at the Ashford Steam Centre during November 1972, and following restoration at Wolverton Works, the vehicle moved to Pecorama (at that time known as Modelrama), Beer, Devon in January 1978. At the time of writing it resides there under full cover of a purpose-built platform canopy.
Carina	S307S	9/1972	Formed part of Sir Winston Churchill's Funeral Train in January 1965. Upon withdrawal, briefly resided at Longmoor Steam Railway and then in 1973 to Lyon, France and used as a static restaurant. To 'Steamtown', Carnforth, Lancashire in 1980. Later stored at Swindon and the only surviving 'Golden Arrow' car still in blue and grey livery (2016). At the time of writing, devoid of any furnishings, it resides at the Bluebell Railway, West Sussex awaiting restoration.
Cygnus	S308S	9/1972	Under management of the Southern Region Pullman 'Division' (1963) *Cygnus* was reserved for Royal Train duty (as required). It was one of the first vehicles' to be repainted in Corporate colours, removing its name with a running number. (Numbers carried were original Pullman Car Company schedule nos. together with a Regional suffix). Moved to the North Yorkshire Moors Railway during Oct 1972. To 'Steamtown', Carnforth, Lancashire for restoration in 1980. Part of the VSOE/ 'British Pullman' operations since 1982.

Lost in transition? Sponge headrests replace the traditional antimacassars, the seating is no longer moveable and the absence of the central partitions leave a lot to be desired: almost all the hallmarks of Pullman de-luxe travel have vanished.

Name/Number	BR Southern Number	Withdrawn	Disposal
Hercules	1969		Listed for Departmental use as *ADB975022*. The vehicle languished in sidings and its conversion never materialised. It was dismantled at Clapham, in July 1973.
Pegasus	M310E	1976	Following 'Nightcap Bar' duty from London Euston, the vehicle was acquired by the Birmingham Railway Museum, Tyseley and was partially restored by 1993, although interior veneers were lifting due to ingress of water. Subsequently sold to Railfilms Limited. During 1999, it received full structural overhaul and rebuilding with many enhancements, including an all-steel body, vestibule doors of a similar pattern to the originals, new interior bar (with one of the original aluminium plaques sourced from Pecorama) and wall panelling undertaken at Blake Group (Stainless Steel Fabrication), Leith, near Edinburgh.

'Convoi Exceptionnel' – S302S (*ex Phoenix*) *on its repatriation by road from Lyon, France to Carnforth, England. Although height restrictions were carefully considered prior to transportation, the vehicle found itself temporarily wedged under a railway bridge in France. In order to free it, the tyres on the transporter were deflated.*

Above: ***During restoration at Carnforth, Lancashire, layers of blue and grey paint were removed to reveal, for the first time in many years, the name Phoenix.***

Above: right: **S306S** *(ex Orion) photographed at Brighton, awaiting disposal, 1973.*

Right: *The fully restored **Orion** photographed precariously being lowered into position at its new home, now known as Pecorama, at Beer, Devon. Today, it is fully under cover of a station canopy and continues to be beautifully and immaculately maintained.*

The end of the line for Car No. 303. Photographed at Micheldever in 1967 with several Pullmans withdrawn from the 'Bournemouth Belle'. It was subsequently dismantled for scrap.

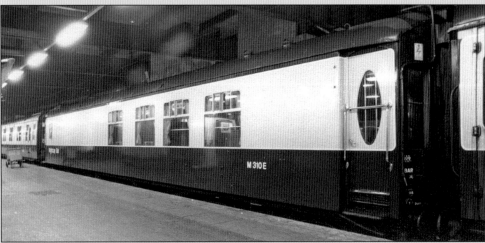

M310E (ex Pegasus) at London Euston station as the 'Nightcap Bar', 15 October 1970. Today, it sports Pullman umber and cream livery, and is noted for its many structural changes made during restoration. On 9 September 2015, HM Queen Elizabeth II and the Duke of Edinburgh travelled in Pegasus as part of a steam-hauled train to celebrate the reopening of the railway from Edinburgh to Tweedbank. Scotland's First Minister, Nicola Sturgeon, MSP was invited to travel with the special party.

From 1 January 1923

First-class Pullman cars ran in the following trains from London and Dover, Walmer, Deal and Sandwich (Timings reflect the 24-hour clock):

DOWN		Sat only			
Charing Cross	depart	11.0	13.25	16.5	19.0
London Bridge	depart	11.7			
Dover (Priory)	arrive	13.45	15.13	17.4	18.38
Walmer	arrive	14.8	15.31	18.2	20.55
Deal	arrive	14.15	15.36	18.8	21.1
Sandwich	arrive	14.25	18.19	21.13	
UP		**Sat only**			
Sandwich	depart	7.10	10.0	16.10	
Deal	depart	7.25	10.15	12.41	16.22
Walmer	depart	7.30	10.20	12.46	16.27
Dover (Priory)	depart	7.48	10.37	13.7	16.47
London Bridge	arrive	9.36	–	15.26	–
Cannon Street	arrive	9.40	–	–	–
Charing Cross	arrive	12.20	15.40	18.30	

The cars were available for the holders of first-class tickets only on payment of a supplementary fare of 2 shillings. Seats could be reserved on application to the Station Master at the starting point, and at the intermediate stations at which the train calls. By April 1924, the Pullman Car Company had agreed with the Southern Railway to gradually repaint the crimson lake liveried 'South Eastern' cars to the then soon-to-be standard cream and umber, as and when they were due for overhaul.[206]

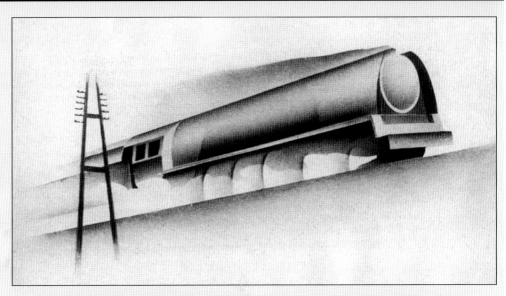

May 1929 to June 1930:

Early Morning Outward Service – with best connections to Italy

(Down and Up services)

London (Victoria East)	depart	9.00	arrive	22.47
Folkestone (Harbour)	arrive	10.43	depart	21.05
Boulogne (Pier)	depart	13.00	arrive	18.56
Paris (Nord)	arrive	16.00	depart	16.00

Afternoon Outward Service

London (Victoria East.)	depart	14.00	arrive	15.30
Folkestone (Harbour)	arrive	15.41	depart	13.40
Boulogne (Pier)	depart	17.53	arrive	11.17
Paris (Nord)	arrive	20.55	depart	8.25

SOUTHERN RAILWAY

"Golden Arrow"

PARIS TO LONDON

SPECIAL BAGGAGE DELIVERY SERVICE.

*B*AGGAGE

registered by "Golden Arrow" to Victoria can be cleared and delivered promptly by Southern Railway Baggage Service, avoiding all waiting on arrival.

The Baggage Service Clerk on the Folkestone-Victoria Train will attend to your requirements on completion of the necessary Customs Declaration Form and Delivery Order.

Waterloo Station, S.E.1.

H. A. WALKER, *General Manager.*

Ctl. 2074 $\frac{5.000}{1/10/35}$

COMPAGNIE INTERNATIONALE DES WAGONS-LITS

GOLDEN ARROW

PULLMAN

Appendix 16. Selected timetables for the 'Golden Arrow', Continental connections and other South-Eastern Section Pullman services

'A City to City Express'

London (Victoria East.)	depart	16.00		
Dover (Pier)	arrive	17.38		
Calais (Pier)	depart	19.50		
Etaples (Le Touquet)	arrive	20.42		
Paris (Nord)	arrive	23.15		
London (Victoria)	depart	9.00		
Calais (Maritime)	depart	6.05		
Boulogne (Maritime)	depart	4.56	13.02	
Etaples	arrive	5.34	7.19	13.32
	depart	5.37	7.22	13.35
Paris (Nord)	arrive	12.10	10.35	16.05
London (Waterloo)	depart	21.00	arrive	9.03
Southampton (Docks)	depart	23.45	depart	7.20
Havre	depart	7.35	arrive	22.35
Paris (St Lazare)	arrive	10.15	depart	19.55

Ostend-Cologne Pullman Express (First- and Second-Class Pullman Cars)

London (Victoria East.)	depart	9.45	arrive	21.15
Ostend	depart	16.10	arrive	15.10
Brussels	depart	17.45	arrive	13.36
Aix-La-Chapelle	arrive	20.26	depart	12.01
Cologne	arrive	22.25	depart	11.00

August 1926 – January 1927:

Newhaven and Dieppe Service (First- and Second-Class Pullman Cars)

London (Victoria)	depart	10.00	depart	20.20
Newhaven (Harbour)	arrive	11.45	arrive	22.15
Dieppe	arrive	14.55	arrive	2.05
	depart	15.24	depart	2.51
Paris (St Lazare)	arrive	17.58	arrive	5.25

Notice given to all travellers: From Newhaven to London, First- and Second-Class Pullman car seats could be reserved at the Bureau de Renseignments (Galerie Supérieure), Gare St. Lazare, Paris; Messrs Thomas Cook & Son, 2 Place de la Madeleine, Paris; the Station Superintendent, Newhaven Harbour, or the Pullman Purser/Conductor on board Channel boat 'Paris' during the passage from Dieppe to Newhaven. (By 1929, Pullman cars were introduced between Dieppe and Paris.)

April – July 1931

'Golden Arrow Limited' – The 'Luxe' All-Pullman Train

London (Victoria)	depart	11.00	arrive	18.35
Dover (Marine)	arrive	12.35	depart	16.57
Calais (Maritime)	depart	14.25*	depart	15.25
Paris (Nord)	arrive	17.35*	depart	12.00

*Five minutes later from 15 May. And on this date the SS 'Canterbury' received non-Pullman passengers for the first time, while the departure from Paris changed to 12.20 with an arrival in Victoria at 19.00.

January 1937

'Golden Arrow Limited'

(First- and Second-Class from Calais to Paris and from Paris to Boulogne)

London (Victoria)	depart	11.00	arrive	17.20
Dover (Marine)	arrive	12.35		
Folkestone (Harbour)	depart	15.44		
Calais (Maritime)	depart	14.30		
Boulogne (Maritime)	arrive	13.10		
Paris (Nord)	arrive	17.40	depart	10.30

By an order of the Ministry of Food, no passenger was to be served with a meal of more than three courses and exceeding 5 shillings in price. All items listed on the Pullman and shipping menus were subject to market availability.

Registered baggage was once again examined at Victoria, and hand baggage examined at the Customs Shed at Dover Marine following passport control. At this time, a French visa was required to visit France.

On 4 May 1947, second-class Pullman cars were withdrawn altogether from the 'Arrow' and replaced by additional first-class Pullmans.

May-October 1949

'Golden Arrow all-Pullman service'

London (Victoria)	depart	10.30	arrive	19.30
Dover (Marine)	arrive	12.5	depart	17.55
Calais (Maritime)	depart	14.14	arrive	15.30
Paris (Nord)	arrive	17.30	depart	12.20

(From 2 October Second-Class Pullman accommodation was reinstated and available in both English and French trains.).

Winter service until May 1952

'Golden Arrow First- and Second-Class Luxe'

London (Victoria)	depart	10.00*	arrive	18.30*
Dover (Marine)	arrive	11.35*	depart	16.55*
Calais (Maritime)	depart	14.38	arrive	15.42
Paris (Nord)	arrive	17.52	depart	12.30

*(One hour later from 7 October)

Winter service until 16 May 1953

London (Victoria)	depart	13.00*	arrive	18.30*
Folkestone (Harbour)	arrive	14.38*		
Dover (Marine)	depart	16.58*		
Calais (Maritime)	depart	18.17	arrive	15.44
Paris (Nord)	arrive	21.34	depart	12.30

*(One hour later from 19 April)

April-December 1946

'Golden Arrow Pullman service'

(First- and second-class from London and Dover; between Calais and Paris first-class only)

London (Victoria)	depart	9.00	arrive	19.20
Dover (Marine)	arrive	10.40	depart	17.40
Calais (Maritime)	depart	14.10	arrive	15.36
Paris (Nord)	arrive	17.50	depart	12.00

Note: Currency restrictions and rationing in force. Travellers to France were not permitted to take with them more than £5 in sterling, and 2,000 francs was the maximum amount of French currency that was allowed to be taken into France.

May to October 1959:

To Paris by 'Golden Arrow'

London (Victoria)	depart	14.00	arrive	19.45
Folkestone (Harbour)	arrive	15.35		
	depart	16.10		
Dover (Marine)	depart	18.13		
Calais (Maritime)	arrive	17.40	arrive	15.56
	depart	18.02		
Paris (Nord)	arrive	21.40	depart	12.36

On 1 January 1963 the Pullman Car Company was fully integrated with the British Transport Hotels Ltd. Passenger receipts, menus and on-board ticketing were now under the auspices of the 'Pullman Division'.

Pegasus, 'Trianon Bar car (III)', was withdrawn from the 'Arrow' during December 1963 and transferred to the London Midland Region. Eventually it was repainted in blue and white livery and bestowed the name 'Night Cap Bar' for use on the overnight sleeper service to Scotland from London (Euston). It was withdrawn in 1976 and stored at Wolverton Works.

By May 1965, second-class accommodation was withdrawn from the 'Arrow'; thereafter the service became officially a composite train of generally three or four first-class Pullmans and second-class ordinary stock.

22 May 1966–27 May 1967[207]

Pullman service to Paris

London (Victoria)	depart	09.30	arrive	18.35
Dover (Marine)	arrive	10.50	depart	17.10
	depart	11.25	arrive	16.30 (Br.T.)
Calais (Maritime)	arrive	12.45*	depart	16.10
	arrive	13.45 (C.E.T.)		
	depart	14.14	arrive	15.42*
Paris (Nord)	arrive	17.25	depart	12.30

*(one hour later until 22 October and from 19 March. Br. T.)

On 6 March 1967, the 'Pullman Division' was merged into British Rail Catering.

29 September 1968–31 May 1969

'First-Class Pullmans and Second-Class'

London (Victoria)	depart	10.30	arrive	19.35
Dover (Marine)	arrive	11.50	depart	18.13
Calais (Maritime)	depart	14.14	arrive	15.42
Paris (Nord)	arrive	17.25	depart 12.30 (Train 19)	

France: The last steam-hauled run of the 'Flèche d'Or' took place on 11 January 1969 with the final Pullman working from Paris on 31 May.

England: Under new management, three of the Pullman cars allocated to the service received an interpretation of the new Corporate grey and blue 'Pullman' livery during 1967 which simply did not suit the vehicles concerned. By late 1969, a blue and grey livery with simplified lining was adopted for the remaining five vehicles, with the train title appearing in place of the car name. Rarely all five ran together, but more often three or four sufficed. The last public service ran on 30 September 1972.

← ««« *The Golden Arrow* »»» →

THE
BIRMINGHAM
Railway Carriage and Wagon Co. Ltd
SMETHWICK.

A final look at the 'Golden Arrow' in June 1972 with all five Pullmans working together. The working is empty stock passing Clapham Junction.

A 1929 chrome Rene Prou table lamp used on French Pullman services.

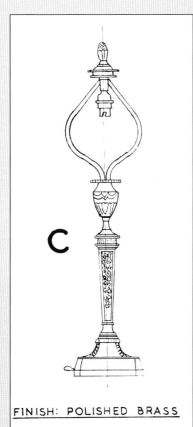

C

FINISH: POLISHED BRASS

Type C

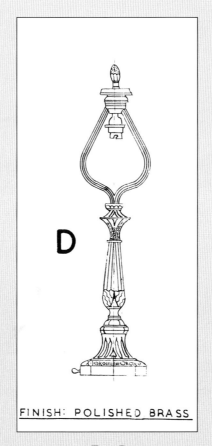

D

FINISH: POLISHED BRASS

Type D

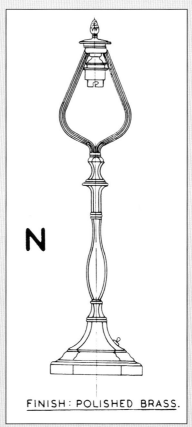

N

FINISH: POLISHED BRASS.

Type N

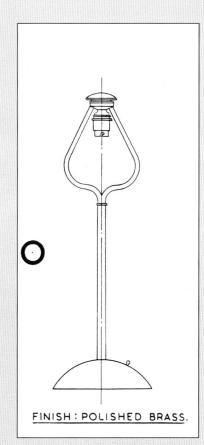

O

FINISH: POLISHED BRASS.

Type O

References

The origins of luxury rail travel on the London to Paris route to 1939

1. Papers of Wagons-Lits historians Philip Jefford and Roger Commault (Private collection). See also: https://www.doverport.co.uk/about/history-and-development.

2. *The National Archives*: RAIL 953/14 London, Chatham and Dover Railway New Express Mail Services to Paris and Brussels, via Dover & Calais, June 1882.

3. *Southern Titled Trains*, D.W. Winkworth (David & Charles, 1988) pp.163-173.

4. See: www.channel-packets.com/ship/nord/nord. Accessed: 18 June 2014.

5. *The Railway Gazette*, 18 March 1910 (Supplement), pp. 1-4.

6. *The Railway Gazette*, 28 July 1911, p.74 and *Railway Times,* 28 March 1914.

7. *The Railway Gazette*, 8 May 1914, p.625.

8. Pullman Company Ltd, Extraordinary meeting notification, Moorgate Street, London, 15 September 1915.

9. Pullman Car Company Ltd memoranda 1 July 1921, Mr Powell to Works Manager Mr Piedot Ref: S2/198.

10. *The British Gazette*, 12 May 1926, 3am issue, p.4. and *Daily Graphic*, 13 May 1926, p.2.

11. *Modern Transport,* 19 February 1927 'Continental Extensions' and Pullman Car Co Ordinary General Meeting, 14 February 1927.

12. *The British Gazette*, 7 May 1926, p.4.

13. Southern Railway Special Notice No.156. C.O.S. Edwin C. Cox, 14 May 1929

14. *The National Archives*. Southern Railway Board Minute Books and *Southern Titled Trains*, D.W. Winkworth (David & Charles, 1988) p.178.

15. *The Railway Gazette*, 21 July 1933, pp.98-99.

16. CIWL horaire 'Flèche d'Or', April 1939 (Editions et Publications W. Fischer)

The post-war revival, 1946-1949

17. *The National Archives*: PRO:RAIL 979/92 SR Traffic Officers' Conference minutes, 23 January 1946.

18. Southern Railway brochure, Cross Channel Services, 15 January 1946, Ctl.2/46034 (McCorquodale Press).

19. *The* National Archives: PRO:RAIL 645/24 SR Hotels & Catering Committee Board minutes, 12 Sep 1946.

20. *The National Archives*: PRO:RAIL 979/92 SR Traffic Officers' Conference minutes, 23 January 1946.

21. Southern Railway brochure, London-Paris Golden Arrow, March 1946, A5950/4549 (McCorquodale Press).

22. Publicity material: Southern Railway *Cross-Channel Services*, 15 January 1946 (Ctl.2/ 46034)

23. *The Railway Magazine*, Sept and Oct 1946.

24. *Trains Illustrated*, No.2, May 1946, pp.10-12.

25. *The Architects' Journal*, 9 May 1946, p.356.

26. *The National Archives:* PRO:RAIL 1188/42 SR: Reintroduction of the 'Golden Arrow', 27 March 1946.

27. *Trains Illustrated*, No.2, May 1946, pp.10-12.

28. *The Railway Gazette*, 17 May 1946, p.544.

29. *The Railway Magazine,* July/August 1946, pp.220-222.

30. *Dover Express*, 19 April 1946 'Return of the Golden Arrow'.

31. Ibid.

32. *The Railway Gazette*, 19 April, 1946, p.438.

33. Ibid and *Dover Express*, 19 April 1946.

34. Ibid.

35. *The Railway Gazette*, 19 April, 1946, p.438.

36. 20. *La Route du Rail*, August -September, 1946 – No.8 (Revue mensuelle illustrée des Chemins de fer français et étrangers), pp.12-3.

37. *Modern Motoring and Travel*, May 1946, p.16.

38. Ibid, p.17.

39. *Dover Express*, 19 July and 18 October 1946 and http://www.ournewhaven.og.uk

40. *Notre Métier* (L'hebdomadaire illustré du Cheminot Française), 10 May 1948, p.1.

41. *The Railway Gazette*, 16 December 1949, pp. 716-7.

42. *The Railway Gazette,* November 1946, p.626.

References

Period of change and uncertainty, 1950-1960

43. 1. *The Railway Magazine*, Vol 76, January-June 1936, p.221 and *The Railway Magazine* Vol 81, July-Dec 1937, p.218.

44. *The Railway Gazette*, 21 July 1933, pp 98-99.

45. The National Archives: AN8/10 (Memorandum dated 12 June 1956 between Pullman and SR General Managers)

46. The National Archives: PRO AN 172/1 (BTC general file: Introduction of Pullman cars on train services, 8 September 1954. Extract from minutes of meeting of Chief Regional Managers, Charing Cross Hotel.

47. Ibid.

48. Southern Region Traffic meeting, 4 May 1956 memorandum (ref: 296/5/6).

49. The National Archives: PRO AN172/1.

50. Ibid.

51. Pullman Car Company Internal memorandum from Mr Stanley Adams, 25 July 1956.

52. The National Archives: AN8/10 Southern Region Traffic meeting. Memorandum dated 1 May 1957.

53. Ibid.

54. Southern Region Traffic meeting - Notes of Discussion, 13 February 1957.

55. Ibid.

56. Haresnape, B, *Pullman - Travelling in Style*, Malaga Books, 1987, p.132.

57. Southern Region Traffic meeting – Notes of Discussion, 13 February 1957.

The final years, 1960-1972

58. *The National Archives* - PRO: AN157/45 SR Pullman Car Services. Memorandum dated 13 May 1959.

59. *Steam Days*, Key Publishing Limited, May 2015, p.17.

60. Hasenson, A., *The Golden Arrow* (Howard Baker, 1970), pp.115-118.

61. British Transport Hotels Ltd letter to all members of staff of the Pullman Car Co. Ltd. 22 December 1962 signed by Mr Frank Hole.

62. British Rail Shipping Services (Southern Region) timetable September 1968, p.2.

63. Winkworth, D.W., *Southern Titled Trains* (David & Charles, 1988), p.188.

64. Haresnape, B., *Pullman. Travelling in Style* (Malaga Books, 1987), p. 150.

65. Kichenside, G., *Orion and the Golden Arrow: the story of a Pullman Car* (Peco Publications, 2014).

66. Leigh, Dell, *The Princely Path to Paris by the Golden Arrow* (Pullman Co publication, The Arden Press, 1926).

The South Eastern & Chatham Railway Company Pullman services – the forerunner of the 'Golden Arrow', 1910-1914

67. *The Railway Gazette*, 7 September 1926, p.295.

68. *The Pullman Car Guide*, WH Smith publication, September 1910, p.3.

69. *The Railway Gazette*, 18 March 1910, p.308. See also the *Locomotive Magazine*, 15 April 1910, pp.79-81.

70. *The Railway Magazine*, March 1910, pp.409-412.

71. Ibid, p.409.

72. *The Railway Gazette*, 11 November 1910, p.520.

73. *The Pullman Car Guide*, WH Smith publication, September 1910, p.2, and The Railway Magazine, March 1910, p.410.

74. Behrend, George, *Pullman in Europe* (Ian Allan, 1962), pp.263-350. Table X

75. *The Railway Gazette*, 18 March 1910, p.308.

76. *The Railway Magazine*, March 1910, p.410.

77. Ibid, p.410.

78. The Soane Museum, London. Correspondence from the Curator of Drawings, 18 June 2013.

79. *The Illustrated London News* and *The Pullman Car Guide*, September-November 1910 and June 1911.

80. See: Buckley, Cheryl, *Designing Modern Britain* (Reaktion Books, 2007); Cohen, Deborah. *Household Gods. The British and their Possessions* (Yale, 2006) and Supplement to *The Railway Gazette*, March 1910.

81. *The Pullman Car Guide*, WH Smith, June 1911, p.6.

82. *The Railway Gazette*, 11 November 1910, p.520 and the Diagrams from the Piedot Collection (former Works Manager of the Pullman Car Company Ltd).

83. Ibid.

84. *The Railway Gazette*, 'Sea Baths in SECR Pullman', 3 November 1911, p.477 and Pullman Company Ltd, Directors' Statement of Account, September 1912, pp.2-7.

85. *The Railway Gazette*, 24 February 1911, p.190.

86. *The Railway Gazette*, 10 May 1912, p.487 and pp.512-513. See also *The Railway & Travel Monthly*, Vol. 5, July 1912 and *The Railway Gazette*, 31 January 1913, pp.136-138.

87. Articles of Agreement between the Pullman Company and the SECR, dated 13 January 1914 (Herbert H Groves, London Bridge SE).

88. Ibid. p.3.

89. Ibid. p.4, and also memorandum dated 16 January 1924 to Sir Herbert A Walker, General Manager of the Southern Railway from Davison Dalziel regarding former South Eastern Section services and special allowances.

90. The Piedot Collection of diagrams and papers, June 1914 (forming part of the Bowering Collection since 1979).

91. *The Railway Gazette*, January-June 1914, p.614.

92. The Memoirs of Pullman Conductor, Mr Walter J Badger (Born 1883, Forest Gate). Employed by the Pullman Car Company 1908-1951.

The Queenborough Pier Pullman dining car service

93. *The Railway Gazette*, 31 March 1911, pp.317-319.

94. The Caledonian Railway named the car after Jane Gordon from the eighteenth century, who was famed for her connections with the Gordon Highlanders Regiment.

The Continental services – seafaring vessels

95. *The Golden Way*, October 1928 (WH Smith), pp.4-9. (The Bowering collection)

97. *The Golden Way*, September-November 1929, Continental Section (The Arden Press), pp.14-21.

97. Correspondence and photographs from the private estate of Mr John Meredith (1946-1949).

98. Southern Railway letter dated 9 December 1926 from Mr Edwin C Cox (Chief Operating Superintendent's Office) to the Pullman Car Company, c/o Sir D Dalziel (Ref: S2/1054 – G.Pad.267)

99. Ibid.

100. *The Golden Way*, September 1933, Continental Section (The Arden Press), pp.7-8. (The Bowering collection).

Pullman cars with brake compartments: *Aurora, Flora, Juno* and *Montana*, 1923

101. The National Archives: RAIL 1204/50. The Pullman Car Co: *Letter from P C Tempest dated 2 August 1922.*

102. Ibid.

103. Pullman Car Company Shareholders Meeting, Moorgate, June 1923. p.9.

104. *Southern Railway Magazine*, Vol XXIV, No. 257, p.207.

105. The *Southern Region Appendices to the Carriage Working Notices*, September 1952.

106. The National Archives: RAIL 1206. *Minutes of the Pullman Car Company Board Meeting, 8 April, 1960* - Disposal of Pullman cars.

The agreement between the Pullman Car Company Ltd and Compagnie Internationale des Wagons Lits et des Grands Express Européens

107. Ashurst Morris Crisp & Co, London. Draft treaty wording: The Agreement between the Pullman Car Company Ltd and Compagnie Internationale des Wagons Lits et des Grands Express Européens, December 1924.

Trial runs for Calais-Paris Service, November 1925

108. *The Railway Gazette,* 20 November 1925, p.648, and 17 September 1926, p.328. Also, *The National Archives:* PRO ZPER 9/42.

109. Perret, Renzo, *Le Carrozze Pullman, La Storia della CIWL* (Elledi, 1982) pp. 16-23.

110. *The Railway Gazette*, 17 September 1926, p.328.

111. CIWL Circulaire No.291 T, Paris, 6 September 1926

112. *The Princely Path to Paris by Golden Arrow*, The Arden Press, September 1926 (First Edition)

113. CIWL Circulaire No.291 T, Paris, 6 September 1926.

The Birmingham-built 'Flèche d'Or-type' cars, 1926

114. The Railway Gazette, 20 November 1925, p.648.

115. The *National Archives:* PRO ZPER 9/42.

The Leeds Forge Co. order, 1926/7

116 *The Locomotive*, 15 February 1927, pp. 53-57

117. Ibid, p.54.

118. *The Railway Gazette,* 4 February 1927, pp. 1-8

The inauguration of the 'Golden Arrow', 11 September 1926

119. *The Railway Gazette*, 3 September 1926, p.272.

120. *The Railway Gazette*, 17 September 1926, p.328.

121. *The Railway Magazine*, September 1926, pp.438-444.

122. *The Railway Gazette*, 17 September 1926, p.328.

123. *The National Archives:* PRO ZPER 9/42 and PRO:ZPER 9/45.

124. *The Railway Gazette*, 17 September 1926, p.328.

The inauguration of the accelerated 'Golden Arrow', 1929

125. *The Railway Magazine*, May 1969, p.250.

126. *The Railway Gazette* (International Railway Congress Number), 1954, p.91 and Pullman Car Company Director's Report, 1947, p.2 and Director's Report, 1949, p.3.

The Southern Railway twin-screw turbine steamer SS 'Canterbury'

127. *The Railway Gazette*, 17 May 1929, pp.743-744.

128. Ibid.

129. *The Golden Way*, The Baynard Press (Continental Edition, June, 1929).

130. Ibid. p.6.

131. *The Golden Way*, WH Smith (March 1930), p.8.

132. http://www.gracesguide.co.uk/SS_Canterbury

London and Paris

133. *This is Europe*, Pullman Car Company Publication (WH Smith, June 1927). Penultimate final publication. Reintroduced in 1947-1956 to a similar format.

134. Ibid.

Bournemouth Air Specials

135. *Railway Magazine,* March and April 1946, p.78.

136. *The Bournemouth Daily*, 29 December 1945.

137. The Badger diaries 1942-1945 (in the possession of the Author).

138. Ibid.

139. Ibid.

140. The *Echo,* 13 November 1945.

141. *Railway Magazine*, July and August 1946, p.252.

The return of the 'Golden Arrow' and 'Flèche d'Or', 1946

142. *Southern Railway Magazine*, Vol. XXIV. No.254, May 1946, p.81.

143. During 1947, the Southern Film Unit released a highly-acclaimed colour film of the train from Victoria to Gare du Nord. The script was written and read by Robert Arlen and the photography by Basil Sangster and Reginald Johnson.

144. *Southern Railway Magazine*, Vol. XXIV. No. 254, May 1946, pp.81-83.

145. Ibid, p.83.

146. See: 'Flèche d'Or' film released by SNCF Section Centrale Cinematographique *Le Magazine du Rail No. 1* (1947).

Mr Walter Badger – *Chef-du-train*

147. *The Tatler and Bystander* (Vol. CLXXX No. 2340), 1 May 1946, p. 137.

148. Ibid.

149. Personal correspondence and diary notes from the Estate of Walter J.W. Badger.

TS 'Invicta'

150. *Dover Express*, 18 October 1946.

151. Ibid.

152. Southern Railway publicity brochure *'Golden Arrow'*, December 1946 (McCorquodale Press).

153. Dover Express, 18 October 1946.

154. Ibid.

155. http://www.doverferryphotosforums.co.uk/ts-invicta-iii-past-and-present. Accessed 18 June 2014

156. Southern Railway timetable, *Cross Channel Services*, 2 November 1947, p.20 and http://www.ournewhaven.org.uk. Accessed 18 June 2014.

157. *Dover Express*, 18 October 1946.

158. Ibid.

159. *Dover Express*, 19 July 1946. Chapter 5 (part 7)

The 'Trianon Bar' car

160. Formerly kitchen car *'Diamond'*

161. Stanley Adams, then Chairman of the Pullman Car Company, was also on the Board of plastics manufacturer De La Rue.

162. *Evening Standard*, Saturday 13 April, 1946, p.5.

163. *The Dover Express*, 14 March 1980.

The new 'Golden Arrow' – Festival year, 1951

164. Pullman Car Co: Board minutes, 5 July 1939, The National Archives: RAIL 1204/2.

165. Pullman Car Co. Board minutes, 5 May 1949, The National Archives, RAIL 1204/2.

166. Southern Region Memoranda, 5 June, 1951 No. 23A/51 (The Bowering Collection).

167. Pullman Car Co. Internal memoranda between F.D.M. Harding and the Chief Engineer, November 1949 referring to a discussion (of unknown date) with Mr R.A. Riddles, Chief Mechanical Engineer of the Railway Executive. Reference: Sp2.CA.

168. *Modern Transport,* 9 June, 1951, pp.6-7 and Hasenson, Alec, *The Golden Arrow* (Howard Baker, 1970).

169. Ibid.

170. *The Railway Gazette*, 8 June 1951, pp. 638-639.

171. Ibid.

172. *Modern Transport,* 9 June, 1951, pp.6-7.

173. Ibid.

174. *Rail Magazine*, Editions Modernes et illustrées, Nos 22 and 23, Fevrier 1979, pp.26-29.

175. *The Railway Gazette*, 8 June 1951, pp. 638-640.

176. Ibid.

177. *The Furniture Record*, 3 February 1951, p.1081.

178. Ibid.

179. *The Railway Gazette*, 8 June 1951, pp. 638-640.

180. Pullman edition of *Londoner's Diary* (Reginald Harris Publications, June 1951, p.3.

181. Kichenside, Geoffrey, *Orion and the Golden Arrow. The Story of a Pullman car* (Peco Publication, 1978).

The little differences that distinguish the 'Golden Arrow' service

182. Southern Region brochure: *New facilities of the Golden Arrow* (McCorquodale Press), Summer Service 1951.

Stewardess of the 'Golden Arrow'

183. *Railway Gazette,* 1954, p.91.

184. *Woman's Mirror*, July 1954, p.49

Service timings

185. Memorandum from the Pullman Car Company to the Southern Region Traffic Office, March 1952.

186. *The Railway Magazine*, May 1969, p.252.

References

The final run of the 'Golden Arrow', 30 September 1972

187. *Railway Magazine*, September 1972, pp. 646-67.

188. *Railway Observer*, 1972, p.446.

Pullman car design, marquetry and the construction of British identity

189. Taylor, A J P, *English History, 1914-1945* (Oxford, 1965), pp.67-8.

190. Buckley, Cheryl, *Designing Modern Britain* (Reaktion, 2007), pp.47-48.

191. Ibid.

192. Stevenson, G, *The 1930s Home* (Bloomsbury, 2008)

193. This company merged with four other French airlines to form Air France in October 1933.

194. Fry, Roger, *Art and Commerce*, Hogarth Press, London, 1926.

195. *Past and Present*, Waring and Gillow publication, London, 1924.

Appendix 1. Extra-fare Pullman car services, 1910-1939

196. Pullman Car Company Accountant's Office, London, 23 November 1962 (Ref: AN. 47979)

Appendix 4. Bill of Fare – a selection: Pullman Car Company/British Rail Catering, 1920-1972

197. Morel, Julian, *Pullman* (David & Charles, 1983), p.168.

Appendix 5. Restricted working of Pullman cars

198. Southern Railway. Restricted Working of Passenger Stock, 1925, p.61

Appendix 7. Bookstall service on the 'Golden Arrow', 1948

199. *Southern Region Magazine*, October 1948

Appendix 8. The 'Golden Arrow' Pullman lapel badge

200. Inter-office memoranda, F Harding, February 1946.

Appendix 9. Pullmans used as 'Supply cars'

201. Southern Railway, Mr Edwin C. Cox, Traffic Manager. Memoranda dated 30 May 1933 (Reference: S.1/1343)

Appendix 10. Pullman cars ('F/G-types') converted into 'Holiday' and 'Camping' coaches (with disposal data)

202. Training vehicle, *No.101*.

203. Original identity of this vehicle was *Cosmo Bonsor*.

204. This car was only withdrawn when conversion of 'K-type' *Car 161* (reverting back to *Fortuna*) was completed.

205. This car was only withdrawn when conversion of 'K-type' *Car 248* (later named *Athene*) was completed.

Appendix 16. Selected timetables for the 'Golden Arrow', Continental connections and other South-Eastern Section Pullman services

206. The National Archives: RAIL 1204/55. Internal memorandum from Davison Dalziel to Thomas Powell (Secretary) 22 April 1924.

207. SC/PO.94/10 British Rail Shipping Services

Acknowledgements

I would like to thank the following without whom this book, *Pullman Profile No.5* would not have been possible: My grateful thanks to the publisher, Crécy Publishing Limited, and to Kevin Robertson.

Considerable help was also given by Brendan Brabazon, Dr Alec Hasenson, Raymond Martin, Charles Farquhar, Sir William and Lady Judy McAlpine, Rhoswen Gruffydd, Ross and Elizabeth Workman, Dr Ettore Redaelli, Bob Patterson, Phil Evans, Dr Siôn Llewellyn, Doug Lindsay, Martin Blackford, Pierre-Yves Toussirot, Jean-Pierre Sineaux, Catherine Pichonnier, Jean Chapotel, Stan Friedman, John Morris, Cerys Lewis, Andrew Overton, Tim Robbins, Joan Gosling, Peter Ives, Gerry Young, Paul Flint, the Chatfield family, the late Esmond Lewis-Evans, the late Joe Kent, the late Roger Commault, the late John Howard Turner and the late George Behrend.

I should also like to acknowledge the help and assistance offered by the staff at the British Film Institute, British Library, The Soane Museum, Museo del Ferrocarril de Madrid, especially Raquel Letón Ruiz (Jefa de Conservación y Archivo Histórico Ferroviario) and Ana Cabanes Martín and library staff; the Bluebell Railway, Birmingham Library, The National Railway Museum, York (Search Engine, particularly Andy Croxton) and The National Archives at Kew.

Finally, my greatest debt is to my children and, above all, my wife. Without William, Rhiannon and Arabella's distractions, I might have completed the book sooner, but I would have been a far less happy person than I am. Without Joanna's support and understanding, the book would never have been published.

A young lady waits in anticipation of her dessert, following a three-course luncheon in the magnificent Pullman car Fingall *now used regularly on the Bluebell Railway's prestige train, 'The Golden Arrow'.*

In preparation for 2019:
Volume 6
The Ocean Liner Express
Pullman Trains

Pullman Society membership details may be obtained from: www.thepullmansociety.org.uk/membership

Photographic Credits

Every effort has been made to attribute all photographic material reproduced in this book correctly. If, in error, I have failed to mention anyone, please accept my apologies as well as my extended thanks.

T=top; M=middle; B=bottom; L=left; R=right

Badger, W (Collection): 134, 136, 141, 145TL, 145TR, 148, 152

Behrend, G (Collection): 11TR, 62BL, 85,

Blackford, M: 42, 163TL

Bowering-Ford, A: 164, 165, 189BR, 190, 192, 206, 207

Brabazon, B (Collection): 6, 11TL, 17, 19, 20, 23TL, 24, 86, 111, 159, 179, 180, 194, 208, 209L, 216

Evans, P: P. 2

Ford, A (Collection): 21, 25, 26, 32, 33, 34R, 36, 37, 40, 44/45, 49, 50, 51, 52, 53, 54, 56, 58, 59, 60, 62TR, 63, 65, 67, 70, 73, 74T, 75,76B, 79, 81T, 82, 83, 84B, 88, 89, 90, 91, 92, 93, 95, 106, 107, 108, 109, 110, 112, 115, 116, 118, 121, 122L, 123, 124, 129, 130, 131TL, 131TR, 132, 137, 138, 142R, 153, 155, 156TL, 156BR, 157TL, 157BL, 160TL, 169T, 181, 189T, 193, 205, 209BR, 210T, 217, 224

Hasenson, A: 23R, 39, 41, 64L, 117L, 117BR, 126, 127, 128, 140, 142L, 149, 154 (Collection), 156BL, 156TR, 157TR, 160BL, 160BR, 161BR, 162, 163TR, 168, 169BR, 210B

Howard-Turner, J (Collection): 144B

Kent, J: 22, 27, 28R, 29, 30, 36, 43, 46, 55, 61L,64R, 66, 71, 72,76T, 94, 113, 114, 131B, 133, 135, 144T, 163BL, 163BR, 178, 182, 184, 185, 186, 187, 188, 191, 198, 202, 204, 209TR

Lindsay, D (Collection): 57, 74L, 125, 146R

Martin, R (Collection): 139, 144B, 146L

McAlpine, W: 157BR

Patterson, R (Collection): 38, 158BR, 160TR, 161TR

Touissirot, PY (Collection): 34L, 81B, 84T, 97, 122R, 158TL, 158BL

A 'King Arthur' class locomotive, No 769 'Sir Balan' at the head of the 'Continental Express' forerunner to the 'Golden Arrow'.

Bibliography

Allen, G. Freeman, *Luxury Trains of the World* (Bison, 1979)

Behrend, George, *Pullman in Europe* (Ian Allan, 1962)

Bryant, J, *Robert Adam, 1792-99: Architect of Genius* (Mitchell Beazley, 1987)

Haresnape, B, *Pullman, Travelling in Style* (Malaga Books, Ian Allan, 1987)

Hasenson, Alec, *Golden Arrow* (Howard Baker, 1970)

Jenkinson, D, *British Railway Carriages of the 20ᵗʰ Century* (Patrick Stephens, 1990)

Kichenside, G, *Orion and the Golden Arrow: The Story of a Pullman Car* (Peco, 2014)

Kidner, R.W, *Pullman Cars on the Southern 1875-1972* (Oakwood Press, 1987)

Morel, J, *Pullman* (David & Charles, 1983)

Mühl, Albert, *Internationale Luxuszüge* (EK-Verlag, 1991)

Perret, Renzo, *Les Voitures Pullman* (Les editions du Cabri, 1983)

Spark, Robert, *Sleepers, Diners & Pullmans* (Trafton Publishing, 1995)

Winkworth, DW, *Southern Titled Trains* (David & Charles, 1988)

21C1 'Channel Packet' at Victoria awaiting departure with the resumed post-war service.

Periodicals

Architectural Review	*Daily Graphic*
Chemins de Fer	*Daily Telegraph*
Country Life	*Dover Express*
La Vie du Rail	*Daily Graphic*
Modern Transport	*Illustrated London News*
Modern Motoring and Travel	*La Route du Rail*
Railway Magazine	*Matin*
Steam Days	*Notre Métier*
The Architects Journal	*The British Gazette*
The Furniture Record	*The Times*
The Locomotive	*Woman's Mirror*
The Railway Gazette	
The Railway & Travel Monthly	
Trains Illustrated	

The National Archives

Pullman Car Company Board Minutes: RAIL 1204/2/5 and others, as listed in the references.

Diaries and Pullman Company booklets and journals:

The notes and diaries of Walter Badger, 1929-1938 and 1949-1952

The notes of Roger Commault, 1930-1950

The Pullman Car Guide, 1913, 1920 and 1926

The Golden Way, 1923-1942 Quarterly and half-yearly editions

The Princely Path to Paris, 1929 and 1930

London Days and Nights, 1928-1934

Wonder Years, 1935-1938

Index

Interior of car 'Carina' with well turned-out Pullman staff. At the front is leading attendant Reg Varney, standing in the suit rear right is Mr E J Morris latterly General Manager of the Pullman car Co. This was the occasion of a VIP special.

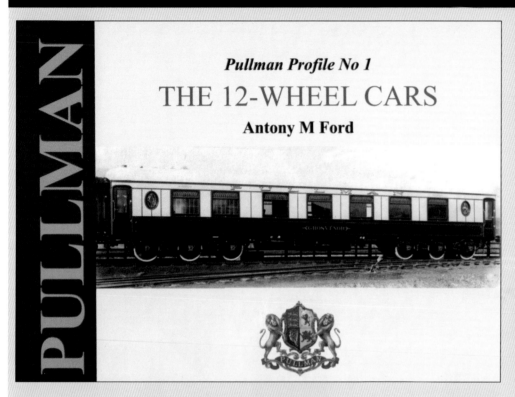

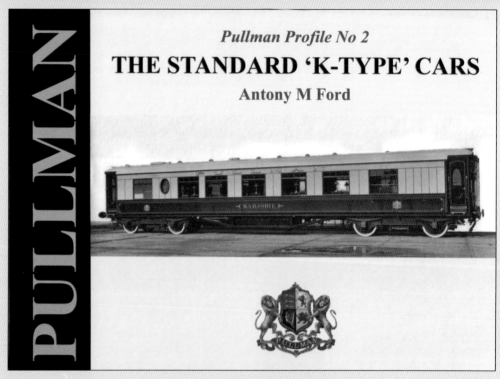

Pullman Profile No 1 The 12-Wheel Cars

Antony M Ford
Hardback, 192 pages
ISBN: 9781906419004 £27.00

The first book in Antony Ford's series, a top quality illustrated guide to the luxury 12 wheel Pullman cars which graced some of the most famous trains of the past. The 12-wheel cars were truly massive vehicles based on solid timber construction and of course running on 6-wheel bogies. Their sphere of operation was principally on the SR and LNER and were in operation well into BR days on such trains as the 'Bournemouth Belle'. All the vehicles of this type are shown in this volume which includes both works, service and withdrawal views and plans.

Pullman Profile No 2 The Standard 'K' Type Cars

Antony M Ford
Hardback, 196 pages
ISBN: 9781906419226 £27.00 **OUT OF PRINT**

This second book includes a huge range of illustrations and photographs depicting the distinctive exteriors and interiors of the best known vehicles built for the Pullman Car Company. Alongside these are many rare builders' photographs showing methods of construction, design innovations including marquetry schemes, carpets, moquettes and other furnishings. This extensive sequence of informative history details each batch of K types built from 1923 to 1927, prior to the advent of the all-steel Pullman car. Captured in this volume is all the glamour and charm associated with the cars, complemented by readable, enthusiastic and well-researched text much of which has not previously been published before.

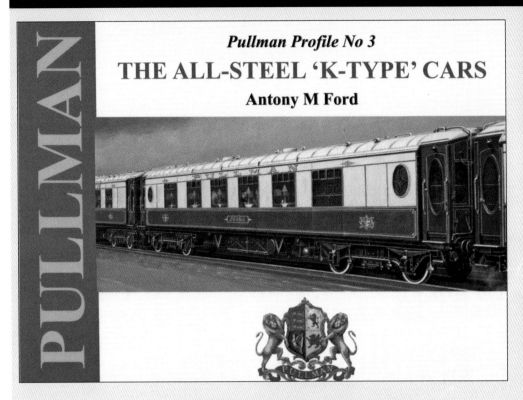

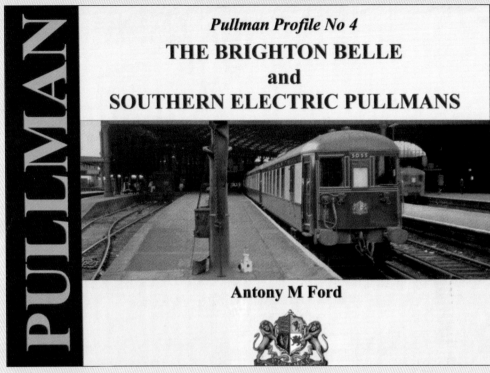

Pullman Profile No 3 The All-Steel 'K-Type' Cars

Antony M Ford

Hardback, 152 pages

ISBN: 9781906419578 £29.95

In the third part of his survey of British Pullman cars, Antony Ford explores some of the grandest vehicles ever built for luxury service. The principal building of the first wave of 'all-steel K-type' cars took place in 1928 when a considerable effort was being made to improve not only first-class, but also third-class accommodation and no-where was this better exemplified. Also included in this finely bound volume are examples of train formations from 1928 to 1967, schematics, disposal and preservation data.

Pullman Profile No 4 The Brighton Belle and Southern Electric Pullmans

Antony M Ford

Hardback, 200 pages

ISBN: 9781909328051   £33.00

In this volume, Antony Ford describes the story of the introduction of the 'Brighton Belle' in the 1930s together with the associate use of Pullman cars in other multiple unit electric trains on the Southern Railway. This is not just a simple history of the electric Pullman trains on the Southern, associated with it is the story of Pullman in the 1930s, its opulence and style and why as the years and decades passed there was still the demand for Pullman travel thirty or more years later.

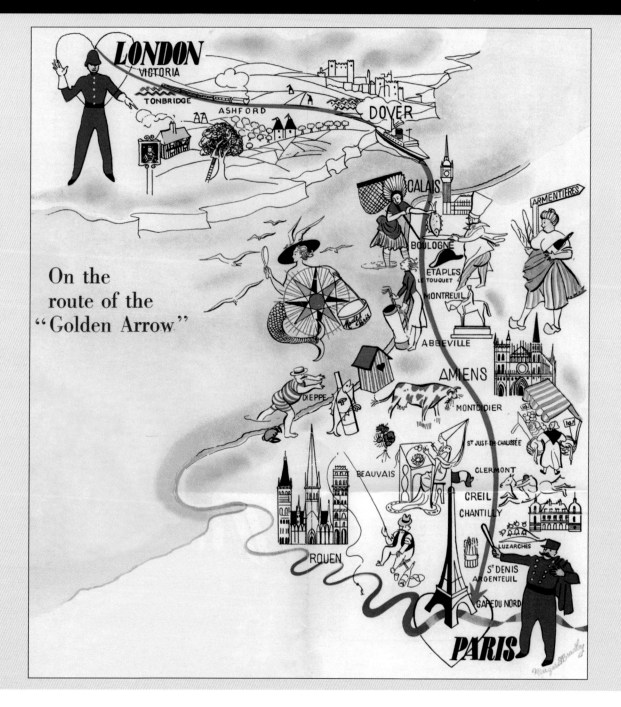